D1246360

Sixty Saints for Boys

Affectionately
Fr Scott
July 31, '94

Sixty Saints
for Boys

Joan Windham

*with illustrations by
Mona Doneux*

Christian Classics, Inc.

Post Office Box 30
Westminster Maryland 21157

1994

First American Printing, 1990
Second American Printing, 1992
Third American Printing, 1994

All rights reserved.
ISBN 0 87061 149 6

Printed in the U.S.A.

PREFACE FOR CHILDREN

All the Saints in this book are Real People who knew, loved and served Our Lord in this World and so now they are happy with him forever in the Next. Most of the things that I have written about really did happen to the Saints, but some of the things that I have written about are just Stories that people tell about them, and these Stories are called Legends. All the Legends *could* have happened if God had wanted it that way, and that, I think, is how most of them started. If the Saint was a Gardening kind of a man then there are Gardening Legends about him. If he was a man who lived in a Starving place then there are Legends about plenty of Food arriving very surprisingly. (But all the same, quite a lot of the Miracles really did happen because God does do things like that for the people who are his best friends.) And so, in this way we find out what kind of a person the Saint *was*, as well as what kind of things he *did*, by reading Legends about him. You know how it is yourself when somebody tells you about something a friend of yours did the other day. Perhaps you then tell it to somebody else, and perhaps you don't *exactly* remember how the thing happened, so you just say what you think it probably was. The next person might alter it a little more and in No Time at All there is a Legend about your friend! It isn't True any more, but it might have been!

I'll tell you something . . . There is a Legend about me. In my garden is a Pond and once I dropped a trowel into it and I nearly fell in when I was fishing it

v

out. A very little boy thought that I *had* fallen in and every time he sees the Pond he says: "Aunt Joan fell in there!" And other people hear him, and although it was some time ago now, a good many people describe exactly what they think happened and how Wet I was and how there were Water Lilies round my neck and all kinds of other stories! But they all believe that I really did fall into the Pond. I didn't: but it is just the sort of thing that I might have done!

CONTENTS

CONTENTS

Sixty Saints for Boys

ST. JAMES

All that we really know about St. James we can find in the Bible, but that isn't very much. However there are a good many stories that people have told each other right from the time he lived, and other stories are written in books. Some of these may quite well be true.

After Our Lord's Ascension the Apostles went about teaching people how to be Christians, and James went to Spain. He was there a long time and he saw Our Lady there. So after years and years, when at last he died, his friends took his body back to Spain and it was buried at a town called Compostella. Well, as soon as people heard about it they began to make Pilgrimages to Compostella. (A Pilgrimage is a journey to some blessed or holy place. People make pilgrimages to Jerusalem and Nazareth and Bethlehem and Lourdes and Compostella and Walsingham and other places.)

Now when the people prayed at Compostella, St. James often used to see them and talk to them. Of course, he had to come from Heaven to do this, but God allowed him to come. And so more and more people went to Compostella to ask St. James to pray for them and the things they needed. And he did, and because he is a particular friend of God's, people were cured of illnesses and their prayers were answered time and time again.

One day, a German man and his wife and son had asked James to pray for a house for them, because they were living in a shed. They had waited and looked everywhere for a house. Well, that very week they found the Very House they wanted.

They were so pleased that they said they would make a pilgrimage to Compostella to say Thank You.

"Wouldn't it be Grand," said the Wife, whose name was Greta, "if we saw St. James himself and could thank him properly?"

And they started off. They were very poor and so they walked. They carried as little as possible, but it came to a Good Deal even so. Greta carried a saucepan and some packages of food and soap as well as her rug and cup and knife and plate. Hans carried an Axe to cut firewood, some sort of matches, and some snares to catch rabbits, and dry clothes for all of them, as well as his rug and cup and knife and plate. Adolf carried some tools and bits of leather to mend their shoes and an extra bag of flour as well as his rug and cup and knife and plate. They couldn't really do with much less. When it rained they stayed the night at an Inn. The Inns were called different names, the George and Dragon, the White Hart, the Seven Stars, the Leather Bottle and the Bird in Hand. (What is the name of the Inn nearest to your house?) Well, one wet evening Hans and Greta and Adolf were tiredly walking along looking for somewhere to Stay the Night when they saw an Inn called the Horse and Groom.

"There!" said Adolf, "let's go there. It looks cheery and warm and we haven't stayed at an Inn called the Horse and Groom."

So they went in and took off their wet things and had a Hot Supper and Hot Wine with Spice in it so that they wouldn't catch Colds. But the Innkeeper was a Wicked Man and hated Pilgrims because they never had much money to spend in his Inn. So when Hans and Greta and Adolf were all asleep in the Warm and Dry, he took a Silver Cup and he hid it in Adolf's Baggage and went quietly away.

Directly after Breakfast they said "Good-bye and Thank You for the warm comfortable night," to the Innkeeper, and set off again. But they hadn't gone far when some policemen galloped after them and told them to stop.

"Why?" said Hans.

"Because the Innkeeper of the Horse and Groom says one of you has Stolen a Valuable Silver Cup," said the Head Policeman.

"One of *us* has?" said Greta in an Astonished Voice. "Of course we haven't. We are Pilgrims going to Compostella, not Thieves."

"Well then you won't mind if we look in your Baggage just to Make Sure?" said the Policeman.

"No, of course we don't mind," said Hans. "Which Baggage?"

"All of it," said the Policeman.

Luckily it was a fine day after the rain, and Greta unpacked her Baggage and the Policeman Searched it.

"Nothing there, Madam," he said.

"Thank you," said Greta, and she began to pack again.

"Now yours," said the Policeman to Hans.

"Nothing there either, sir."

"Thank you," said Hans, and began to pack again.

"Now yours, my lad," said the Policeman to Adolf.

"Hey!" he said. "What have we here?" and he pulled out the Silver Cup! "So you *are* Thieves and the Innkeeper is right!"

It didn't matter what Hans and Greta and Adolf said, and the next morning Adolf was hanged up on a tree with a rope round his neck, and all their Goods and

Chattels were given to the Innkeeper to Console him. Hans and Greta went sadly on to Compostella, where they told St. James what had happened and thanked him for finding them the House. But they didn't see him.

On their way home, Hans said he wanted to go and see the tree where Adolf was hanged, and when they got there Adolf was still there. But when they stood and cried sadly, Adolf said:

" Don't cry, Mother and Father, I am quite all right and I was waiting for you to come. St. James has been here all the time and has fed me and cheered me up! "

Hans was so astonished that he ran to the Town to find the Judge, but Greta stayed with Adolf. The Judge was just going to have dinner. He was going to have Roast Chickens and Bread Sauce and Brussels Sprouts and chipped Potatoes. And because he was going to have Two Whole Chickens he was only going to have a little Fruit afterwards. There were Melons and Oranges and Apples and Strawberries and Bananas and William Pears for him to Choose.

When Hans rushed into his house he put down his Carving Knife and said:

" What's all this? "

" Adolf isn't dead at all! " said Hans all out of Breath with having run so fast.

" Nonsense! " said the Judge, who luckily remembered about Adolf. " He was hanged Thirty-six days ago."

" But he *is* alive! " said Hans. " He talked to me! "

" He is no more alive than those Roast Chickens are! " said the Judge. And an Extraordinary Thing happened. The Chickens got up off the dish, in their Feathers and all, and the Cock began to Crow and the Hen to Cluck!

" *Well!* " said the Judge, staring at the Chickens. " Well, I *say!* "

4

"Come and see Adolf *quickly!*" said Hans, who was so excited about his son that he scarcely noticed the miracle of the Chickens.

The Judge went with Hans, and a whole crowd of people followed them and they found Adolf listening to Greta while she told him what they had done at Compostella!

So Hans and Greta and Adolf happily went home, but the Judge sent the Police to catch the Innkeeper and hanged him instead.

St. James's Special Day is on July 25th, and people called Hamish or Jack or Jacob can all have him for theirs, because they are all One and the Same Name.

ST. JOSEPH OF ARIMATHAEA

Once upon a time there was a man who was a Good and Just Counsellor, and his name was Joseph, and he lived in a place called Arimathaea, and he was one of Our Lord's Disciples. (A Disciple is a person who follows and learns from another person. Our Lord had hundreds of Disciples, but only Twelve Apostles.) We don't really know very much about Joseph, except that he was a Nobleman and Rich, but I'll tell you what we do know. After Our Lord had been crucified and had died the Roman soldiers just left Him on the Cross. The Disciples thought what a terrible thing this was, and how dreadful for Our Lady, too, but they were afraid of the Roman soldiers, and of the Jews who had wanted Our Lord to be crucified, and so they didn't do anything about it. So, late in the evening, Joseph, because he was Rich and therefore Important, went secretly (so that the Romans and the Jews wouldn't know) to Pontius Pilate and asked him Please could he take away Our Lord's Body to bury it? Now Pilate hadn't really wanted to crucify Our Lord at all, and he was feeling very sorry about it, but he did not believe that Our Lord could be dead yet. He thought that Joseph was trying to help Him to escape. So he sent for the Centurion, whose name was Longinus, and he asked him if it was true that Our Lord was dead. Longinus said, " Yes, I saw Him die." Then Pilate said that Joseph could take away the Body and bury it.

So Joseph and another Disciple called Nicodemus took Our Lord's Body down from the Cross. Now

6

Joseph's garden was near the place where He was crucified, and in the garden was a new cave in the rock that Joseph had got ready for himself to be buried in when he died. By the time they had got Our Lord down it was very late at night, and he did not know of anywhere else near at hand, so he hoped that his own new cave would be nice enough for Our Lord, and he thanked God for the honour of being allowed to give it up. So Joseph and Nicodemus put Our Lord's Body safely there, and they rolled a great Rock to the door of the cave so that no one could get in in the Night. Then they went sadly home. Now all that is perfectly true, but there are lots of other stories about the things that Joseph did afterwards that are not in the Bible, and I will tell you some of them.

A year after Joseph had given his own new cave to be a burial place for Our Lord, St. Philip, who was one of the Apostles, sent Joseph and eleven of his friends to Britain to tell the British people about Our Lord. Because, of course, there were no Christians there yet, and no one had even Heard of such a thing.

Now there were a lot of Tin Mines in Cornwall (and there still are) and people used to come from round about Palestine to buy Tin. So Joseph and his Eleven Friends sailed in one of the Tin people's boats, and after a time they landed in Cornwall, which is in the bottom left hand corner of England. They brought with them a very Precious Thing. It was the Silver Cup that Our Lord had used at the Last Supper when He put wine into it and said, "THIS IS MY BLOOD." Do you remember? The cup was called the Holy Grail.

Lots of people collected round to Stare at Joseph and his Eleven Friends, because they had different Clothes and they could not speak the British language. But they went on to a place nearby, to Glastonbury, and they made a Camp, and they settled down and got friendly with the people, and soon they could speak it fairly well.

Everyone who used to visit their camp used to look at their Chapel and say:

" What's that place? "

" It's a Chapel."

" What's a Chapel? " asked the Visitor.

" A place where we Worship God," said Joseph.

" Can I see? " asked the Visitor.

" Of course you can," said Joseph.

And always, when they went into the Chapel and saw the Holy Grail the people would want to know about it, and Joseph or one of his Eleven Friends would tell them. But they were not allowed to touch the Holy Grail, because of its being so Precious. And so, because they couldn't *see* the Christians' God, some of the English people thought that He must be in the Cup.

" That's why Joseph won't let us touch it," they said.

" Well," said one of them, " let's Steal it just for one day, and then we'll be able to see God."

After that so many of the English people tried to get into the Chapel, and so often, that the Christians had to take it in Turns to Stand Guard, and at last Joseph said to them:

" We can't go on like this. One of these days some-body really will Steal the Holy Grail, and it is much too Precious to be handed round the Villages for every-one to Stare at and Handle. What do you all think that we had better do? "

They thought and they wondered, and at last one of them said:

" Couldn't we Bury it in a Safe Place? "

The others all thought that this was a very good Idea, and so they buried the Holy Grail by a well at the bottom

8

of a little mountain called Glastonbury Tor. It was a winter's day and Joseph stuck his tall Walking Stick into the ground to Mark the Place. And now a wonderful thing happened! You remember that it was a Winter's day? Well, the walking stick grew Roots and Leaves and Flowers and turned into a Hawthorn Tree all in the same afternoon! And what is more, instead of flowering every Summer like Hawthorns always do, it flowered every Winter!

Well, Joseph and his friends travelled on and taught the people about being Christians, and they built them Chapels, and they never got back to Glastonbury, somehow. Nobody else knew where the Grail was buried, and they thought that the Hawthorn Tree was Joseph's Stick, and that it was very Surprising, but they never thought that it was Marking anything.

But for Hundreds of years people looked and searched for the Holy Grail. It was one of those Special Things that King Arthur's Knights of the Round Table tried to do, and one of them, called Sir Galahad, is supposed to have seen it once, but we don't know if he really did, because it is all so very Long Ago. But as far as we know, it never has been found. Or perhaps somebody found it and never knew what a Precious Thing it was.

Anyway, after years and years some Monks came and built a Monastery, with a Famously Beautiful Chapel, round Joseph's Thorn Tree so that it was in their Garden and they looked after it for Ages until it got Very old. At last one of the Gardening Monks said to the Abbot:

"Father Abbot, I am afraid that St. Joseph's Thorn Tree won't live much longer, it is Hundreds of years old. Do you suppose that I might take one or two Cuttings so that we'll still have some of it when the Old Tree dies?"

"I don't see why not," said the Abbot, rubbing his chin with his thumb, "it would be a great Pity to lose it altogether after All these Years."

So the Brother Gardener made Two or Three Cuttings and they had just started to grow nicely when Oliver Cromwell's soldiers arrived!

I don't know if you know about Oliver Cromwell, but he was one of the Heads of the Puritans who were Extraordinary people, and they only thought Three Things.

One was that they thought that the Church was Bad, and that all the Beautiful Churches were Bad too.

Two, they thought that Kings were Bad to have.

Three, they thought people couldn't be Happy as well as Good, and Sundays must be Solemn and Sad, and that Churches must be Plain and Ugly, and that nobody must Laugh or Sing (because you couldn't be Good as well as Happy) and Worst of All they thought God was terrible and Frightening, and was always watching to see if He could Catch them out.

So you can see what Extraordinary people they were, can't you? (As a matter of Fact there are still some of them about, poor miserable things.)

Well, Cromwell's soldiers went about Smashing the lovely old Churches and Burning them. Haven't you seen Statues and things in old Churches with their noses bashed and their fingers broken off? Well, now you know who did it.

When the soldiers got to Glastonbury they pulled down the Famously Beautiful Church, and then they went into the Monastery Garden and saw the Thorn Tree.

"What's this?" they shouted. "St. Joseph's Thorn? Nonsense, of *course* it can't flower in the Winter! What Wickedness to tell such lies to the poor people!" And they Chopped it down and dug up the roots and made a Bonfire of the whole lot! *But* they didn't find the little Cuttings that the Brother Gardener had made! So we still have St. Joseph's Thorn Tree. And one or two Cuttings have grown at Kew Gardens, so that all will be well if anything happens to the one in Glastonbury. And it really does flower in the Winter!

St. Joseph of Arimathaea's Special Day is on March 17th, and anyone born on that day can have him for their Special Saint, specially people who live in Glastonbury. (And who else has March 17th for his Special Day? Yes, St. Patrick of course! So anyone called Patrick Joseph is a really Special person.)

ST. PETER

(The Legend of Westminster)

Once upon a time, a very long time ago indeed, there were Two Kings in England. One was called King Ethelbert and one was called King Sigbert, and King Ethelbert was King Sigbert's Uncle and he called him Uncle Ethelbert.

Neither of them were Christians, because, in those days, nearly everyone was a Pagan. (You know what a Pagan is by this time, I'm sure.)

Well one day King Ethelbert got Talking with the Bishop of London and was Converted. He was so pleased at being a Christian that he wanted to do something to Celebrate. (Celebrating is doing something special to Mark the Occasion. Like having a Sugar Cake on your Birthday, or handing round the chocolates if anyone has been Extra Good.)

"What can I do to Celebrate?" King Ethelbert asked the Bishop of London.

"It all depends on how Rich you are," said the Bishop of London.

"I'm Fairly Well Off," said King Ethelbert, looking Rather Shy.

"Well, we badly need a New Church in London," said the Bishop. (Bishops are always saying that they badly need new Churches.)

"Oh, Goody!" said King Ethelbert, shaking hands with the Bishop of London, "I'd *love* to build a New Church! An Enormous one!" he said, getting quite

Excited. "The most Enormous one in London! I'll build a Cathedral! When can I begin?"

"We haven't even thought where it'll be, yet," said the Bishop of London, very pleased at being given a Cathedral when he'd only asked for a Church.

"I want to build it by the River," said King Ethelbert, "because then it will Show from a Long Way Off." (In case anybody doesn't live in London and so doesn't know, the River there is called the Thames.)

So they built a Magnificent Cathedral by the River Thames at the East side of London, and when it was built King Ethelbert said to the Bishop of London:

"Which Saint shall we give the New Cathedral to?" (Because you know, don't you, that every Church in the Whole World has either Our Lord or Our Lady or some Saint for its Special Person?)

"St. Paul was very good at converting Pagans like you were," said the Bishop of London, "why not Saint Paul?"

So they had St. Paul for their Saint. And the Bishop put on all his best Vestments and his Mitre (which is a Bishop's Hat that he wears in Church), and his Crozier (which is a Bishop's stick with a hook on the end for Catching Sheep because of the Good Shepherd) and they Consecrated and Dedicated the New Cathedral.

Now when a New Church is consecrated the Bishop comes and blesses it in a special sort of way to make it God's own particular place, and a proper place to have Mass in. And he blesses the Altar and puts Relics of a Saint in it and then he Dedicates (which means gives) the Church to whichever Saint has been chosen.

So the Bishop of London came in all his Vestments and things to the New Cathedral and he knocked on the door with his Crozier and the Sacristan said:

"Come in!" And the Bishop went in. They did

this because it was the first time that the Church had
been used for Christians to pray in. When he was in,
he saw that the Sacristan had sprinkled some sand
just inside the door and so he drew a Cross on the sand
with the stalk of his Crozier. (Bishops still do all these
things.) Then he put Twelve Crosses all round the
walls and then he sprinkled everything with Holy Water
and he blessed all the little Altars and he put a Relic
under the stone in the big Altar and blessed it and did
heaps and heaps of other things, and when he had
finished it wasn't just the New Church by the River
but it was St. Paul's Cathedral in London.

Now one of the people who came to see St. Paul's
Cathedral was King Sigbert who, you remember, was
the Nephew of King Ethelbert. And he was so delighted
with it that he became a Christian too!

" What shall *I* do to Celebrate? " he asked the Bishop
of London as they stood on the steps of St. Paul's
Cathedral.

" It all depends on how Rich you are," said the Bishop
of London.

" I'm Fairly Well Off," said King Sigbert, looking
Rather Shy.

" Well," said the Bishop, " we've just got a new
Church, so I don't know what to suggest, I'm sure! "

" But *I* wanted to build a Church too! " said poor
King Sigbert, looking rather as if he wanted to cry
because he was so disappointed. " I *want* to build a
Church, a lovely one by the River and all! "

" But we'll never have enough people to fill *two*
Enormous Cathedrals," said the Bishop of London.

" Well, I'll make a place for Monks then, an Abbey,"
said King Sigbert, " it will have a Beautiful Church
belonging to it, and then perhaps some Monks will
come and live there! "

" All right," said the Bishop of London.

" Let's go and choose the place now," said King Sigbert.

" Well, it mustn't be too close to St. Paul's then," said the Bishop; " what about making it on the Other Side of the River? "

" No," said King Sigbert, " it will take too long to get a boat and everything, I want to start *now*! " (Blackfriars Bridge wasn't there in those days.) " Let's just go along the River Bank until we find a Nice Place! "

So they walked and walked away from the East side of London over the little bridge of the River Fleet (that Fleet Street is built on top of) and along the Sandy bit called the Strand. The Bishop of London began to get tired, and he Lagged behind. His poor old Feet began to hurt him.

But King Sigbert was so anxious to find a Good Place that he kept hurrying along. Then he kept remembering that it isn't Polite to keep Hurrying Along and leaving the Bishop behind even if you *are* a King. So he had to go back and walk beside the poor Bishop of London. But in a little while he walked faster and faster and there he was in front again!

At last, right on the West side of London they came to a May Tree. It was a lovely one, with all its Blossom out and it smelled lovely in the sun. It was round a corner of the River from St. Paul's, too, and King Sigbert said:

" *Here!* Here's where I'll build my Abbey! Can I build it here? "

By this time the poor old Bishop of London was Quite Exhausted, so he said:

" Yes, yes, of course you can! " and he sat down with his back against the May Tree and Mopped his Brow. (Which is rubbing your forehead with a Hanky.)

So they built King Sigbert's new Church there by the

May Tree and every day he came to watch the Work-men. He helped them to carry Ladders and watched them sawing and hammering and polishing, and asked them what they were doing This for, or what they wanted That for, until they wished he'd go home to his Palace and Rule his People. But King Sigbert was so Inter-ested and Excited that he sent to ask his People if he could stay until the Church was finished, and they said that he could.

At last the Great Day came and the Last Bit was put on the very top of the Tower and the Last Statue put on the Last Altar and everything was in its Place. And it was called Westminster because it was a Minster at the West side of London. (A Minster was a monastery Church, especially if it was a Cathedral as well. And some very old Monastery Churches are still called Minster, like York Minster and Beverley Minster, al-though there are no monasteries belonging to them now.)

" Which Saint shall we Dedicate it to? " King Sigbert asked the Bishop of London.

" Well, I'm in favour of one of the Early Christian Martyrs myself," said the Bishop. " St. Lawrence, say, or St. Stephen."

" *I'd* like St. Peter," said King Sigbert. "Then we'd have St. Peter at one end of London and St. Paul at the other. Let's have St. Peter! "

" I'll think it Over! " said the Bishop of London Rather Grandly, " and we'll have the Consecration and Dedication next week! " and he went home. King Sigbert hoped that he could have St. Peter, and went and said a Special Prayer about it.

Now all that part of the Story that we have just read you can find in any History book. But the Exciting Part that I'm going to tell you now only seems to be in a Very Few books.

ST. PETER

That night, when nearly everyone was in bed, a Tall Man with a Beard came walking through Lambeth and Stangate (which are on the other side of the Thames). He walked right up to the River Bank opposite to King Sigbert's New Church and then he looked This way and That way to see how he could get across.

Just then a Fisherman who was sitting fishing in his Boat looked up and saw him.

" Good evening! " he said, " why are you standing on the River Bank looking This way and That way when it is so Very Late at Night? "

" I want to go to the New Abbey," said the Tall Man with a Beard, " and I want you to row me across! "

" Why do you want to go to the New Abbey so Very Late at Night? " asked the Fisherman. " It isn't even Consecrated yet! And if I spend my time rowing you about, what about my Fishing? I won't have any Fish to sell in the Morning! "

" Take me across, and I'll see that you don't lose any Fish," said the Tall Man with a Beard.

So the Fisherman wound up his line and stuck the Fly into the Handle of the Rod so that it wouldn't Blow About and Hook things. Then he moved his Creel and Landing Net to make room for his passenger, who sat down quietly in the Stern.

" People usually Wobble about when they get in," said the Fisherman, " and they Tip the Boat. I must say that you did it very nicely."

" Oh, I'm used to Boats," said the Tall Man with a Beard.

" Fisherman yourself, I shouldn't wonder," said the Fisherman rowing hard.

" That's right," said the Tall Man with a Beard.

When they reached the other side he got out of the boat without Tipping it and said:

" Now will you please wait for me and take me across again when I come back? "

"Well, don't you be long then!" said the Fisherman in a Surly sort of voice, and he settled down to wait in the Cold.

In a little while he saw a bright light in the Abbey. It was just as if someone had switched all the lights on. But they couldn't have because they didn't have Electric Light in those days.

The Fisherman was Rather Nervous.

" What *is* happening? " he said to himself. " It can't be on Fire because the light isn't Red enough! " The light got brighter and brighter, and then got Very Bright indeed!

The Fisherman was Frightened and hid under his Big Top Coat.

After a long time he heard the Tall Man with a Beard say:

" Hullo! Wake up! "

" I wasn't asleep! " said the Fisherman crossly, coming out from under the Top Coat. " What was that light that I saw in the New Abbey? "

" Did you see a light? " said the Tall Man. " I'm hungry, have you got anything to eat? "

" No! " said the Fisherman grumpily.

" Not even any Fish ?" asked the Tall Man.

" Look here! " said the Fisherman, " here I sit half the Night while you play tricks with the lights in the Abbey, and then you ask me if I've got any *Fish!* Nice lot of Fish I'm likely to get now, with the Day Breaking and all! " He banged the oars into the rowlocks and started off very Fast and Jerkily.

" Never you mind," said the Tall Man with a Beard, " have you got a net? "

" It's in that little Cupboard thing under where you're sitting," said the Fisherman.

The Tall Man got it out and let it down in the River, and by the time they had got back to the Lambeth side there were so many Fish in the net that it Nearly Broke!

The Fisherman was very Surprised, but he didn't say anything, and he waited to see what would happen next.

The Tall Man picked out the Biggest Fish and gave it to the Fisherman.

" Take this to the Bishop of London," he said, " and tell him that St. Peter gave it to you for him."

" Are *you* St. Peter? " said the Fisherman, all Astonished.

" Yes," said the Tall Man with a Beard, " and tell the Bishop that *I* have consecrated the New Abbey, and

that it is Dedicated to *me* like King Sigbert wanted. If he doesn't believe it, tell him to look in the Minster and see. I want him to say Mass there this very morning, so tell him as soon as you can before he gets up. You can keep the rest of the fish for your Trouble," and St. Peter vanished away!

So the Fisherman went to the Bishop of London's Palace and banged at the door.

" Who's that? " asked the Bishop of London, poking his head out of the window, " and what do you want at nearly Three o'Clock in the Morning? "

The Fisherman showed him the Big Fish and told him what St. Peter had said.

"Rubbish!" said the Bishop of London, "you've been Dreaming! Besides, I am going to Dedicate Westminster Abbey to St. Lawrence next week!"

"But it's *been* Dedicated!" said the Fisherman, "it has really! St. Peter did it himself! Do come and see!"

So the Bishop of London and the Fisherman walked together along the River Bank and over the River Fleet and along the sandy bit called the Strand to Westminster.

They went into the New Church and there, just inside the Door, was a Cross marked in some Sand!

"Dear me!" said the Bishop, "this is all very Odd!"

And they looked and saw the Twelve Crosses on the Walls and there were little drops of water everywhere where the Holy Water had been sprinkled!

"I do believe you are right after all!" said the Bishop of London.

"I know I am!" said the Fisherman.

So later in the Morning the Bishop said Mass in the new Abbey Church and in the Sermon he told everybody that St. Peter had come himself to Consecrate and Dedicate the Church!

A very long time after that, when the Church was getting rather old and shabby, King Edward the Confessor (who was a Saint) tidied it up and built a lovely new Tower. And that Tower is called St. Edward's Tower to this Very Day. And then, when it had been made all tidy again, King Sigbert's wish came True. Because a whole houseful of Benedictine Monks came to live there, and made it into St. Peter's Abbey, at Westminster, and you can see it any day you like, if you live in London. The Monks had a very big Garden for their Abbey to grow their Cabbages and Altar Flowers and things, and it is still one of the biggest

Flower Markets in the World. Only it is called Covent Garden now, instead of Convent Garden, like it used to be.

The Special Day belonging to this story is the Feast of St. Peter and St. Paul which is on June 29th. So the two biggest Churches in London both have the same day. There are Hundreds of Boys who are called after St. Peter and St. Paul, and even Girls are called Petronella and Petrina and Pauline and Paula.

ST. ANDREW

The only things that we really *know* about St. Andrew are in the Bible for anybody to read, and so I needn't tell you about *them*. But the Story that I am going to tell you is one that people used to tell each other and talk about Hundreds of years ago, and by now no one knows how much of it is True and how much of it is just a Story.

Well, one day Andrew was walking along the edge of the bottom part of France when he came to a town called Nice. (Which is a place where heaps of people go in the winter because it is nice and Sunny.) And he went into a Hotel to have some Lunch. When the waiter came along he said to Andrew:

"I take it, Sir, that you are a Stranger in these Parts?"

"Well, yes, I am," said Andrew. "Why do you want to know?"

"Well, I wanted to warn you, Sir," said the Waiter, putting a dish of Macaroni Cheese in front of Andrew (it was Friday), "there are Seven Devils who stay just outside the Town on the way to Cap d'Antibes, and they kill all the People who go along the road."

"What on earth for?" asked Andrew in a Surprised voice, and he put some salt on to the edge of his plate.

"Because they want the People's Souls," said the Waiter, flicking Andrew's table with his dinner napkin. "They choose the Wicked looking ones who haven't had time to go to Confession. I just wanted to Warn you."

ST. ANDREW

"Do you think that *I* look Wicked?" asked Andrew anxiously.

"No offence, I'm sure, Sir," said the Waiter Rather Nervously.

"And none taken," said Andrew kindly.

Andrew finished his Macaroni Cheese; said his Grace; folded up his Dinner Napkin; paid his Bill and started off along the road towards Cap d'Antibes.

When he came to the City Gates he shouted in a Very Loud Voice:

"Devils! Come here, I want to speak to you!"

The Devils looked at each other.

"What shall we Appear As?" they said. "Let's look Very Frightening."

"Do you suppose he is afraid of Dogs?" asked one.

"He might easily be," said another.

So they turned into seven Different Kinds of dogs, all Black and Snarling. There was a black growling Retriever; a black barking Aberdeen; a black slinking Greyhound; a black snapping Poodle; a black bristling Bulldog; a black menacing Great Dane; and a black treacherous Collie. And they all charged down the road at Andrew, looking as Frightening as they could!

When the front one (it was the bristling Bulldog) was only about a yard away Andrew said:

"Stop! In the Name of the Lord!"

The Devils all stopped very suddenly, and some of them skidded in the Dust. Andrew was much more Frightening for them than they were for Andrew!

"I command you to go away from here and *never* come back!" said Andrew.

And immediately the Seven Dogs vanished!

The people of Nice were so Astonished that they all became Christians at once, and Andrew had a Very Busy time Baptising them and asking them to Tea

23

to tell them how glad he was that they had stopped being Pagans.

When they were all settled down nicely Andrew thought that he had better be getting on to Cap d'Antibes. So one morning he set off, and everyone waved Good-bye.

As he came to the Gates of Cap d'Antibes he met a Funeral Procession, and he stopped the Chief Mourner to ask who was dead.

" It is my Only Son," said the Chief Mourner, " and now I shall never see him again! " (The people of Cap d'Antibes were Pagans and didn't believe in Heaven.)

" How did he die? " asked Andrew very sympathetically. " I am so very sorry for you."

" Well he just went outside the Other Side of the town for a walk," said the Chief Mourner, mopping up some Tears, " and Seven Black Dogs killed him! "

" *Seven Black dogs!* " said Andrew in a Tremendous Surprise; " were they all Fierce and all Different Kinds? "

" I don't know, I wasn't there! " said the Chief Mourner. " And anyway, what does it matter what they were like? "

" What will you give me if I make your son alive again? " asked Andrew.

" I haven't got anything very valuable," said the Chief Mourner, and as he was speaking he pulled his Overcoat round his Rich Diamond belt. " I'm a Very Poor Man."

" What about your Son, isn't *he* Valuable? " asked Andrew, who *had* seen the Diamond belt.

" Oh, you can have *him*! " said the Chief Mourner, " he was never much good to me. But can you really make him alive? "

" God will, if I ask Him to," said Andrew, and he Blessed the Chief Mourner's son, and he sat up and became a Christian and a disciple for Andrew; which was Very Useful because there was always such a lot to do.

Then Andrew went and found the Seven Devils and asked them what they Meant by it.

"You never said we mustn't come to Cap d'Antibes," said the Head Devil, "you only said to go away from Nice, and we did!"

"Well, go back to your Own Place then," said Andrew Sternly (He was sorry he hadn't thought of saying that before), "and never come back Anywhere!"

And that was the end of them!

Soon after this Andrew came to a place and converted the Wife of the Governor. The Governor, whose name was Ægeas, was so angry that he sent some soldiers to arrest Andrew. Then he sat on his Chair of Office and Glared at him.

"What d'you mean by it?" he growled. "Eh?"

"Well, she wanted to be a Christian, so I let her," said Andrew. "She just found out the Truth."

"Rubbish!" said Ægeas the Governor, "tell that to your Disciples! Now to-morrow morning at ten o'clock sharp you must come and offer a Sacrifice to the Gods in the Temple!"

"I offer a Sacrifice to God every morning," said Andrew; "I offer a Spotless Lamb which, after it has been given to all the people, is still Alive and Whole!" (He meant the Sacrifice of Mass, of course, but Ægeas didn't understand him.)

"Don't be Absurd," said Ægeas. "That is quite impossible. Explain to me what you mean!"

"You will never understand unless you become a Christian," said Andrew. "I wouldn't explain such a Holy Thing to a Pagan who might laugh at it. Will you be a Christian like your wife?"

"I *won't!*" screamed Ægeas in a Furious Temper because Andrew wouldn't tell him about the Sacrifice. "I'll Torture you until you tell me!"

And he ordered that Andrew should be scourged. After that he said: "Now will you tell me what you meant, and offer Sacrifice in the Temple?"

"I've already said that I do offer a Sacrifice every morning," said Andrew.

"Very well. You shall be Crucified like you say your God was," said Ægeas. He was trying to Frighten Andrew into telling him.

"Thank you," said Andrew. "That is the Greatest Honour that I could have. I will be proud to die in the same way as Our Lord."

"Well, just for that, you shan't!" said Ægeas spitefully. "I'll have your Cross made like an X, and so, you see, you *won't* die the way that you want to!"

"Our Lord doesn't mind the Shape," said Andrew.

And so he was crucified on a Cross made like an X. And it is still called St. Andrew's Cross.

Did you know that St. Andrew is the Patron Saint of Scotland? And Scotland's Flag is a Blue one with a White St. Andrew's Cross on it.

St. Andrew's Special Day is on November 30th, and there are heaps of people called after him, especially in Scotland. Anyone whose Birthday is on that day can have St. Andrew for their Special Saint as well as the one that they are named after.

ST. THOMAS

O nce upon a time there was a man called Thomas and he was one of Our Lord's Apostles. We don't know a great lot about him except what St. John tells us in his Gospel, so I'd better tell you what he says, first.

You remember after the Resurrection (when Our Lord had come alive again after being crucified), that He went to see the Apostles when they were all together? It was on Easter Sunday evening, when they were all sitting in one room. The doors were locked because they were afraid that the crowds of people who had wanted Our Lord to be crucified might want *them* to be, too.

Suddenly, while they were all sitting sadly there (I expect they were thinking and talking of Our Lord), there He was! No one had opened the door or anything, but He just came.

At first the Disciples were Rather Frightened because they didn't quite know whether it was Our Lord or not. So He showed them His hands where the nail marks were, and then they were all very glad that He had come back.

Now Thomas was not with them when Jesus came, and so the other Disciples said to him:

" We have seen the Lord."

But he said to them:

" Unless I actually see in His hands the marks of the nails, and feel the place in His side where the spear went in, I will not believe it was really Our Lord."

And eight days after that, they were all together indoors again and this time Thomas was with them. And Jesus came just as He did before, the doors still being shut, and He said to Thomas:

" Come and see my hands, Thomas, and come and feel my side, and don't be Faithless, but be Believing."

And Thomas looked at Jesus and he said:

" My Lord, and my God." Because he really knew, now.

And then Our Lord said:

" You have believed, Thomas, *because* you have seen me. Blessed are the people who have *not* seen me, and yet have believed."

(Have *you* seen? And do you believe? Well, you are one of those people that Our Lord was talking about. It is easy to believe a thing when you see it, isn't it?)

And that is all that St. John said about St. Thomas, when he was writing about all the things that happened in those days.

But there is another Story about him, and it is this . . .

One day, soon after Our Lord had gone back to Heaven, Thomas was walking in the Market Place and Wondering what he would Buy. He was just going to buy a Rubber Horse to go in the Bath of a Little Girl whose Uncle he was, when he saw a young Indian Man who was looking at all the Stalls with a very Worried Face.

" I suppose he can't find what he wants to buy," thought Thomas, "I'll just ask him, in case I might know of a Shop for him."

Then he said:

" What are you looking for, Young Man? "

" Well," said the Indian Man, " King Gundoferus of India wants me to find him someone who can help

28

him to build a New Palace. He's tired of the one he's got now, and all our Palace-builders have been used up because the King does not like the sort of Palaces they build."

"Now that's a Funny Thing," said Thomas, "as it happens, *I* can build Very Good Palaces. Shall I go back to India with you?"

Thomas was an Architect, did you know?

"Well, it would be a Very Good Thing," said the Indian Man, "only Christians aren't Very Popular Just Now in India. But I won't tell, and no one need know if we are very careful."

"All right," said St. Thomas, "I'll come." And they started off.

When they got to King Gundoferus' Palace in India it was Just On one o'clock. King Gundoferus met them at the door.

"How do you do?" he said, "it is just lunch time, the Second Gong was ringing as you came up the drive. We'll talk about the New Palace afterwards."

Well, before they'd had time for Much Discussion King Gundoferus was Called Away on Urgent Business. So he left £100,000 for Thomas so that he could be getting on with building a Very Expensive New Palace.

"I'll be away for three weeks," he said, "so I expect you'll be Getting on Nicely by the time I come back."

Well, instead of starting to buy Bricks and Marble and Gold for the New Palace, Thomas began building one in Heaven for the King out of kindnesses and things, so he gave *all* the money to Poor People who hadn't got any, and he made heaps of the King's subjects into Christians, and he mended the Hospital Roof which was leaking on to the Ill People inside, and he

Let Off some people who Simply Couldn't pay some very heavy Taxes.

When King Gundoferus came back in three weeks, he Sang Happily all the way home because of his Lovely New Palace that Thomas was making for him. And then he was Very Angry Indeed.

" You have used all that money on False Pretences! " he Roared. " I gave it to you for my Lovely New Palace, and you have Wasted it All! "

And he put Thomas in the Deepest Darkest Prison Cell while he thought of a Really Horrible way to kill him.

Now it happened that that evening the King's brother Died, and what with the Funeral and So On, the King forgot about Thomas for a few days. Well, one morning while he was out for his Walk, he met that very same brother who had Died!

" Goodness me! " said King Gundoferus in a Surprised Voice. " What *are* you doing here! "

" God made me Come Alive again to tell you that you mustn't kill Thomas," said the Brother.

" Well, but he Wasted all that money and he never even Started the New Palace," said Poor Cross King Gundoferus.

" Oh! yes he did, though," said the Brother, " because when I was in Heaven I saw a Gorgeous Palace, all Gold and Silver and Rich, and when I asked whose it was they said that it was one that Thomas had made for you."

" Was it really? " said King Gundoferus, All Astonished. " Let's get him out of Prison and see what he says about it."

So they got Thomas out. He was Rather Thin and Untidy with being there so long, but the King did not mind that.

ST. THOMAS

" I've seen that Palace that you made for Gundoferus,"
said the King's Brother, "and I want to buy one too."

" Perhaps it is the Only One there Is," said King
Gundoferus, " but if it is, you can share mine, if you
like."

" Thank you," said the King's Brother.

" That will be all right," said Thomas, " there will
be lots more, only you have to pay for them with
Kindnesses and Goodnesses, like giving things to Poor
People and mending Hospital Roofs and Keeping God's
Rules. It is better to have a Palace to wait for you in
Heaven, because however Stupendous a one you have
here, you can't take it with you when you die. So
you'd both better be Christians like me, and save up
Kindnesses and things for your New Palaces."

So they did.

St. Thomas's Special Day is December 21st and it
is the Shortest Day in the Year. I don't know why St.
Thomas had to have it, but I don't expect he minds.
And anyhow, in Australia it is the longest day.

St. Thomas the Architect

Build me a palace, St. Thomas, please,
And plant me a garden with flowers and trees.
I'll help my mummie and do as I'm told,
(Could I have door-knobs made of gold?)
I'll be good at school and give things away,
(Could I have some of my friends to stay?)
I'll wash my face and my ears as well.
(Could the trees have a beautiful smell?
Could I have puppies and parrots and cats?
And shiny floors with welcome mats?
If I learn to pray as hard as you,

31

Could I have bowls of hyacinths, too?)
And shall I be weeks in Purgatory first
All bothered and hot, with a terrible thirst,
Or can I be one of the martyrs and go
Straight to Our Lord, who loves me so?
Ask Him to let me, St. Thomas, please,
And get ready my palace, with flowers and trees.

ST. DENIS

Once upon a time there was a man called Denis and he lived in Greece and he was an Astronomer. An Astronomer is a man who knows about the Stars and the Sun and the Moon. He knows why they move round and which Star's Turn it is to be in the sky. People who live here and in the States never see Orion's Belt in the Summer. But people who live in South Africa do not see it in the Winter. Do you know Orion's Belt? Well, do you perhaps know the Great Bear? (Some people call it the Plough.) If you know how to find the Great Bear you can always tell where the North is even in the dark, because it shows you the North Star. (I believe that someone just now thought " Well, it's nothing to do with Denis, anyway. And I don't *know* what it's all about." But it sounds Interesting, don't you think? I am sure, if you are up late enough, that someone will show you the Great Bear. Or perhaps they will show you the Dog Star. Or Mars, a Red Star, or Venus, a Green Star. Ask and see! Perhaps you would rather see the Little Bear, or the Milky Way or try to count the Pleiades? What about the Twins, or Cassiopeia combing her Hair? Didn't you know that the Stars had names? Well, how would we know which was which, if they didn't?)

Anyway Denis Knew about Stars and Comets and Earthquakes and Eclipses and all that, and one thing puzzled him very much. One day there was a Total Eclipse when there shouldn't have been. So he wrote to a Friend of his who was an Astronomer too and asked him if he had seen it.

" Yes," wrote the Friend, " I did, and there was an Earthquake too. And on the Same Day there were no Stars seen in Egypt, even although there were no clouds. It is quite Impossible but it *did* happen. And another thing," said the Friend in his letter, " all these things happened at the same time that Jesus of Nazareth was crucified. Do you remember, a man called Paul was here a little time ago and told us about Him. I didn't take much notice at the time, did you? "

No, Denis hadn't taken much notice, he had been too busy being an Astronomer.

" It must have been one of the Gods who did it," he thought. (Denis was a Pagan, and so was his Friend.) " It couldn't have happened unless one of the Gods did it. I wonder which one? "

He walked up the street where he lived in a town called Athens and he looked at the Statues of the Gods that were there. Each statue had its name written underneath. There was Zeus, the chief of the Gods, and Phoebus the Sun God, and Artemis the Goddess of the Moon. Then there was Ares the God of War, and Ceres the Goddess of the Earth and the Harvest. Denis shook his head. None of these could have made Earthquakes *and* an Eclipse *and* a storm. He went on. There was the statue of Poseidon the God of the Sea, and of Hermes the Messenger of the Gods, and of Eros the God of Love.

" It must be a God we have never heard of," he thought, and then he had an idea.

" This God we don't know must be stronger than all the others," he thought, " and yet he hasn't got a Statue. I'll put up a Statue to him." And he went to a Carver that he knew and said:

" Please make me a Statue of a very Strong God who can make Eclipses and Earthquakes and Storms."

34

"Certainly," said the Carver. "What does he look like?"

"I don't know," said Denis. "I never thought of that."

"Well, I can't make a Statue of someone when I don't know what he looks like, now can I?" said the Carver.

"No, I don't suppose you can," said Denis. "I know!" he said. "Make a square stone thing and on it you can carve

'To the Unknown God'

Then the God, whoever he is, will know that we haven't forgotten him, even if we don't know who he is!"

So that is what the Carver did, and they put the square stone up in the street with the other statues and Denis went home to his wife whose name was Damaris, and settled down to being an Astronomer again.

Now, after a time Paul came back to Athens and while he was waiting for Silas and Timothy to come he wandered about the town looking at things. Everywhere he went he saw Statues of the Gods, and it made him crosser and crosser as the days went by. And whenever he could he argued with the people about it. At last someone said:

"Why don't you come up the hill to the place where all the clever people live? There are doctors and priests and astronomers and lawyers and people like that. They will know how to argue with you better than we do." So Paul went up the hill and the clever men came out to see who it was.

"What is it?" they said. "Who is it?" "What is he talking about?" "He sounds like a foreign missionary."

At last, one of them went up to Paul and said:

" Will you please tell us what you are talking about? If it's something New we would like to know about it."

And Paul looked at all the clever men and he said:

" Well, as a matter of fact I am feeling a bit Annoyed because, although you are Clever people, you seem to have done a Silly Thing. You are very religious people, I know, because I've been looking at all your Statues and yet, do you know, I actually found a stone with

' To the Unknown God '

written on it? Now if you don't know who he is, how can you worship him? And if you *do* know, why say he is Unknown? The God you mean is the God who made the world and everything in it. He cannot be a Statue. He made all the people and all the Nations from one Family. He made the Spring, the Summer, the Autumn and the Winter. He made the Day and the Night, the Stars and Sun and Moon. He made the hundreds and thousands of people and then he waited for them to find him. He was never very far away."

And so he taught them about God the Father and about God the Holy Ghost and he told them about God the Son who became a Man so that we might know him and so that he might save us from all the sins and sillinesses we had done. And he told them about the Crucifixion of God the Son and the Eclipse and the Earthquake and the Storm that happened at the same time. And some of the people had heard it all before, but some of them hadn't.

Then as Paul looked round at the crowd, he saw Denis whom he had met some time ago. And after his sermon he went to Denis and said:

" Denis, could I come and have some Supper with you ? "

" Of course you can," said Denis. " Damaris was shopping this morning so there will be plenty for all of us." And they started off down the hill to walk to Denis's house.

As they walked along Paul said:

" Denis, what *is* all this about the Unknown God? "

" Well," said Denis, " you see, he is a God who does not live with the other Gods, as far as I know, and one that we know nothing about. He is very strong and mighty."

And Paul said:

" Is he a Man or is he a Spirit? "

" He is Man *and* Spirit," said Denis, " but he is too Great and Wonderful for us to know like the other Gods. That's why I had that Unknown Statue. Did you know that it was I that had it made? "

" No," said Paul. " But Denis, this Unknown God is the very God that I teach about. He is the God who came from Heaven and became a Man."

But Denis could not believe this yet, and while they were still talking about it a Blind Man came along the road and Denis said to Paul:

" If in the Name of your God you say to this blind man ' See ' and he *does* see, then I will believe everything that you have been telling me." (If you say anything in the name of anyone else you say it *for them*. If you are too busy to go and buy a railway ticket, I could go and buy it for you In Your Name. So if you say something in the Name of God it means that, whatever it is, you *know* that God will do it. But what about the Commandment " You must not take the Name of God in Vain? " Well, that means that you mustn't say " In the Name of God " for a nonsense, or for a naughty and wrong thing. Because God wouldn't do a wrong thing, so it would be a Sin for you to take his Name for

it. Suppose somebody went to a house and stole a pound of butter and the owner of the butter caught him.

" Why are you taking my butter? " he would say.

" I am taking it in the Name of Joan Windham," he might say. " It isn't for me, or anything to do with me."

Well, I would be *Furious!* Because I wouldn't steal anybody's butter, and I wouldn't tell anyone else to do it. Do you understand? So when you say " In the Name of the Father and of the Son and of the Holy Ghost," do you ever stop to think what it means? If you say or do a thing in God's Name, it is something that God would like to do, or would like *you* to do.)

So when Denis said that to Paul about the Blind Man, Paul said:

" Yes, of course I will."

" But," said Denis, " you mustn't use any Magic Words (because you might know some). *Only* in the Name of your God. Then I'll know he is True."

" I'll tell you what," said Paul, " I'll write down the words and *you* shall say them. Then you will be sure that there is no Jiggery Pokery."

" That is a very Good Idea," said Denis.

So Paul wrote on a piece of paper:

" In the Name of Jesus Christ I tell you to See," and he gave the piece of paper to Denis. So Denis took the paper and he went up to the Blind man.

" Blind man," he said, " in the Name of Jesus Christ I tell you to See."

" *Oh Thank you,* Sir! " said the Blind Man. " It has been twenty-three years since I saw anything. Now I can see the Sky and the trees and the people and the houses and the birds. Oh Thank you *very* much, Sir! "

" There! " said Paul. " What did I tell you? "

" I believe in everything you have taught," said Denis. " May I be a Christian? "

" Yes," said Paul. " Shall we wait until after supper and then we can tell Damaris all about it too."

So after supper Paul talked to Denis and his wife Damaris and they asked him questions until Paul was sure that they knew what they thought.

Then they were baptized and were Christians. Not very long after this Damaris caught her Death of Cold and after her funeral Denis went to learn to be a priest.

St. Denis's Special Day is October 9th, and people in every Christian country are called after him. St. Denis is the Patron Saint of France, and anyone called Denise or Deniston or even Tennyson can have him for their own Saint.

ST. ALEXANDER

Once upon a time there was a forest in Roumania (it is still there for all I know) but anyway at the time that I am talking about there lived in the forest a man called Alexander, and people sometimes called him Alex for short.

Alexander was a Charcoal Burner and he used to collect little twigs and thin branches from the trees in the forest and he made little fires and burnt the sticks very slowly so that they turned into black sticks called Charcoal. (If he was in too much of a hurry they turned into White Ashes instead and he would have to begin all over again.)

People use charcoal for quite a lot of things. They draw with it, and make fires with it, and use it for medicine, and make shoe polish with it. So you can see what a useful job Alexander had.

The place where Alexander found the best sort of sticks was right in the middle of the forest, so to save time, he lived there all alone in a little house that he had built for himself. He was very poor because people paid him very little for his charcoal and he always had black smudges of charcoal on his face and hands. (Most people who work with coal or chimneys or charcoal get Black and Dirty. People who work with flour or lime or cement get White and Dusty. But it all washes off and is the sort of dirt called Clean Dirt.)

So Alexander looked after his little fires by himself all day and he learned to be very Patient because if he was Impatient his charcoal would turn into ashes. In a quiet job like that the birds and the animals get used to the person who is working and take no notice. Alexander saw Baby squirrels playing, and mother foxes taking their cubs to roll in the sun and all kinds of things that we never see. It made him think how quiet and patient God must be.

"Here is this enormous forest," he thought to himself, " and it is full of living things; plants and animals and birds and insects. They all lead busy lives, not one of them is lazy and yet very few people even know that they are there! There must be hundreds of them that are too shy even for me to see. And yet God knows all about them and what they do all day. He never frightens them however near he is because he is so Still."

While Alexander was quietly living in the forest and burning his charcoal and thinking about God and watching the Birds and Animals there were great Goings On in the town where he sold his charcoal. And this is what was happening:

At first there had been very few Christians in the town, but as time went on there were more and more until at last the priest said that they really ought to have a Bishop of their own instead of belonging to a Bishop called Gregory who lived a very long way off and scarcely ever had time to come and see them. So it was decided that Bishop Gregory should come and that everybody should say which priest they wanted to be the new Bishop. Well some wanted This priest and some wanted That priest and some didn't know whom they wanted but they didn't want either of Those. At last they collected seven priests who wanted to be the Bishop and they wrote and told Gregory that they wanted him to come and choose.

The Town Hall was all ready with a Throne at the end of it for Bishop Gregory and chairs and seats for all the people. When everyone was settled the First man who might be the Bishop came in. He was tall and thin with a big nose and a very Grand expression. He looked at the crowds of people as if they were too Common for Words. The people who wanted him to be the Bishop clapped and cheered as he went and stood in front of Gregory.

" Do you think that you would be a good Bishop? " asked Gregory.

" I am sure I would," said the man.

" I think that you are too Proud," said Gregory. " Next please! "

The Second man had silk clothes and a jewelled crucifix, and he had a rosary made of real rubies in his hand.

" Would you keep all those lovely things for yourself, if you were the Bishop? " asked Gregory.

" Of course I should. They are my own property," said the man, and he held them a little tighter.

" You are too Covetous, I think," said Gregory. (Covetous is selfish and miserly.) " Next please! " said Gregory.

The Third man had the gayest coloured clothes and a smiling face and beautiful curly hair. He winked at all the people and the ladies clapped their hands because he was so handsome.

" Do you want people to go on thinking that you are handsome and clever when you are the Bishop? " asked Gregory.

" But of course! " said the man, and he looked quickly at the people to see if they were listening. " Even a Bishop must have his bit of fun."

" I think that you are too fond of Pretty Ladies," said Gregory. " Next please! "

The Fourth man had black hair and a frowning face. He stared at the people angrily and then went and stood in front of Gregory. The people who wanted him clapped for him but he shook his head at them and they stopped.

" If you were the Bishop, would you be Strict with the people and punish them severely if they broke the rules? " asked Gregory.

"I would," said the man. "They are a lazy, sinful lot, but I'd not put up with any of their nonsense! " And he glared at Gregory.

" You get Angry too easily," said Gregory. " Next please! "

The Fifth man was very fat indeed, but he looked kindly at the people and he waved his hand at the ones who wanted him. As he stood in front of Gregory he pulled a buttered bun out of his pocket and began to eat it. " Excuse me! " he said.

" Couldn't you have waited until after the Choosing before you ate your bun? " asked Gregory.

" Not me! " said the man, " I wouldn't miss my tea for any man on earth. It keeps a man good-tempered to be fat."

" I think that you are too Greedy," said Gregory. " Next please! "

The Sixth man was thin and mean-looking, he did not look happy. He stared at all the priests who had already seen Gregory. (They were standing at the back of the Throne and waiting to see who would be Chosen.)

" Well," said Gregory, " what is the matter? Aren't you happy? Don't you want to be Bishop after all? "

" No good me wanting," said the man. " I've no good looks like that man over there, or riches like that one, or a nice house like that one, or a kind family

43

like that one. I never get the things that Other People have."

"You are too Envious to be happy," said Gregory. (Envious is being so jealous of other people's things that you haven't time to see what nice things you have yourself.) "Next please!" said Gregory.

But no one came.

"Next please!" said Gregory, looking round. "I thought that you said that there were seven people who wanted to be the Bishop," he whispered to the Mayor who was standing beside him. "I've only seen six."

"NEXT PLEASE!!" shouted the Mayor, and all the people laughed. Then the door banged and in came an untidy man with ruffled hair and his shoes undone. He was yawning and rubbing his eyes.

"Sorry, my Lord," he said to Gregory. "As I was the last one I thought that I'd have a nap while I was waiting and I didn't hear you call."

"Do you always have naps when you can?" asked Gregory.

"Always, my Lord," said the man solemnly, "a man can't have too much sleep, I always say."

"I think that you are too Lazy," said Gregory.

All the people rustled and coughed and sat up and shuffled their feet. They stared at Gregory and waited for him to say which of the seven priests would be the Bishop.

"Well," said Gregory, and he looked round at all the people, "I am sorry but I don't think that any of them would do for a Bishop."

The people started talking among themselves and then someone shouted:

"But we must have one of them! There isn't anyone else!"

"No," said Gregory. "They may not be so bad as ordinary people go but they're no good for Bishops. You couldn't have a Bishop who was Proud or Greedy or Lazy or any of the other Seven Deadly Sins, now could you?"

"You're too Choosey," said the people. "You can't have a Perfect man."

"No," said Gregory, "but he ought to try to be Perfect, and these men don't."

All the people started arguing again, and in the noise Gregory said to God:

"Please, God, if you really want a Bishop here, will you choose one for yourself? It is very difficult for me with all these seven, and the people are getting so cross."

Just then someone shouted:

"You'd better have Alexander the Charcoal Burner if you can't think of anyone better!"

All the people laughed because they couldn't imagine having sooty, raggy Alexander for a Bishop!

But Gregory knew that this was God's answer to his prayer and so he held up his hand for the people to stop laughing and said:

"Who is this Alexander?"

"I was only joking," said the man who had shouted. "He is a Charcoal Burner and he lives in the forest."

"Will somebody please go and get him?" said Gregory.

The people all stared. What *was* Gregory thinking about? Did he really mean to see if Alexander would do? Yes, he did. So Alexander was brought along. First he washed the black marks off his face and hands, then he went to Bishop Gregory and knelt and kissed his ring. Then he stood up and waited to see why the Bishop had sent for him.

" Alexander," said Gregory, " do you think that you would be a good Bishop? "

" *Me*, my Lord? " said Alexander; " no, I have no learning, I don't know anything at all."

" Would you like a Rosary made of Rubies? "

" Why, no thank you, my Lord," said Alexander, " I have a very nice wooden one, it will last me my lifetime."

" Do you like Parties and Pretty Ladies? "

" I don't know any," said Alexander. " I've never been asked to a Party myself but a bit of fun now and then is good for everybody." He wondered why Gregory was asking him all these questions in front of the townspeople.

" Do you think that the Townspeople are a lazy sinful lot? " asked Gregory.

" Oh no, my Lord, please don't think that! There's good in everyone if you look for it." Alexander had quite forgotten how mean the people were in paying for their charcoal.

" Have you had your Tea yet? " asked Gregory.

" I don't have it as a rule," said Alexander, " only when it is raining and I can't burn my charcoal. I eat when I am hungry and that does me nicely."

" Are you happy? " asked Gregory. " Have you everything that you want? "

" I'm very happy, my Lord," said Alexander. " I love my work, I have enough to eat, I have my own little house and God is good to me."

" Would you change your work for something quite different? " asked Gregory.

" I would if God wished it," said Alexander.

Gregory stood up. He walked down the steps of his throne and put his arm round Alexander's shoulders.

" Here is your new Bishop," he said to the people.

ST. ALEXANDER

At first they all sat with their mouths open. Surely it could not be true! Surely the Bishop was having a joke with them! Then, as they began to think, they saw that Alexander was just the opposite to all the other seven, and they looked at Alexander. And looking at him they loved him.

So Alexander the Charcoal Burner became a Bishop and he was one for years and years but in the end he was a Martyr.

St. Alexander's Special Day is on August 11th. And people called Alec or Alex or even Sandy may belong to him. There are lots of them in Scotland.

ST. CYRIL

O nce upon a time there was a boy and his name was Cyril and he was Twelve and his family were Pagans. Now some Pagans do not bother the Christians at all because they don't care One Way or the Other, but others hate Christians because they are jealous of them and think that they might have something *they* haven't got. Cyril's family were the Hating kind.

One day when Cyril was coming home from School he heard a lot of voices talking in the Christian Church. He was an Inquisitive boy, and so he put his head round the door to see what was going on. He saw a crowd of people of all Ages and all Sizes listening to a priest and asking questions. He slipped in and sat near the door to listen.

"None of these people seem to know much," he thought. "What silly questions they ask. Christians don't seem to know what they think." After a time he felt Brave and he said:

"Please may *I* ask a question?"

"Of course," said the Priest.

"Well," said Cyril, "why are these Christians so Ignorant?" (Ignorant is not knowing anything.)

"Because they're Pagans," said the Priest, smiling.

"But they're in a Christian Church!" said Cyril.

"Well, so are you, come to that," said the Priest.

"But *I* only came in to see what was Going On," said Cyril.

"So did they," said the Priest, and all the people laughed quietly to each other and then began asking

48

questions again and the Priest answered them. Cyril listened for a while, but he was so Surprised at finding a Christian Church full of Pagans that he couldn't Pay Attention so he went home to Tea.

After a few days, he called in again at the Church and listened and began to ask questions himself. He became more and more interested and at last asked the priest if he could be a Christian.

" Why? " asked the Priest.

" Because Christianity Makes Sense," said Cyril. " It really does, and I should like to know Our Lord better. I feel as though I know Him a bit already."

" I expect you do," said the Priest, " and yet he has known you very well indeed ever since you were born."

So Cyril was Baptised and then, after a lot more Questions and Answers, he made his First Communion. He was so happy that he could scarcely believe it.

But one day somebody who had seen him going in and out of the Church told his father about it.

" Cyril a Christian? " said the father. " No, that isn't possible. He is a sensible child and very obedient. But we'll soon find out."

Now in a few days' time there was a great Feast Day for the Pagans, and they all went to their Temples and offered sacrifices to their gods. But Cyril asked to be excused.

" I don't want to go," he said.

" Why? " said his father. " Come along. It doesn't last very long and then you can go swimming or what-ever it is that you want to do."

" Well," said Cyril, " I might as well tell you now that I am a Christian and have been one for some Months."

His father was very Angry and very Upset, and told Cyril he must find somewhere else to live because he

would not let him live at home any more. So Cyril
went out into the town to find Somewhere to live
and he asked people he met if they knew of anywhere
for him.

In less than No Time the Governor of the town heard
all about what had happened and sent for Cyril. " Because," he thought, " if I am kind to him he may become
a Pagan again and he most certainly will not if I behave
as his father did."

So when Cyril came the governor gave him a comfortable chair and a nice meal and explained how silly all
this Christian business was.

" Why worship a man who was simply a wise Carpenter," he said, " and a foreign one at that, a Jew?
You were interested and you liked all the other people
you met in the Church, and so you wanted to be like
them. Isn't that right? "

" It was at first, perhaps," said Cyril, " but now that
I have got to know Jesus I can't just think of him as a
foreign carpenter because I know He is God."

" My *dear* boy! " said the Governor, quite shocked.
" What an Extraordinary remark! Now you take my
advice and forget all about it. Then you can go back
to your Mother and your lovely home, eh? "

Cyril thought about his Mother. He loved her and
when he had last seen her she was crying because he
had been Turned Out.

" But I *can't!* " he said sadly to the Governor, " because I'm not just Pretending. I really do know that
Jesus is God and however much I said he wasn't it
wouldn't make it any different."

" Well," said the Governor, " the pity of it is that
there is a Law about Obstinate Christians. You know
that? "

" Yes," said Cyril. " I am not afraid of being Dead,

because I'll be living in Heaven, but I expect I'll be afraid of Actually Dying."

"I expect you will," said the Governor, "and that will bring you to your Senses, I hope."

So he ordered his Minions to light a very hot and blazing Bonfire. And he tied Cyril's hands behind his

back and told a man to take him to the fire and stand him where it was Much Too Hot. After a minute or two he called him back and when Cyril was standing in front of him again he said:

" Well? "

" It was not Kind, to do that," said Cyril. " I mean to bring me back."

" Why? " said the Governor.

" Because I'd just got ready to be a Martyr and God was helping me to be Brave. Now I'll have to start all over again, and it isn't easy. Kill me quickly and let me go to God."

So they threw Cyril into the middle of the Bonfire and in a very short time he saw Our Lord and knew that it was All True.

But the crowds of people who had been watching were sad, and cried to see a little boy being Martyred so bravely, and that made some of them find out Why. So, you see, Martyrs do not only save their own Souls, but Other People's.

St. Cyril's Special Day is May 29th. There are two or three other St. Cyrils, but you can read about them another time.

ST. STEPHEN

Once upon a time there was a man called Stephen, and he was the Pope. Once upon the same time there was an Emperor called Valerian. (I don't know whether Valerian was called after the flower or the flower was called after Valerian, but it doesn't really matter, and anyway I always call the flower Kiss-me-quick.)

Valerian wanted to have a War with someone, because he had been training his soldiers for years, and they were quite Excellent, and it seemed such a Waste not to use them. But try how he would he couldn't find anyone who would fight with him, and he was in Despair! You remember that Pagans like Valerian was said that there were lots of Gods? Can you Imagine? They had a God of the Sun called Apollo and a Goddess of the Moon called Diana, and a God who made Thunderbolts and things called Vulcan, and a God of War called Mars. Well, Valerian and his Minions (Minions are people who run about and do things) had been praying and praying to their God of War called Mars and burning Incense for him so that he would find them someone to fight with. But nothing happened, and you know why, don't you? Yes, because there is only one God, and there isn't such a person as Mars. It was rather like knocking and *knocking* on a door and waiting and *waiting* for someone to open it, and it is so sad for you because there is no one there, but you don't know that, and so you go on knocking.

At last one of the Minions said:

" What about that old Stephen who calls himself a Pope? The Christians say that if he prays to their God he often has his prayers answered."

" I don't Hold with Christians," said Valerian, " and I've been meaning to capture Stephen and his people for simply Ages."

"Well," said the Head Minion, " supposing we catch him and make him pray to Mars for us. If Mars still doesn't answer we can Kill Off old Stephen." (You do remember that Stephen was the Pope, don't you?)

" What an excellent Plan! " said Valerian, all Pleased. " Whoever captures Stephen can have his house and all his things. And whoever captures any of his friends can have any of their things! "

The next day the Minions started looking for Stephen because he was the most Important Christian, and they found him writing in his study.

" Come along, Stephen! " they said rudely, " you've got to come with us."

" Why? " asked Stephen, looking up from his writing.

" Because Mars won't listen to us, and Valerian wants you to come because you are good at Praying."

" Not to Mars, I'm not," said Stephen, and he picked up his pen again.

" Now then! " said the Top Minion, " orders is orders, and the Emperor Valerian's orders are that you are to go to him."

" Oh," said Stephen, " you didn't say that before." And because the Emperor was the most Important Person in the Land, and to avoid trouble, Stephen went with the Minions Quietly so as not to make an agitation among the Christians.

When they got to Valerian they found that he was waiting for them in the Temple of Mars, and crowds of Pagans had come to see the Pope of the Christians Praying to the God of War.

Valerian explained to Stephen what it was he wanted.

"You must ask Mars to make people want to fight us," he said; "we want a War."

Stephen knew that he was sure to be Killed anyway, because Valerian didn't hold with Christians, but he loved Our Lord very much, and he couldn't possibly pray to a False God.

"Go on!" said Valerian. "We are all waiting!" And the Minions who were holding Stephen pushed him down until he was kneeling in front of the Statue of Mars, and the people laughed to see the Pope of the Christians kneeling to one of their Gods.

Stephen made the Sign of the Cross and began to pray:

"Please, dear God," he said, "you see what is happening to me, and I am sorry I am kneeling in front of Mars, but I can't help it. *Please* could you do something to show these people that you are the only real living God, and that Mars is only a False God? I would not trouble you, only there is nothing that I can do myself alone."

And God listened to Stephen, and what do you think He did?

All of a sudden there was a great Cracking and Tearing and Rumbling noise, and all the people looked up just in time to see the roof fall in and the heaviest piece fell right on to the Statue of Mars and squashed it into little crumbs! Most of the people were killed, but not Valerian or Stephen.

Stephen got up and brushed the dust off his clothes and walked home. All the way he was thanking God for His wonderful help. "And surely," he said, "that must show the Pagans who is the Real God."

55

ST. STEPHEN

Next Day was Sunday, and all the Christians, of course, went to Mass, but they hadn't got proper Churches because of Valerian and his Minions, and they used to have their Churches down in the Catacombs. (Do you remember the story of St. Philomena? In case you don't, the Catacombs were big underground caves and passages, and the Christians used to have their churches and chapels down there and their Baptisms and their Marriages, and they were buried there, and sometimes they even lived there. And because it was underground and Dark they used a lot of candles, especially on the Altar, so that the priest could see what he was reading. And that is one of the reasons why we have Candles on our Altars, even in the bright daylight, to remind us how much luckier we are than the Early Christians.)

Stephen had just got up to the Sermon, and he was telling the people about Baptism when in came Valerian's Minions!

" What do you mean by walking off like that? " they said angrily. " First you Ruin our temple, and then you make us look for you all over again! Come along at once!"

"I can't," said Stephen. "I am in the middle of Mass."

" *We* don't mind," said one of the Minions.

" But God does, and so do I, and so do all the people who have come to Mass," said Stephen, " and so I am afraid that you will have to Wait."

Now when Stephen mentioned God the Minions felt a bit nervous. They remembered what had happened to Mars, and so they stood rather Grumpily at the back of the Cave, and they watched Stephen go on with Mass and give the people Holy Communion and then finish.

57

"I say," whispered one of the Minions, "I think that there might be something in what all these people believe. It looks as if they really love their God."

"Stephen isn't a bad old man, really," said one of the other Minions, "it is a pity that Valerian hates the Christians."

"We will have to kill him, whatever we think," said the first Minion. "Valerian is sure to Torture him, after yesterday."

"I know what," said one of the Minions, "let's kill him here. It would be nicer for him, and then we can leave his body for his people to bury." And that is what they decided to do. So when Mass was finished the Head Minion went up to Stephen.

"I am sorry, Sir," he said, "that we interrupted your Mass, but we really do have to kill you because Valerian is our Emperor and he says so."

"Oh, yes," said Stephen, "I quite see that."

"But we thought," said the Minion, "that perhaps we could kill you here and now, with your own people, so that you needn't go back to Valerian."

"How kind of you!" said Stephen. "May I just go to Confession first?"

"Anything you like," said the Minions, and they waited while Stephen went to Confession. When he was ready he went and sat on his Pope's Throne and the Minions came very Politely and cut off his head, and all the people cried. But Stephen went straight to God and thanked Him very much indeed for letting him die so quickly and easily.

"Well," said God, "you are a good old man, Stephen, and you were really very Brave, what with one thing and another. Do you know that those Minions are going to be Christians because they stayed to Mass?"

"*Are* they?" said Stephen. "*Well* now!"

ST. STEPHEN

St. Stephen's Special Day is on August 2nd. And although he is not by any means the only St. Stephen, I thought that I'd tell you about him because most books are about one of the others. Is your Birthday on August 2nd?

ST. LAURENCE

Once upon a time there was an Archdeacon called Laurence, and he lived with his Mother whose name was Patience. An Archdeacon is a Top Deacon (like an Archbishop is a Top Bishop and an Archangel or Arch-Angel is a Top Angel). A deacon looks after things generally for a Bishop and that is what Laurence did. He looked after all the Money of the Church and he Handed it Out to anyone who hadn't got any. There wasn't very much in the way of Treasure because the Christians were always having their Money Taken Away from them by Greedy Pagans. (Pagans are people who don't want Anything to Do With Our Lord.) And in those days there were a Good Many People who were All Against Christians. Another Job of Laurence's was to look after all the poor ill Christians and the Widows-and-Orphans. The Church had lots of these and she had them for her Treasure instead of Money because she liked them better.

Now it happened one day that the Governor (who was a Pagan, and did not Hold with Christians) heard about Laurence and his Job, and he said to himself:

" Why should those Christians have any Money? I believe they must have got Thousands of Pounds hidden away somewhere." (They hadn't really, but the Governor Thought that they Might.)

So he sent for Laurence and he said:

" I hear you are the Keeper of the Church's Money."

" Yes," said Laurence, " I am. And I look after all the Poor Ill ones and the Widows-and-Orphans."

"Never mind them," said the Governor, waving his hand at Laurence. "I only want to know about the Money. Where did you get it from?"

"Well," said Laurence, "they all come up with their little lot, and when we put it all together it makes a Bigger Lot."

"Oh," said the Governor, "well, you can't have it any more because I want it to pay some Bills. So give it up."

"But it belongs to the Church, not to me," said Laurence, "*I* can't give you someone else's money, now, can I?"

"Well, if you don't," said the Governor in a Frenzy, "I'll take you Prisoner for being a Christian, and *then* what will you do?"

"I'll just have to Lump it, I suppose," said Laurence. (Lumping it is when you have to Put Up with something that makes you Heavy and Sad, like a Lump of something.)

"Well," said the Governor in a Smoothing kind of voice, "just let me *see* the Treasure. Only *see* it." (Then he was going to Steal it!)

"All right," said Laurence, "I'll show you the Church's Treasure, only it will take two days to Collect it All into One Place."

"Mind you collect it All, and don't have a Secret Store, then," said the Governor, and he went off to Lunch, rubbing his hands with Glee, and Chuckling Fat Chuckles.

Then Laurence's Guardian Angel put a Good Idea into Laurence's head; the Good Idea was a trick to play on the Governor!

So Laurence went round to all the Christians in the Town and collected all the Ill People and the Poor-and-Raggy People and the Widows-and-Orphans that there were, and they all went and sat in the Governor's Garden and Waited. Laurence went into the house and called the Governor:

" Where are you, Governor? "

" Upstairs changing my shoes," shouted the Governor, " who is it and what do you want? "

" It's Laurence with the Church's Treasure," said Laurence, very Loud, " are you coming down? "

" Oh, it's you, is it? " shouted the Governor. " Well, you'll have to wait till I do up this button, it's Rather Stiff."

So Laurence waited.

Soon the Governor came downstairs.

" Well? " he said, puffing out his cheeks, " where's your Famous Treasure? I've got some Sacks to put it in. You didn't Really think that I only wanted to See it, did you? "

Laurence laughed in his sleeve, and pointed out of the Window.

" There's the Treasure of the Church! " he said. " Our Lord's favourite things are Poor-and-Raggies and Widows-and-Orphans, so the Church has them for her most special thing, too."

The Governor flew into a Black and Thundering Fury. He had quite thought that he was going to get a great deal of money!

He called his Minions (Minions are people who run about and do things), and told them to throw Laurence into prison. So they threw him in, and left him.

That night, when Laurence was asleep in prison, God gave him a dream, and this was the dream:

He saw Our Lord walking about among all the Ill People that he looked after, and Our Lord said:

" Laurence, would you like to come and live with me, now? "

"I'd love to more than Anything," said Laurence, "but what about all my Ill People?"

"I'll look after them for you," said Our Lord, "but if you come, I'm afraid you'll have a Horrid Time to-morrow."

"Why?" asked Laurence.

"Because you will be Burned Alive until you are Dead," said Our Lord. "The Governor is angry with you for playing a Christian trick on him, but it won't last very long and then you can stay with me for ever and ever and ever."

"I do hope I'll be Brave," said poor Laurence, and then he woke up.

After Breakfast the Prison Keeper came in and said:

"Laurence, the Governor wants you."

"All right," said Laurence, and he went with the Prison Keeper.

"Good morning, Laurence," said the Governor, "I've decided what to do with you."

"Good morning, Governor," said Laurence, "I know: you're going to Burn me Alive until I am Dead."

"How did you know that?" said the Governor, All Astonished.

"Because Our Lord told me, in a dream," said Laurence, "so be quick, please, because I want to go to Heaven."

The Governor took him out into the Garden where Laurence had played the trick, and there was a huge fire all ready laid! Beside it was Patience, Laurence's Mother, who had heard what was going to happen and had come to pray for him and Cheer him Up.

"You're going to be Roasted," said the Governor, "unless, of course, you like to stop being a Christian and be a Pagan, like me?"

"Roasted *alive*?" asked Laurence. He felt very

Frightened, because, although he knew that he would be in Heaven in a little while, when he thought of being Roasted Alive, he thought he Simply Couldn't be brave. I wonder if *I* would be Brave, or if *you* would? It's never easy, being a Martyr.

Anyway, they put Laurence on a thing like a Bed without any mattress or bedclothes, and they put it over the Fire, which one of the Minions had lit.

"Please, dear Lord, make me Brave so that I won't say I'll stop being a Christian," said poor Laurence, "because I don't *want* to say it, but if it hurts too much, I might."

Suddenly he felt Very Brave and he said to the Minions:

"Do you know, I think that I am cooked enough on this side, would you please Turn me Over? I'm sorry to be such a bother, but I'm too Burnt to do it myself."

Our Lord *had* made him Brave, hadn't he?

So the Minions Turned him Over and he said:

"Good-bye, Mummy, I'm just going."

"Good-bye, darling," said Patience, "I won't be very long coming after you." And Laurence died and went straight to Heaven and Our Lord met him.

"You *were* Brave!" said Our Lord, "I know that it hurt Frightfully."

"That's the worst part of being a Martyr," said Laurence, "but I'm glad I was one, now," and he went and talked to all the Other Martyrs and they told him all the things that had happened to *them* before *they* got to Heaven.

As soon as Laurence had gone, the Governor said to Patience:

"What did you mean when you said that you would not be long going after him? You don't mean to say that a Sensible Woman like *you* is a Christian?"

64

" Yes, that's why I'm sensible," said Patience.

" Well, I'm sorry, but there's No Alternative," said the Governor, and he called his Minions again and they threw Patience into Prison so hard that she broke her neck and she got to Heaven very soon after Laurence.

St. Laurence's Special Day is on August 10th, and I know a lot of people called after him, especially one whose Other Name is Michael. And St. Patience's Special Day is May 1st, and more than a few people are called after her, too.

ST. FELIX

Once upon a time there was a man who was a Syrian, because he lived in Syria. (Where does a Frenchman live? And an Arab? And an American? And a Swiss? And a Norwegian? Right.) Well this man was a Syrian because he lived in Syria, which is next door to Palestine.

Now the Syrian had two sons, and one of them when he grew up was a Soldier, and the other, whose name was Felix, was a Priest. He was the special priest belonging to the Bishop and he went with him everywhere. He found places to eat in and to sleep in when the Bishop was visiting round the Churches and he looked after the Bishop himself because he was very old.

At this time the Emperor did not like the Christians and, as so often happened, there was a Persecution. (Persecuting is treating people cruelly and attacking and hunting them.)

Well, the persecution was so bad that the people said that their old Bishop must go away and hide in the mountains until things were better again.

" But I can't leave you," said the poor old Bishop. " It wouldn't be Right."

" Yes, you must go," said the people, " because we would rather have you Alive in the mountains than Dead down here with us. So do go, my Lord, and then we will tell you when it is safe for you to come back. Felix will look after us for you. He knows all your ways."

66

So Felix packed up a few things for the Bishop and one of the Christians took him in his fruit and vegetable van to the mountains, where he started off with his bundle to find a cave or somewhere to live.

After a few days the Emperor's Soldiers came to the town.

" Where is the Bishop? " asked the Captain.

" We don't know," said the people, and it was quite true because they didn't know exactly where in the mountains the Bishop was by now.

Felix came out of the school to see what all the noise and crowd was about.

" Who is that? " shouted the Captain, pointing at Felix.

" I am Felix," said Felix.

" What work do you do? " said the Captain. " You are a Priest and you know where the Bishop is! "

" I do my own work," said Felix, " and I don't know where the Bishop is."

" Take him away! " shouted the Captain, " all Priests are Scoundrels. He'll tell us soon enough when he has been in prison for a bit! "

So the Soldiers took Felix away and scourged him and chained his hands together and threw him down the steps into a dark damp prison cell.

Felix lay at the bottom of the steps. He felt very ill and for a long time he kept his eyes shut and did not move. Then he thought:

" What a good thing that the Bishop went away! The poor old man would have died if all this had happened to him." And he thanked God for letting him be the one to save the Bishop for the Christians.

One night, after Felix had been in Prison for a while, he woke up and saw an Angel standing near him. He sat up and rubbed his eyes. Then he looked again because he thought that he might be dreaming. But he wasn't.

" Felix," said the Angel, " the old Bishop is in a very bad way. He is dying of cold and hunger in the mountains and God wants you to go and help him."

" Of course I will," said Felix. " Does he want me to go at once? "

" Yes," said the Angel, and he stood watching Felix.

" I am ready then," said Felix, and he stood up and took a step toward the Angel. And at that very moment the chains fell off his hands and he was free!

" Good," said the Angel. " I was wondering if your Faith was strong enough for you to start without asking about your chains."

" Well," said Felix, " if God wanted me to go at once, he wouldn't make it impossible for me by leaving me chained up, would he? "

" No," said the Angel, " but some people wouldn't have thought of that."

As they started up the steps of the prison cell the doors opened in front of them and the Angel took Felix to where the Bishop was. Then he gave him some milk and some bread and went back to Heaven.

Felix knelt by the Bishop. He was dreadfully thin and so cold that Felix thought that he must have died. Then he thought:

" But God wouldn't have sent me all this way for nothing," and so he started to rub the Bishop's arms and legs to warm them.

" Use my hands, Lord," he said, " and save the poor old Bishop for us please. Use my hands to warm him and make him better. I can't do it alone, so here are my hands. Use them, Lord, quickly! " And all the time he was praying he kept on rubbing and rubbing because God only helps us if we help ourselves too.

68

He doesn't care much for lazy people, or spineless ones.

Soon the Bishop felt warmer and not so stiff and Felix wrapped him up in his cloak and went on rubbing. Then he lit a little fire and put the jar of milk down beside it to warm. When he was so tired that he could scarcely rub any more, the Bishop opened his eyes and said:

" Hallo, Felix, when did you come? "

" An Angel showed me where you were," said Felix, " and I came about two hours ago. I thought at first that you were dead."

" I thought I was, too," said the Bishop, and he sat up.

Felix gave him the warm milk and some of the bread. Then he carefully picked up the Bishop and carried him home. And his cook, who met them at the door, cried because she was so sorry to see him looking so ill and so glad to see him at all.

Felix himself went to his own little house, and on his way he met a man who told him that the Emperor was dead and that there was no more Persecution. So he went about seeing to the schools and doing a lot of the Bishop's work for him because he was so old and ill.

But as soon as the new Emperor had settled down he started the persecution again and Felix had to be careful. One day he was walking along when he met some soldiers who had been sent to catch him. The soldiers stopped him and said:

" We're looking for a man called Felix. Have you met him on your way here? "

" No," said Felix, " I haven't met him," and the soldiers thanked him and went on down the road.

" Goodness! " thought Felix, " that *was* a Narrow Escape! But it won't be long before they find out!

Please God help me not to be found, because there isn't another priest round here for the people and they do need one! "

He ran and ran away from where he saw the soldiers and at last he came to the edge of the town and he saw an old ruined wall. He climbed sideways along it and found a Crack in it just wide enough to squeeze through. The other side was all bricks and loose stones and there was a dry well there too. He climbed down into the well and lay in the grass and ferns at the bottom and panted very hard because he had run so fast and because he was frightened that he might be caught.

Soon he heard the soldiers running back and heard them shouting to each other as they ran.

" He was Felix himself all the time! " shouted one.

" Of course! " said another. " I can't think why we didn't notice that he was a priest."

" We were in such a hurry to ask him that we didn't look at him properly," said the first one.

By then Felix could hear them stop by the wall and look at it.

" Don't let them find me, Lord, please don't! " he said.

" He came along here," said one of the soldiers. " I can see where he stepped on that brick." And they began to climb sideways along the Ruined Wall following the scratches that Felix had made on it when *he* had climbed.

Felix's heart made such a noise that he thought that it sounded louder than the soldiers' footsteps and he rolled over and lay on his face to try to quieten it.

The soldiers stopped at the Crack in the wall.

" Here! " said the front one. " Here's where he went through! Now we've got him! "

" No," said the soldier who was next along the wall, " he couldn't have gone through here because look at the Spider's Web! "

" *Well* now! " said the front soldier, all astonished, " that does show that he couldn't have gone through the Crack, because he would have broken the Web. And even if he did go through before the web was made, no spider could spin such a thick web again in such a short time."

And they all went back along the wall to look for Felix somewhere else.

Felix waited until they had gone and then he climbed out of the well and went to look at the Crack in the wall that he had squeezed through. There, filling it right across, was a most beautiful Spider's Web like a round net and the Spider herself sat in the very middle waiting for some flies to get caught in it!

" Oh *thank you*, dear God! " said Felix, smiling at the Spider. " What good ideas you do have! "

Felix stayed behind the wall among the rubble for six months. A Christian woman who had seen him squeezing through brought him some food every day.

After that the Persecution ended for a long time and Felix came out of his hiding place and went to see the people. When he told them about the Spider's Web they cheered and waved their hats and said that God had made a miracle. Then they carried Felix to the Church and they all sang the Te Deum. (Which is a Thanksgiving hymn for God.)

St. Felix's Special Day is on January 11th, and I know two people who are called after him. One of them lives in Yorkshire and the other one lives in Oxfordshire.

SSB–F

ST. MAURICE

Once upon a time there was a Roman Soldier and his name was Maurice and he was a Christian. Now at this time there were so many Christians among the Roman Soldiers that the Governors and So Forth had stopped killing them. They had a much better idea.

"We will make all the Christians into a Regiment," they said, "and then no one will interfere with them and they won't interfere with anyone else."

So that is what they did, and there was a great Christian Regiment (or Legion, as the Romans called it) and there were 6,660 soldiers and 6 officers in it and Maurice was the Head of them all.

Nowadays we still have the same idea, and there is a Jewish Battalion in the Army, and the Irish Guards are nearly all Catholics. It is a very good idea. Now Maurice's Legion was called the Theban Legion because most of the soldiers came from a place called Thebes. And they were very good soldiers indeed because they were happy and they knew their Duty to God and their Duty to the Army.

One day one of the Generals sent for the Head of the Theban Legion and said:

"Maurice, there is a battle to fight over the Mountains and we must be ready to go the day after to-morrow."

"Yes sir," said Maurice, and he saluted smartly and went back to his regiment.

He saw to the soldiers' packing and reminded them to fill their water-bottles and their food tins and he

72

helped them to roll their blankets and things into the right shape to carry comfortably. By the Day after To-morrow they were all ready, Smart and Shining, and they marched out to fight the Battle that was over the Mountains in some place or other.

For days and days they climbed up the mountains (the name of the mountains was the Alps) and it got colder and snowier the higher they got (they were very glad of the rugs that Maurice had made them take) and at last they began to go down the other side into Switzerland and it became warmer as they marched down the hill.

At last, one evening when they were camping for the night, the Emperor, who was leading the Army, spoke to them all and this is what he said:

" Listen to me, all you men! To-morrow we will be far enough down the mountains to start fighting the Swiss. This is a most Important Battle for Rome and I think the most sensible thing we can do is to pray to Mars the God of War so that he will help us."

All the Legions of the Army cheered and said they would except the Theban Legion. The Christian soldiers looked at one another and made Surprised and Asking faces at each other. At last some of them went to Maurice who was their Head.

" What shall we do to-morrow? " they said. " We can't possibly pray to Mars. Or do you think that perhaps we'd better Pretend to, just to Keep the Peace."

" Good gracious no! " said Maurice. " We can't possibly! Anyway, there are 6,666 of us, so they can't very well shoot so many! But I think that the best thing would be for me to see the Emperor myself in his tent and put the matter before him. We don't want to do anything Unsoldierly by refusing to obey him when we are one of his Crack Legions."

73

So Maurice went to see the Emperor that evening when they had all had their supper.

The Emperor was sitting near his camp fire and looking at a Map of Switzerland by the light of the flames.

" May I speak to you, Sir? " asked Maurice.

" Certainly," said the Emperor. " Is everything all right with your Legion? "

" Yes, Sir, they're splendid," said Maurice. " But there is one thing."

" Yes? " said the Emperor.

" We can't join the rest of the Army in the Prayers to Mars to-morrow morning," said Maurice. " You see, you are so Busy, we thought perhaps you hadn't remembered that the Theban Legion is the Christian Legion."

" I know quite well that you are the Christian Legion," said the Emperor. " But it will do you no harm to join with the others in Prayers for our Success in Battle."

" If that's what you need, sir," said Maurice, " then we will gladly pray for your success, but to our own God and also to Holy Michael the Archangel, who will defend us in the Day of Battle."

" *No*," said the Emperor. " You all pray together to-morrow morning. That is an Order. And anyway, what are you Quibbling about, man, when we are going to fight the Swiss Christians? "

" Believe it or not, Sir," said Maurice, " but that is the first we have heard of who it is we are going to fight. I am afraid, Sir, that that finishes the matter. The Theban Legion will not fight to-morrow! "

" *What!* " shouted the Emperor; he jumped to his feet and his map fell into the fire, but he was too Angry and Astonished to notice. " Do you realise, my good Maurice, that that is Mutiny? "

74

"I am afraid I do, Sir," said Maurice, "but I am sure you will understand my position, Sir."

"That has nothing to do with it!" shouted the Emperor, and he angrily tried to save his burning Map. "Now look what you've made me do! It was the only decent map of Switzerland I had!"

"Very sorry, Sir," said Maurice. "You do understand that my Legion will not be going with you tomorrow, Sir? We are your Soldiers, Sir, and are ready to defend our country and to help our neighbours; we are not Traitors and we are not Cowards. But we cannot deny the Faith and the Law of Our Lord."

"Oh, *go away!*" said the Emperor, and he fished the remains of his Map of Switzerland out of the fire.

Maurice went back to the Theban Legion and told them what had happened.

"Of course," he said, "I couldn't really say anything else." And the Legion agreed with him.

In the morning when all the Legions were ready to march down and attack the Swiss the Emperor called one of the other Legions and said to its Leader:

"The Theban Legion has refused to worship Mars and has refused to go into Battle with us. Therefore I order you to kill one man in every ten all along the rows!"

This was quite a usual thing for the Romans to do and no one was very surprised. So that was what was done and all the rest of the Christian soldiers stood Stiff and Proud and prayed for the souls of their friends. Now one in every ten came to about 666 men and that is a great many.

"Now," said the Emperor, "will the rest of you march with us to attack the Christians in Switzerland?"

And all the Legion shouted "No!" So Maurice and all the rest of his 6,666 men were all killed then and there and the rest of the Army went on down the mountains into Switzerland.

What a wonderful thing it must have been in Heaven when the whole of the Theban Legion with Maurice at the Head, marched in to see God.

The place where this happened is called St. Moritz to this very day and people go there for Winter Sports. I wonder how many of them remember the Theban Legion.

St. Maurice's Special Day is on September 22nd, and people all over the world are called after him. Morris and Maura both count, too.

ST. ADRIAN

Once upon a time there was a Fair and Handsome young man called Adrian, and he was very strong and tall, and he was Twenty-Eight.

Now Adrian was a Roman Soldier and a Centurion and very Military-Minded, and all his officers thought the world of him. In case you don't know what a Centurion is, it is a Roman Soldier who is Top over one Hundred ordinary soldiers. (Like *century* is a hundred years, and a *centipede* is supposed to have a hundred legs, only it hasn't really. It has a good many, all the same.)

Well, one day Adrian's C.O. sent for him. (C.O. is short for Commanding Officer.)

" Good morning, Adrian," said the C.O.

" Good morning, Sir," said Adrian, standing up very Stiff and Proud and saluting.

" I want you to take some Prisoners out into the prison yard, and punish them," said the C.O. " Scourge them first, and then, if they won't behave, Spike their tongues so that they can't talk! "

" Yes, Sir," said Adrian, saluting again. " May I ask, Sir, why they are in Prison, Sir? "

" They are some of those tiresome Christians," said the C.O. " I have never come across such Obstinate people in all my life."

So Adrian went down to the prison yard to see about things, and when the Prisoners (thirty-three of them) had been scourged he asked them whether they would now stop being Christians and worship the Roman Emperor instead.

78

But they all shouted:

" No! Long live Christ the King! "

Adrian saw that it was no use, and so he ordered the soldiers to Spike the prisoners' tongues so that they couldn't teach anyone else to be Christian.

" How very brave they are! " he thought, as he watched the soldiers sticking Iron Spikes into the prisoners' tongues. " They must *know* that they are right, or they wouldn't be able to bear it. And, after all, what does it matter," he thought, " once you're dead, you're dead, and that's that." (Romans didn't believe that people had Immortal Souls.)

" Stop! " he suddenly shouted to his soldiers. " I wish to speak to some of the prisoners, and I want them to be able to answer me." Then he went up to the prisoners and said:

" *Why* do you put up with all this? Will it make any difference to you once you're dead, do you think? "

Then a tired old man said:

" No eyes have seen, and no ears have heard, and neither has anyone even been able to Imagine the wonderful things that God has got ready for the people who love Him."

" Is that really True, though? " asked Adrian.

" As true as True," said the tired old man.

" Well, then," said Adrian, " I am a Christian! " and he waited among the prisoners to have his tongue Spiked with them. But the soldiers finished doing the prisoners and left Adrian out!

" Why have you Left me Out? " asked Adrian.

" Because Soldiers aren't allowed to do things to their Superior Officers, Sir," said a Soldier, saluting Smartly, " but I am afraid, Sir, that we must arrest you and take you before your C.O."

" Certainly," said Adrian, and two of his soldiers

marched him off, and everybody stared because of his being so Tall and Handsome.

"What *is* happening?" asked the C.O. as Adrian marched in with the two soldiers.

"I am now a Christian, Sir," said Adrian.

"You must have got sunstroke, my poor Adrian," said the C.O. kindly, "would you like some Leave?" (Leave is a sort of holiday when soldiers are allowed to leave the barracks and stay with their families or something for a few days.)

"I haven't got sunstroke, Sir, it's raining," said Adrian. "I've turned into a Christian, that's all!"

"That's *all*, did you say?" said the C.O. "Well, you can go to Prison, then, till you learn some sense!"

"I have learnt some sense and that is why I am a Christian," said Adrian.

"Don't answer back!" said the C.O. crossly, and Adrian was marched away again and was loaded with chains, and was put in prison with a lot of other Christians.

Now Adrian had a very nice wife called Natalie, and when she heard that her husband was in Prison she ran there to see how he was.

"I *am* so glad you're here, darling!" she said to Adrian.

"*Glad?*" said Adrian, "why on Earth?"

"Well, because I am a Christian, too, only I couldn't tell you in case you were angry," said Natalie.

"Of all the Extraordinary Coincidences!" said Adrian, "but I am afraid they won't let me go home again now."

"No," said Natalie, "but I'll bring you all some Dinner and Sponges and Soap and things, so as to keep you happy until you are Martyrs. Only do be careful not to let anyone know about me being a

Christian, because then I'll be here too, and you won't get your little Comforts."

So Natalie went home and collected a lot of things. She was glad that Adrian was going to be a Martyr because it was so lovely for *him*. But she hadn't been married very long and her house was all nice and new, and if Adrian was dead she couldn't Afford to live there alone. So poor Natalie was sad as well as glad.

When she had got together a good Parcel of things she went round to some friends' houses and asked them to cook things as well. And they did. And every day Natalie and her friends used to go to the Prison and take the prisoners their Breakfasts, Dinners, and Teas.

But one day the Roman Emperor went to the prison to have a look at the prisoners.

"How's this?" he said angrily to the Gaoler, "these people look very fat and well. What is the meaning of it, eh? They ought to be half starved and dirty."

"I am very sorry, Cæsar, I'm sure," said the Gaoler in a Frightened voice, "but all their Sisters and their Cousins and their Aunts come with food and things for them, and one poor gaoler can't keep out a Whole Pack of Women!"

"Well, I won't allow it!" said the Emperor. "Not another woman is to come into the place! See to it!" and he strode out.

When Natalie and her friends heard this they didn't know *what* to do.

"They'll all starve if we don't go!" they said sadly.

"I know!" said Natalie, "let's cut off our Hair and dress up like Men!" And they did, and the Gaoler let them in, all Unsuspecting.

The next day Adrian was taken to the Emperor, who ordered all his Bones to be Broken one by one on an Anvil, like Blacksmiths have.

When Natalie heard this she ran to the Prison and asked the other Prisoners to pray for Adrian.

" Because," she said, " he isn't like us who have been Christians for Ages. He has only just turned into one, and I'm *so* afraid that he might Deny Our Lord without knowing how wicked it is." (Denying people is when you won't have anything to do with them.)

Then she ran back to Adrian. But by this time Adrian had had all his Bones broken and he couldn't stand or even sit up.

" Poor Adrian!" said Natalie kindly, " poor brave Adrian! Would you like a Drink of Water? "

Adrian said that he would.

" If they do anything else to me I might stop being Brave," he said, " it is horrible being all Broken."

" Ask Our Lady to help you," said Natalie, " you'll soon be in Heaven now."

So Adrian did and then the door opened and in came the Gaoler.

" All the prisoners must have their Arms and Legs Chopped off!" he said. " Ha! Ha! that'll teach you to be Christian! "

" Please," said Natalie to the Gaoler, " may my husband be the First? "

" Why? " asked the Gaoler.

" Because then I can go home and not have to wait so long," said Natalie. She didn't really mean that. She wanted Adrian to be First because she thought that he might get too Frightened if he saw all the others being Chopped.

So Adrian was carried to the Anvil (like Blacksmiths have) and his Arms and Legs were chopped off, and then he found that he was in Heaven.

There he saw Our Lord. He had been wondering

where he was, because he didn't know about things
very well. There hadn't been time to teach him before
he went to Prison and all that.

"Well, Adrian," said Our Lord, "you bore up like
a Proper Soldier. I *am* sorry that you had such a
terrible time, but if you go along to Our Lady she
has got a Special Treat for you!"

Adrian went to Our Lady and knelt down in front of
her (because she is a Queen).

"When the Pope gives you your Special Day, Adrian,"
she said, "I'll tell him to give you my Birthday. So
you'll have a *very* Special Day because you were so
wonderfully brave!"

When Natalie died, Adrian met her, and she was
given the same day because of husbands and wives
being One Person.

There are lots of Adrians for Our Lady's Birthday
on September 8th, but the people called Natalie are
very Lucky indeed, and I'll tell you why. "Natalie"
means "Birthday," and lots of girls who are born
at Christmas are called Natalie because of its being
Our Lord's Birthday. So you see that the Natalies
have Our Lord's *and* Our Lady's Birthdays for their
Special Days.

ST. GEORGE

Once upon a time there was a Soldier called George. He was very good at being a Soldier, so the General kept sending him away to fight battles with different people all over the World.

One time he was sent away to a Town to arrange about a Battle, and when he got there there was no one to be seen!

"Dear me!" said George, "this is Most Upsetting! Fancy having a Town without any People in it!"

So he wandered about the empty streets until he came to the Church. He was just going in when he heard a funny sort of Sniffing Noise coming from inside! He very carefully peered through the door—The Church was full of people crying!

"Still More Upsetting!" thought George. He went inside and saw a Man near the door who had on a Green Tail Coat with Brass Buttons. He was walking about with his hands behind his back and Keeping an Eye on things.

"What *has* happened?" asked George. "My name is George, in case you wanted to know."

"Well," said the Man in Green, "we'd better go outside while I explain," and he passed George some Holy Water on the ends of his fingers. They went out through one of those doors that turn round and round and sat in the Sun on the Church steps.

"It's like this," said the Man in Green. "There's a Pond just outside the Town and in it there lives a very Gobbling kind of Dragon. And every single day there ever is it has to have one live thing to eat. It has been here a year and two months and five days. First it ate all the Cows and Horses, then the Sheep and Pigs, then the Dogs and Cats, then the Turkeys and Geese, then the Cocks and Hens, then all the Wild Animals, and *now*," the Man in Green whispered in a Frightened Voice, " it is eating all the Children! "

" Whose Children? " asked George. " Because no one wants theirs to be the Ones, I suppose."

" That is the whole trouble," said the Man in Green, " we have to do Eena Meena Mina Mo every time and it takes simply ages. The awful thing about to-day, though, is that the King's Daughter is The One."

" Where is she now? " asked George.

" Tied up to a Flag Pole waiting for the Dragon to feel hungry," said the Man in Green.

" Why on *earth* don't you Kill the Dragon instead of feeding it? " asked George. The Utter Incapability of the people Passed his Comprehension.

" Well, we aren't very good at killing Dragons," said the Man in Green in a sad voice.

" Well, if you *really* can't, why on *earth* don't you ask God to, then? " said George. " You all go to Church and Sniff very loud and never even say one word to God about it when there He is waiting to tell you what to do."

" Well, that *is* a Good Idea if ever I heard one," said the Man in Green. " How did you think of it? " and he ran back into the Church through the Twirling Door and said in a Loud Voice:

" Come out, Everyone! George wants you."

Everybody stopped sniffing and looked round.

" Who is George? " they all whispered to each other, and they all whispered back:

" I don't know."

So they all came out to see.

George told them the Good Idea about asking God to help them with the Dragon and they were Absolutely Astonished! They'd never had the remotest idea of doing such a thing.

" Just think of God being there all the time and you never even thinking of Him! " said George in a disgusted voice.

" Do you believe that I could kill that Dragon all By Myself? " asked George.

" Of course you couldn't! " all the People shouted.

" Well, suppose I do, then what? " said George.

" Well, if you *do* then God *must* have helped you, like Faith Moving Mountains and things."

" I'm glad you've managed to think of that at Last," said George, and he went Rather Gingerly towards the Pond.

First he untied the Princess from the Flag Pole. She was crying because she was afraid that what with all this talking the Dragon might reach her first. Then George began to walk round the Pond very fast, whistling a very loud tune to make the Dragon come out of the Pond. It did. George ran round the Pond and the Dragon followed him. George went faster and faster, and when the Dragon was going at a pretty good rate George stopped suddenly, and as the Dragon whizzed past he cut off its Head with one Blow!

" There, you see," he said, wiping his Gory Blade on his pocket handkerchief, " it's perfectly simple! I asked God to give me a Good Idea and He did! "

The King was so pleased that he made a New Rule then and there. And this was the New Rule that the King made up:

SSB-G

THAT EVERYBODY MUST ALWAYS ASK GOD
TO HELP THEM OUT OF BOTHERS. BECAUSE
HE ALWAYS DOES.

And all the People cheered and said they would.
And they did.

A little while after that George's general sent him
to another Town to Arrange about another Battle.

" And mind you attend to business this time," said
the General, " and don't go killing Dragons and things
all over the place."

" All right," said George, " but it was only one Dragon
and I killed it by the Pond." And he started off.

When he got to the new Town George found that
they were All Against Christians. Now George always
had a Red Cross painted on his White Shield, so, when
they saw this, the People knew that he was a Christian
and they took him Prisoner. They took him to their
King, who was in a Bad Temper that day because he
had knocked his elbow on the table at Breakfast time
and it still hurt. And they said:

" Your Majesty, here is a Christian Prisoner, what
shall we do with him? "

" If he's that George who Killed the Dragon, you'd
better keep him," said the King, rubbing his elbow.
" He'd be useful in case one came here. But I *won't*
have him a Christian; send him to the Judge."

The Judge was a Cross Old Man with a pale straggly
beard and beady eyes. He hated Christians and always
had them killed, but he thought he'd give George
one chance because of the King wanting to keep
him.

" Say you Hate God," he said, Glaring at George.

" But I don't," said George in a surprised voice.

" Well, *say* you do, anyway, or I'll have you killed,"

said the Judge crossly, " and you won't be Killed Suddenly, but Very Slowly."

George did not want to be Killed Slowly at all, but he thought to himself:

" If I go on saying that I *don't* Hate God, and the Judge has me Killed, I'll be a Martyr and go straight to Heaven. I hope being Killed Slowly won't take too long."

So he said to the Judge:

" It's no good, I won't say it, and, what's more, I'll say the Opposite. I Love God. So there! "

" Now you *have* done it," said the Judge. " Here, you Men, take him and kill him Very Slowly."

So they took George and Killed him very slowly, and it was horrible and hurt frightfully. But as soon as he was Dead he flew straight up to Heaven and there was God waiting for him and smiling.

" Good! " said God, " I've got a Lovely Place all ready for you. I'm sorry you've had such a Horrible Time, but I'll make up for it now."

St. George has a Specially Nice place in Heaven because of being a Martyr, and his Special Day is April 23rd, and there are Hundreds of People called after him, even when their Birthdays aren't in April.

ST. CHRISTOPHER

Once upon a time there was a Giant. He was twice as high and twice as wide as the biggest man you have ever seen. He was very, very strong, and could do much harder work than anyone else because of being so big, but he only lived in an ordinary-sized house, so he wasn't very happy because he had to stoop all the time so as not to bump his head. The one proper-sized thing he had was an Enormous Chair. It took up a lot of room in the Dining-room, but the Giant did not mind that because he liked sitting in it so much.

One day, he was sitting in his house on the Enormous Chair and he thought this thought:

" I wish I were a King! I am so very Big and Strong that I could win *all* the Battles with *all* the other Kings. And I would be the most Special and Important of them all, because I am so Big."

Then he thought another thought, and this was the Other Thought:

" If I can't be a King myself, I shall go and do Strong Things for the Most Special and Important King there is, and that will be nearly as good."

So he got up out of the Enormous Chair, and he pulled up a young May tree for a walking stick, and he cut off its roots and branches, and started out to find the Most Special and Important King there is.

He asked everybody he met:

" Which is the Top King? The one who isn't Afraid of Anything? "

And everybody said that King Mundus was.

So the Giant went and worked for King Mundus, who had a Palace made of Silver, with china floors, and Gold doors and furniture, and Purple Velvet Curtains. The King and all his Courtiers dressed in Fine Raiment, and the King had a Diamond Walking Stick.

There was an Enormous Army at the Palace, but it never fought anyone because King Mundus was the Top King, so he didn't need Battles. But he used the Army to help him to go hunting for Elephants, but he never killed them; he kept them to ride on afterwards. Really, King Mundus was the Bravest King that the Giant had ever seen. Even when Lions Sprang Out at him when he was out hunting Elephants, he just used to hit them with his Diamond Walking Stick, and they fell down dead.

One day they were riding along in a Procession with the Giant and the King all Stiff and Proud in front; and some of the soldiers were singing behind them. In the song was something about Satan, and every time the soldiers sang the word " Satan " King Mundus turned Rather Pale.

" Why do you turn Rather Pale when they sing ' Satan '? " asked the Giant, " I thought you said *you* were the Top King, and so you oughtn't to be frightened of anything at all."

" But King Satan is more Top than all the Kings, even me," said King Mundus.

" Well," said the Giant, " why didn't you tell me that before? I said that I wanted to work for the Most Special and Important King there is, and you aren't if you're frightened of Satan. Good-bye."

So the Giant went off to find King Satan. He didn't have to go very far because, coming to meet him, he saw another Procession. Riding at the head of it, and rather a long way in front, was a very Proud and Grand King. He had a black horse and he was dressed all in Black Velvet except for his Silver Crown, and he was so Haughty and Stiff, that even the great big Giant felt Rather Frightened, but not *very.*

" What do you want, and why are you here? " said this Grand Person.

" I am a Giant, and I am looking for King Satan, so that I can work for him, because he is more Important than the Top King."

" Well, I am King Satan," said the Grand Person, " you needn't do very hard work. Just ride along beside me and look Stiff and Proud."

So the Giant turned round and rode beside King Satan, and after them followed the Procession of Soldiers and Judges, and Sailors, and Workmen, and Kings and Queens with crowns on, and all sorts of Elegant People, all galloping their horses to try and keep up with King Satan and the Giant.

They hadn't gone very far when they came to a Church with a Crucifix outside it.

" I don't think we'll go past here, I don't much like Crucifixes," said King Satan.

The Giant thought this was Rather Funny, but he didn't say anything, and they all turned round and went another way. Soon they came to another Church with another Crucifix, and the same thing happened.

" Are you *frightened* of a wooden Cross? " said the Giant. " If not, *why* don't you like going near one? What are they for, and who is the man on them? " (Because the Giant was not a Christian, and he had never heard of Our Lord.)

" Well, yes, I am afraid," said King Satan, " because the man is Christ the King, Who is stronger than I.

But never mind all that, come along with me, and I will make you Very Grand."

"Well, I can't go with you if you are not the *Very* Top King," said the Giant, "I *must* go and work for King Christ. Good-bye."

So the Giant went away to look for Christ the King, Who was stronger than King Satan, who was stronger than King Mundus, who said he was the Top King.

One day he found a Wise Old Man who lived all alone in a little Hut in a Dark Forest near a Deep River without a bridge.

"Do you know where I can find Christ the King?" the Giant asked him. "You see, I want to work for him because he is stronger than King Satan, who is stronger than King Mundus, who is the Top King."

"You can only work for him if you fast and pray as well," said the Wise Old Man.

"Well, I can't," said the Giant, "because if I fast I won't be so strong, and I don't know how to pray."

"Well, there *is* another way," said the Wise Old Man. "Do you see that Deep River? Nobody seems to be able to cross it without falling in. Now, you go and live beside it and Carry people Over, because you are so Strong. It won't be too deep for you, will it?"

"Of *course* it won't be too deep for me," said the Giant, "but I want to work for Christ the King, I don't want to go carrying a lot of silly people over the River all the time. Why can't they have a bridge?"

"Because the river runs so fast that it washes the bridge away every time," said the Wise Old Man. "Besides, you *will* be working for Christ the King, because He *specially* told me what He wanted you to do. But you won't be allowed to see Him until later; no one ever is."

So the Giant built himself a house on the bank of

the Deep River, and whenever anyone wanted to go across, they used to ring a Clanging Bell that hung on a tree that was just outside, and the Giant would come out and say:

"Do you want to cross the River?"

And they would say:

"Yes, please."

And the Giant would say:

"Well, jump up!" and they would jump up on his back and he would carry them over. But if they were too old and couldn't jump up, he would lift them.

One night, right in the middle of the Night, the Bell rang: "Clang! Clang! Clang!" And before the Giant had time to get out of bed and put on his dressing-gown and bedroom-slippers, a voice said:

"Carrier! Will you carry me across the River?" But when he got outside there was no one there! The Giant thought this was very funny and he went back to bed.

"It must have been a Dream," he thought.

As soon as he had gone to sleep again the Bell rang: "Clang! Clang! Clang!" and before the Giant had time to put on his dressing-gown and bedroom-slippers a voice said:

"Carrier! Will you carry me across the River?"

But when he got outside there was no one there *again!* The Giant thought that this was very funny and he went back to bed again. "That must have been a Dream, too," he said to himself.

ST. CHRISTOPHER

As soon as he had gone to sleep again the Bell rang:
" Clang! Clang! Clang! " And before he had time to
get out of bed and put on his dressing-gown and bed-
room-slippers a voice said:
" Carrier! Will you carry me across the River? "
When he got outside there stood a little boy.
" Hullo! " said the Giant. " Was it you the other
times? " But the little boy only said:
" Are you *sure* you can carry me? "
The Giant laughed because it was such a very little
boy, and he was such a very big Giant.
" Of course I can! " he said, and he lifted the little
boy right up on to his shoulder, because he was so
small and light. Then he took his great walking-stick,
made of a May tree, in his hand, and stepped down into
the Deep River. Suddenly the wind began to blow and
the water got deeper and deeper, and it flowed so fast
that it nearly knocked the Giant over.
" Are you *sure* you can carry me? " asked the boy.
" Of course I can! " said the Giant, and the stones
at the bottom of the River began to roll along, and
they nearly tripped him up. The little boy felt heavier
than he looked, and it was certainly difficult to
walk.
" Are you *still* sure you can carry me? " asked the
little boy.
" Of *course* I am sure! " said the Giant Rather Crossly.
He wished the little boy wouldn't keep *on* asking him;
it interrupted him when he was trying not to fall down.
He thought that the little boy was afraid of being
dropped, but he didn't look a bit frightened. It rained
so hard in the poor Giant's face that he could scarcely
see, and the little boy got heavier and heavier, and
the Giant's shoulders ached and ached.
" *Now* are you sure? " said the little boy, and the

water began to carry the Giant away, it was so Deep and Swift.

"No, but I'll try and manage," said the Giant, and he tried so hard that, in spite of the wind and rain and thunder and lightning, he at last got to the other side, and then the Storm stopped! He was so tired and out of breath that he just put down the little boy and lay down on the River Bank and shut his eyes. After a minute he opened them again and said:

"I have *never* carried anything so heavy in all my life! Who are you? Why weren't you frightened? Even *I* was, rather, in that Very Deep part."

"I am Christ the King, Whom you wanted to work for," said the little boy, "I wasn't frightened of the Storm because I made it myself. I was very heavy because everybody gives Me their Troubles to carry, so, of course, you were carrying them as well. Now you really are My servant because you have never worked so hard before, and so I will show you something Special. Stick your walking-stick into the ground."

The Giant did, and what *do* you suppose happened? Well, you remember how he had cut off all the roots and branches to make it into a stick? Well, it grew in the ground and made new branches and leaves and flowers all in one minute! The Giant saw it do it.

When he turned round to ask Christ the King (Who had been pretending to be a little boy so that the Giant wouldn't know him) about it, he had gone away!

After that the Giant was always called Christopher, which means Christ-Carrier.

Have you ever noticed that in a lot of motor-cars, near the driver's seat, there is a little blue and silver picture? Sometimes it is all silver. Well, if you look at one closely next time you see one, you will see that it is Christopher carrying Christ-the-King-pretending-to-be-a-little-boy. We put the picture on our cars because Christopher still looks after us in Traffic or on journeys. So now he is the Special Saint for Travellers, and his Special Day is July the 25th. Now I expect you have noticed that there ought to be Two Special Days in this story, so I will tell you when the other one is. It is the Last Sunday in October, and it belongs to Christ the King.

ST. NICHOLAS

O nce upon a time there was a Bishop, and his name was Nicholas, and he lived Seventeen Hundred years ago, which is a long time.

Well, one year, there was a Famine. (A Famine is when there is absolutely Nothing Left to Eat Anywhere, and so people have to eat Grass and roots of trees boiled into Soup, and things like that.) Well, in this Famine, Nicholas was travelling over some mountains to look for some food for his people, when he came to a Small Hotel, all by itself in between two mountains. It was nearly Night by then, and he thought he had better sleep there, and go on in the morning. He was very hungry and he would have loved to have had some Supper, but he knew that there would not be any because of the Famine.

But when he was settled by the fire in the Hotel, the Hotel Man came in and started laying the table!

" Are you going to give me some Supper? " asked Nicholas.

The Hotel Man laughed and said that he had a Secret Store of food down in his Deepest Darkest Cellar, and that Nicholas could have some, if he liked. Nicholas was very pleased, he *was* so hungry! He hadn't had anything to eat, except some Dock Leaves and Sorrel, since the day before yesterday breakfast time.

Soon the Hotel Man brought in a dish with a silver dish cover over it and put it in front of Nicholas' place. Then he gave him a square green plate, with white edges, to eat off.

"Help yourself!" he said, and he lifted off the dish cover. Inside was some very nice-looking Salted Meat (like ham is) with Dumplings round the edge.

"I am sorry I can't give you any potatoes," said the Hotel Man, "but there aren't any left, because of the Famine."

"Never mind, I like dumplings," said Nicholas, and he looked at the supper again. Then he smelt it. Then he looked at the Hotel Man, who was humming a little tune and pretending not to notice.

"Where did you get this meat? There isn't any left in the whole land," asked Nicholas.

"Oh, it's just some I had in a Secret Store in the Cellar," said the Hotel Man, and he flipped the table with the dinner napkin which he kept hanging over his arm.

"Is this all there is, or is there some more?" said Nicholas.

"There is a little left in a tub in the cellar," said the Hotel Man. "Haven't you got enough there? Shall I go and get you some more?" And he picked up the dish.

"No, leave the dish, and show me where you got it from," said Nicholas.

"I'd rather you didn't go all the way down there," said the Hotel Man, "I'll bring it up."

"Take me down *at once*!" said Nicholas, very Loud and Fierce and the Hotel Man said, "All *right*! I am not deaf, " in rather a frightened voice.

So they went down and down the very steep steps into the Deepest Darkest Cellar. There stood the Tub! It was painted green and it had Iron Rings round it. It had a wooden lid.

"Bring me a light, please, I want to see in it!" said Nicholas.

The Hotel Man brought a candle, in a blue candlestick, and Nicholas lifted up the lid and looked inside. It was half-full of Salted Meat, just the same as the meat upstairs. Then he blessed it (like he could because he was a Bishop), and what *do* you suppose happened? It really was the Most Surprising Thing that the Hotel Man had ever seen! Out jumped three little boys! The wicked Hotel Man hadn't got any more meat for his customers, so he had killed the little boys and Pickled them and Peppered them and cut them into little Squares and popped them into his Salt meat tub.

Nicholas took them away with him and gave them back to their mother, who had been looking for them everywhere. When they told her what had happened, of course she told all her friends, so everybody said that Nicholas was the Special Saint for Children,

because of the little boys. His Special Day is the 6th of December, near Christmas, and if you say " St. Nicholas, St. Nicholas, St. Nicholas," very quickly and very often, you will see that it turns into " Santa Claus," and they are both the same person!

ST. PAUL AND ST. ANTHONY

Once upon a time there was a boy called Paul (not the Paul who used to be called Saul, but another one), and he was sixteen years old. He lived in Egypt with his sister, whose name was Maurice, which is a funny name for a girl. Their father and mother had been killed because they were Christians, and they thought that at Any Moment they might be killed themselves.

So one day Maurice said to Paul:

" I don't think that we'd better live here any more."

" Neither do I," said Paul, " it's no good just Waiting for someone to come and kill us. I'll tell you what. You go and stay with Granny because she lives a long way off, and I'll go somewhere else."

" Where will you go? " asked Maurice.

" I haven't thought yet," said Paul.

So Maurice went to stay with their Granny and Paul started off into the Desert to find a Good Safe Place. And as he went along he told God all about how difficult things were nowadays and how he hoped that Maurice would arrive at their Granny's house safely.

" Please will *you* Look After her? " he said to God; " she isn't used to travelling alone."

And then he said:

" And please will you Look After me, too? I'm not very good at Deserts, and I don't want to get Lost. I'll tell you a thing," said Paul to God, " I *would* like to have a Job. The sort of Job that helps Maurice and

103

Granny and Grandpa and all my Relations and all my Friends and all the Other People who might need to be helped."

"Well," said God, "it would have to be a Tremendous job if it was going to help all those people."

"I know," said Paul, "but I wouldn't mind that if it *did* help them."

"Very well," said God, "you had better be a Hermit."

"What is that?" asked Paul.

"Well," said God, "there aren't any yet, you will be the First One. But soon there will be lots of them. You see, Paul," said God, "no one person can help Everyone, like you want to. But I can. So if *you* will tell me about the people that you want to help, I will do it for you. But it will take you nearly *all* your time to pray for so many things for so many people. And you will want to have some time just to talk to me yourself, too, won't you?"

"Yes," said Paul.

"It will mean living all alone," said God, "and never seeing people or even hearing them. You will just be a sort of Living Prayer for Other People."

"Well, I will do it," said Paul, "if you will please help me. It does not matter where I live, does it? I might just as well live here in the Desert. In fact," said Paul, "it seems a very Good Place to live All Alone in."

So he found a place where there was some Water in a sort of well, and a Cave near it to live in. And there he lived, praying for Other People until he was an old, old man. And he had never seen or heard another person all that time.

But meanwhile, just as God said there would be, there were some more Hermits in the Desert, and one day the Oldest of them, a Proud Old Man, had a Dream that God sent him. And the Dream was this:

ST. PAUL AND ST. ANTHONY

He dreamed that God came to him and said:

" Anthony, you think that you are the Oldest and Holiest Hermit in the Desert because you are Ninety years old. But you are not, Anthony. There is an older and holier one called Paul, and he is more than a Hundred, and has been a Hermit twenty years longer than you have. Now, I want you to go and Visit him! "

" But, Lord, I am an Old man," said Anthony, " I am Ninety. I am too Old to go looking for people in the Desert."

" No, you are not," said God, " I will help you, and I want you to see my Good Old Paul."

So in the morning when he woke up, Anthony took a big stick to help himself along, and started off to find Paul. He was very slow because he was so old, but God showed him the way, although there wasn't any Path. At last, after days and days he came to Paul's Cave and Well and he went up to the door that Paul had made to keep out the Weather.

But when Paul saw that someone had found out where he lived after all these years he shut the door in Anthony's face and said:

" Go away! I am a Hermit. I am not supposed to see anyone ever again or even hear anyone's voice! So please go away! If you want a drink you can take some out of the Well! "

But Anthony said:

" *Please*, Paul, let me in! God sent me to visit you. I am a Hermit too, and I would be very grateful, Paul, if you would let me in! "

So Paul opened the door and let Anthony in. They were delighted to see each other because each of them thought that the other was a Good and Holy man. And so they were. Both of them.

" Well," said Paul, " and how are things getting on in the World nowadays? I suppose they have Invented a lot of New Things and so on? "

" Yes, they have," said Anthony, " the young people are very Go-Ahead and all that. They never listen to us Old Ones. But God loves them just the same I'm sure."

" It's nice to meet someone who knows what's going on," said Paul. " I feel quite an Old Fogey beside you. What other Modern things do you know? "

" Well, I wouldn't call them exactly *Modern*," said Anthony. " You are the first stranger that I have seen for Seventy Years."

" But it's all News to me," said Paul, " because I've been here for Ninety years."

" Well," said Anthony, " I lived alone for years and years like you, until lots of other Hermits came and lived round about. So we all lived together in a sort of Bigger Place called a Monastery. And the Hermits who live together are called Monks. I am the Head One because I am the Oldest."

" That *is* a Good Idea! " said Paul, " and how do you live and what do you do? "

And so they chatted of this and that and were very happy. But when it was Supper Time Paul looked Rather Anxious.

" What is the matter? " asked Anthony.

" Well," said Paul, " God has very kindly sent a Raven with half a Loaf of Bread every day since I was Eighty and got too old to do my own Cooking. I wonder if that will be enough for you? "

" I wouldn't think of eating your supper! " said Anthony, " anything will do for me! "

" There isn't anything else except water," said Paul, " but we'll each have half when it comes! "

But when the Raven came he brought Two Whole Loaves of Bread!

So they had a good supper of Bread and a good drink of Water from the Well and then Paul said:

"Do you know, Anthony, years and years ago Our Lord told me that when it was time for me to die he would send someone to bury me. So I've just been thinking, that must be why he sent you!"

"Oh, but," said poor old Anthony, "I've only just found you and you are my friend! Don't go and leave me yet, Paul!" and he prayed that he would die, too, so that they could go on with their talks in Heaven.

"Never mind, Anthony," said Paul, "think how lovely it will be for me, and anyway it won't be long before we are together again, because you are Getting on in Life yourself. But one thing I *would* like. *Please* would you go back across the Desert and get that Cloak you've got at your Monastery. The one that the great Bishop Athanasius left there once. I would so like to be buried in it!"

Anthony was very surprised that Paul knew about the Cloak, but he set off across the Desert again to fetch it for his friend Paul. He was very Old and Feeble and he had Hills and Valleys and Stony places and Steep places to go over. At last he got to the Monastery, so tired that he felt that he couldn't go another step. The other Monks were delighted to see him again.

"Where *have* you been? We have been very Anxious about you," they said.

Now, since seeing and talking with Paul, Anthony wasn't a bit Proud any more, and he said:

"I have seen a man like Elias the Prophet and like John the Baptist in the Desert and like St. Paul in Paradise and his name is Paul the Hermit."

And then, although he was so tired, he started off
again at once with the Cloak because he wanted to
see Paul again before he died. But one day when he
was nearly there, he saw something Unusual coming
towards him.

"What can it be?" he thought, "it looks like a
Procession. But you don't have Processions all suddenly in the Desert!" He stopped and waited.

Soon there came past him a crowd of Angels, and
among them Anthony saw some of the Apostles. And
right in the Middle of them all was Paul!

Then Anthony knew that his friend had died and
that he had seen him on his way to Heaven.

"But still," he said to himself, "I must go and bury
his body now that he doesn't want it any more!" and
he hurried along.

When he got to Paul's Cave he had a little rest and
a drink of water. Then he got up and looked round
for a Spade or something to dig the grave with.

"I wonder how Paul planted things without a Spade
or even a Trowel?" he thought. Then he remembered
Paul telling him about the Raven. "Of course!"
he said to himself, "he hasn't planted anything for
more than Twenty Years. He only had Bread and
Water."

While he was wondering what he could do he heard
a sudden Padding Noise behind him! He turned round
and there were two great Lions coming towards him!

"Oh, dear!" he thought, "troubles will never Cease!"
And he quickly went into the Cave and shut the door.
Then he watched the Lions through a Crack.

They went up to Paul's body and, close beside it,
they began to dig with their paws. They dug and dug
until they had made a Proper Grave and then they
went away!

Anthony came out of the Cave.

" I wish that I hadn't been frightened of them," he thought to himself, " but how could I know that they were Kind ones? "

So he wrapped Paul's body up in St. Athanasius's cloak and buried it. Then he went back into the Cave.

" I wish I could find something of Paul's to keep for a Memento," he thought, " but he was so poor that he doesn't seem to have had anything." Then in a corner he found Paul's own old cloak. It was so Worn and Patched that, if you had seen it, you'd hardly have known what it was.

But Anthony folded it up and took it home with him and always afterwards he wore it on Special Days like Christmas and Easter and things, because it was the most Valuable thing that he had got.

St. Paul the Hermit's Special Day is on January 15th, and St. Anthony's is on January 17th, quite close to it, because of them being Old Friends.

ST. HUMPHREY

Once upon a time there was an Abbot in Egypt, and his name was *not* Humphrey. One day this Abbot thought that he would like to go and see how all the Hermits in the Desert were getting on, and so he set out after dinner for a few days' Travel Round.

He visited first one and then another, and then he found a dead Hermit and buried him, and he spent the night in the dead Hermit's Cell, which was very Convenient. The next day he went Further into the Desert, and at last he came to a Cave. He peered inside. No one there! He went in and looked round carefully, because of robbers. It looked clean and swept, and there was a plant in a pot growing near the door. The Abbot felt the ashes of the fire, and they were Warm, and then he saw a plate and a jug of water.

" Someone lives here! " he said to himself, " and whoever it is can't be far away. I'll wait until he comes back."

So he sat on a stone just inside the door, and began to say his Office (which is prayers that priests say every day).

Soon he heard trampling, and cows mooing and a dog barking, and he looked out, and there was a man dressed like a monk coming along, driving some cows, with his dog running behind him.

When he got to the Cave the man stood Stock Still with Surprise!

" Who are you? " he asked. " I haven't seen a stranger for years and years! "

"I'm just an Abbot, doing some Visiting," said the Abbot. "Is there anything that I can do for you?"

"I am very Happy," said the Hermit. "God is very good to me."

"If I may say so," said the Abbot, "you are a funny sort of Hermit, having Pot Plants and Animals and things."

"Well," said the Hermit, whose name was *not* Humphrey, "I have them because God made them, and when I look at them I think how beautifully they are made. Sometimes things are even more beautiful inside than outside, and they are so neatly Fastened Off and Lined and all that. And if they are so wonderful then God who made them must be much more Wonderful. And if they are beautiful then God who made them must be much more Beautiful. So that all the things that I see about me make me think of the Glory of God. Even Air."

"Why air?" asked the Abbot, in an Interested voice.

"Well, air is soft and invisible, and it doesn't look like anything, or feel like anything. It is so soft you can't feel it at all. *But* if I push a Tree I can't move it. God can move it about with Air. He can even blow it right over! And He doesn't have any sort of Machine to make the wind, like we would have to have. He just uses what's there."

"*Well*, now!" said the Abbot, "I never thought of that myself. What about the cows?"

The Hermit looked at the cows. "They wandered in here one night," he said. "I expect that God sent them in out of the cold. In return for that I look after them, and in return for that they give me milk. I give the milk to other Hermits, so that they can drink it and live to love and praise God. It all comes from God, and it all goes back to Him."

"I like your sort of Hermit," said the Abbot. "How do you manage for the Sacraments?"

"One of the nearby Hermits is a Priest," said the Hermit, "and we go to him on Sundays and holidays, and he says Mass."

"Good!" said the Abbot. "Well, I must be getting along. Good-bye, and God bless you!"

And he went off further and further into the Desert. After going along for seventeen more days he saw a man with long Hair and a Beard and dressed in a Rag.

"Oh, dear!" said the Abbot, "now this really *is* a Robber!" And he hid behind a rock and waited for the Man dressed in a Rag to pass by. But as he came up to the rock he said:

"Come out! my Lord Abbot. Don't be afraid of me because I am here for the love of God."

"Well, now," said the Abbot, "I never would have thought it, I'm sure." And he came out and Stared politely at the Man.

"Who are you, please?" he asked.

"I am a Hermit, and my name is Humphrey," said the man, "would you like to come and spend the night with me?"

"Thank you," said the Abbot. "I am pretty tired."

Humphrey lived in a Cell under a Palm Tree, which had dates growing on it. When they got there they found that it was so small that one of them would have to sleep outside, because there was not enough room for two. They decided that it would be more polite if they both slept out, and they did, and they had Dates for supper, and then they talked and talked.

"The last Hermit I visited," said the Abbot, "wasn't a *bit* the same as you. He had plants and things because they made him think more about God. You don't seem to have anything at all."

"I haven't got much," said Humphrey. "I eat what I find, mostly dates, and I drink water from the little well over there."

"But you haven't even got a cup or a plate or a bed!" said the Abbot.

"I have got a Cell for the winter, and when it rains," said Humphrey. "God is very good to me."

"That is what the other Hermit said," said the Abbot, "but why are you so *very* poor?"

"Well, Our Lord was very poor," said Humphrey.

"But not so poor as that," said the Abbot.

"No, but I am so much less Important than Our Lord," said Humphrey, "so it seems to me that I ought to be poorer and have less things. Also, if you haven't got anything you can't lose anything, and Robbers never come. If I have things then I have to look after them and think about them sometimes, and that makes me have less time to think about God."

"Well, now!" said the Abbot, "I never thought about that myself. How do you manage about the Sacraments, all these miles out in the Desert?"

"As a matter of fact," said Humphrey, looking Rather Embarrassed, "An Angel brings me Holy Communion every Sunday. My Guardian Angel, it is."

"Does he *really?*" said the Abbot, all Astonished. "God must love you very much."

"I love God very much," said Humphrey, "but I shouldn't think that He has much reason to love me."

"Shouldn't you?" said the Abbot, and they went to sleep.

When the Abbot woke up in the morning he thought that Humphrey looked Very Ill Indeed, and he said so.

"I know," said Humphrey, "I am going to die to-day, and God sent you here so that you could hear my confession and then Bury me."

The Abbot got the breakfast ready (it was dates and water), and he went and sat sadly beside Humphrey. He hadn't known him very long, but he liked him very much, and he rather thought that he would like to be a Hermit who had nothing at All for the love of God.

Then Humphrey said:—

" I'll tell you something, my Lord Abbot. After I die and I am with God, if anyone remembers me and says a prayer for me, or gives food to the Poor for me, I will ask God to bless him. Our Lord told me that He would do anything that I asked him, once I had finished my life here."

" Supposing that a man is too poor himself to give food to a Beggar," said the Abbot, " won't you pray for him? "

" Well, if he burns some Incense and prays for me, that will be enough," said Humphrey.

" But supposing he is too poor even to get any Incense," said the Abbot, " won't you pray for him? "

" Well, he can just remember me and pray for me," said Humphrey, " and I will pray for him."

" I do wish," said the Abbot, " that I could stay here in your place when you have gone."

" No," said Humphrey, " you must go and tell the others about praying for me, so that I can pray for them."

And then he made his Confession, and the Abbot gave him a very short Penance because he was so Ill. And when he had said his Penance Humphrey left his poor old body behind like an old coat and he went to God. And the Abbot buried his body near the Palm Tree with dates on it, and he thought that he would stay and be a Hermit in Spite of what Humphrey had said, but just as he had Decided the Palm Tree with dates on it drooped and died, and fell on the Cell and flattened it out!

Which did show that God wanted the Abbot to go back and tell the others. If he hadn't gone back we would never have known about Humphrey, would we?

St. Humphrey's Special Day is on June 12th, and it is quite true that if people remember him in their prayers he will ask God to bless them. I think that lots of people called Humphrey have never even heard of Saint Humphrey, which is very Sad. But perhaps I am wrong.

ST. MARTIN

Once upon a time there was a boy called Martin, and his father was a Retired Roman Soldier and his mother was very Kind and they were all Pagans.

One day, when Martin was on the way back from school, he saw a whole lot of people going into a big Building.

" I wonder what they're doing? " he thought. " Perhaps it is a Concert or something. I think I'll go in too, and see."

So he went in and sat on a bench near the door and waited to see what would happen.

Now, as a matter of fact, it wasn't a Concert at all, but a Christian Church, and everyone was there for Vespers, and as Martin watched and listened he got very Interested. He was so Interested that at the end he went and asked the Priest what it was all about.

When the Priest had told him, Martin was so very much More Interested that he said that he wanted to be a Christian.

" Well," said the Priest, " I can't make you a Christian now because you aren't a Grown-up, and your Father and Mother mightn't like it."

" I'll go and ask them," said Martin, and he hitched up his Satchel and went home.

" Mummy," he said while he was having Tea, " do you know what? "

" What, darling? " said his mother, putting some more sugar in her cup.

"I'd like to be a Christian. Would you mind?"

"I don't think I'd mind, darling," said his mother, "as long as you know what you're doing."

"Oh, *good*!" said Martin happily; "I was afraid that you and Daddy might Object."

"I don't exactly Object," said his Father, "but you are Rather Young, you know, Martin. I want you to wait until you are Older, and then you can if you still want to."

"All right," said Martin, "but may I go to the Christian Church and Learn about it meanwhile?"

"Oh, yes," said his father, "you can do that."

So Martin did, and soon he knew as much as the Christians did, but he wasn't a Christian yet himself.

When he left School Martin joined his father's old Regiment in the Roman Army, and the Roman Emperor's name was Julian.

One bitterly cold day Martin was riding along with his Regiment. Everyone was shivering, and, although their horses were tired, they made them Trot because all the Bobbing Up and Down kept them warmer. There was a Cutting Wind, and the soldiers wrapped their thick cloaks round them and wished that they were toasting their toes in front of a nice warm Fire.

Suddenly Martin saw, a little way ahead, a Poor-and-Raggy man leaning against a tree so as to keep out of the Cutting Wind. Martin looked in his purse. Nothing there! (He was none too Well Off himself.)

"I say, you chaps!" he shouted to the soldiers in front, "has anyone got any money for that Poor-and-Raggy man by the tree? I'll pay you back when we get home, if one of you will give him something!"

"Don't be silly, Martin!" answered one of the soldiers in front, "what do you want to go wasting your money for? You haven't any too much yourself! The man will soon be dead in this Cutting Wind, so it would be a terrible waste to give him anything at all!"

By this time Martin had got up to the Poor-and-Raggy man.

"What *can* I give him?" he thought, "he must be perished with cold!"

Then he had an idea. . . .

He took off his Thick Cloak and cut it clean in half with his sharp sword!

"Here, Sir!" he said to the Poor-and-Raggy man. "This will keep you warm. You aren't very big, and it will cover you up nicely. I can't give you the whole cloak because if I caught Pneumonia (which is a Coughing Illness) my Commanding Officer would be shorthanded!" And Martin spurred up his horse to catch up the others, who all made a Mock of him because they said that he looked ridiculous with only Half a Cloak. Which, no doubt, he did.

That night Martin had a Dream.

He dreamed that Our Lord came to him with a lot of Angels. The funny part was that Our Lord was wearing Half a Cloak! While Martin waited to see what would happen next, Our Lord turned to the Angels and said:

"Do you know where I got this Half Cloak? I got it from Martin, who gave it to me when he isn't even a Christian yet!"

When Martin woke up in the morning he thought this thought:

"I'd better hurry up and be Baptised! I do want to be a Proper Christian for Our Lord!" So he went to a Priest and was Baptised at once.

After a time he thought that he would rather be

a Priest and serve people instead of being a Soldier
and killing people. So he went to the Emperor Julian
and said:

"Please may I stop being a Soldier now? I've been
one for several years!"

Now Julian was an Apostate, which means that he
had been brought up as a Christian, but that when
he was a Grown-up Emperor he turned his back on
Our Lord and turned into a Pagan and worshipped
the Roman Gods. That, of course, is a *terrible* thing
to do. Pagans who are born Pagans can't help it, and
are not wicked at all because of it. But Christians
who turn into Pagans commit one of the Worst Sins
there are. Because they have *known* Our Lord and
have laughed at him and left him. And that is an Evil
and a Frightening thing. As well as turning into a Pagan,
Julian used to persecute the Christians and kill and
imprison them.

(If anyone reading this book is called Julian, he
mustn't mind at all about being like the Emperor
Julian. Because there is a very nice Saint called Julian
who built a Hospital by a River and then made himself into a Ferry Man to Ferry the ill people over in
a Ferry Boat. And once one of the Ill People was Our
Lord pretending to be a Leper, which was a Beautiful
Surprise for Julian. So never mind about having the
same name as Emperor Julian the Apostate.)

Well, now, we must go on with Martin.

When Martin asked the Emperor Julian if he could
please stop being a soldier, Julian laughed.

"Ha! Ha!" he laughed Nastily, "I know why you
came to-day about it!"

"Why do you think I came to-day?" asked Martin
in a Surprised Voice. "I didn't really come to-day for
any particular reason."

" Oh, yes, you did! " said the Emperor Julian, wagging his finger at Martin, " it is because there is a big battle to-morrow, and you are a *Coward*! "

" But I've been in heaps of battles before," said Martin, " we are always having battles, it seems to me! "

" Well, never mind about the other battles," said Julian crossly, " I say that you are a Coward *this* time! "

Now no one likes being called a Coward, specially brave Soldiers like Martin, so Martin said Rather Huffily:

" Very well. I'll *prove* to you that I am not a Coward. I'll march in the Very Front of the Army without my Helmet or my Shield or my Breastplate or my Sword. The only Armour that I'll have will be the Sign of the Cross, and you'll see, I won't be wounded! "

" The Sign of the Cross won't help you, Coward Martin," said the Emperor Julian, " but I'll take you at your word! "

And he gave orders that Martin was to march in Front of the Army without his Helmet and things.

But in the morning the Enemy sent a message to say that they would Give In without a Battle. Which just shows that God was looking after Martin!

Heaps of other Interesting Things happened to Martin. He did become a Priest, like he wanted to. And then, when he was Older Still, he was the Bishop of a place called Tours in France, and the people loved him so much that he has been called St. Martin of Tours ever since. One thing Important that he did was this: He built the first Monastery in France, near Poitiers.

St. Martin's Special Day is on Armistice Day, November 11th, and there are heaps of people called after him besides the people who have Birthdays on that day. And because there isn't a story about St. Julian in this book, people called after him may have this story for theirs. Because I did just Mention him. St. Julian's Day is January 9th.

ST. PATRICK

Once upon a time there was a man called Patrick and he was Welsh but most of the time he lived in Ireland.

One day when he had been teaching the Irish people how to be Christians, he thought this thought:

" Supposing that after all my Work some of the Irish People do not get to Heaven after all, it will be a Terrible Disappointment to me. Besides, it will not be very nice for the people who get Left Out."

So he climbed to the top of a great stony Mountain which had on the Very top an enormous Rock called The Rick. Patrick climbed up on to The Rick and sat himself down and said:

" I will spend the Whole of Lent up here praying that All the Irish People will get to Heaven in the end, no matter how long they may have to stay in Purgatory beforehand."

So he prayed and prayed and prayed, and by nearly the end of the Forty Days of Lent he was so Hot and Tired what with sitting on The Rick and praying and all that, that although he was a Grown Man he began to cry! He cried a lot and his clothes got quite wet with all his Tears, and *still* God hadn't answered him about the Irish people going to Heaven. So at the end of the Forty Days and Nights of Lent Patrick said to himself:

" Well, I suppose I must just stay here and go on praying." So he did.

After a few days St. Michael said to one of the Angels:

" I wish Patrick would get off The Rick; I want it for something."

ST. PATRICK

" Shall I go and tell him? " said the other Angel, whose name was Victor.

" Yes, do," said St. Michael.

So the Angel Victor went to The Rick and comforted Patrick and took off his wet cloak and spread it on the sunny rock to Dry, and he said:

" Because you have prayed so long and so hard, as many Irish People as would fill the space between Here and As Far Out to Sea as you can see will go to Heaven. And will you please get down off The Rick, because St. Michael wants it for something."

This made Patrick feel a little better and he thought that he would try to Drive a Bargain, so he said:

" Well, I have been crying so much that my eyes are Sore, so I can't see Very Far Out to Sea."

So then the Angel Victor said:

" Very well then, you can have as many people as would fill As Far as you can See on Land, as well. So now will you please hurry up and get off The Rick? Your cloak is quite dry."

Patrick made a Surprised Face and said:

" Is that all? After I have been sitting here and praying for More than Forty Days? "

" Well," said the Angel, " you can have seven more people every Saturday until the End of the World."

" *And* my Twelve Friends who help me in my Work," said Patrick.

" All right, *and* your Twelve Friends," said the Angel Victor, " now get off The Rick! "

" No, I don't *think* I'll get off yet," said Patrick, " what else can I have? "

" Well, you can have Twelve People every Thursday as well as the Saturday ones," said the Angel Victor, " and now go on, do, I can't wait here all day."

But Patrick was very pleased at the way he was Driving

his Bargain and getting more and more People for Heaven, so he said:

"No. I won't go until I have something else too."

"*What* else?" said the poor Angel, who was getting Tired of all this.

"That Ireland will always be Catholic," said Patrick.

"All right, you can have that too, *and* whoever sings your Special Hymn, will be saved, *and* whoever does Penance in Ireland. Surely that is enough?"

Patrick was enjoying his Bargaining very much by now, and his cloak felt Warm and Comfortable, so he said:

"No." Just like that.

"Well, we'll have to Turn you Off by Force, then," said the Angel Victor, "and the Forces of Heaven are very Strong, remember."

"No, wait!" said Patrick, "don't do that! But I won't go (unless God himself tells me) until I have One More Thing. Only One more!"

"Well, what *do* you want?" said the Angel Victor crossly. He was sick of all this Arguing.

"I want," said Patrick, very slowly because he was asking for such an Enormous Thing, "I want, on the Day of Judgment, to be the Judge of the Irish People, under God of course."

"But you CAN'T!" said the Angel Victor, all Horrified and Shocked at Patrick. "Don't be Silly, and *come down*, there's a good man."

Patrick smiled a Big Smile.

"No," he said, "unless you go back and ask God to let me do that I'll stay here for Ever and Ever until I am dead and then I'll leave someone else here instead of me and so you will never be able to have The Rick."

The Angel Victor flew away to God and told him what Patrick had said.

ST. PATRICK

"Well," said God, "he has been praying very well for a very Long Time, so I suppose I'll have to let him. I do not want him turned off by Force because I like him."

The Angel Victor flew back to Patrick.

"All right," he said, "you can."

"Good," said Patrick. "Now I'll get down." And he went away, laughing at his Bargain.

And that is why the Irish People love St. Patrick, because on the Last Day, when he is Judging them, they feel sure he will let them all go to Heaven!

After Patrick died the Irish people built a Chapel on The Rick and they called the Stony Mountain Croagh Patrick and so it is called to this very day. And once a year Thousands of People climb up there for Mass. They have to start After Supper the day before and Climb Up the Stones all night in the Dark so as to be there in Time.

St. Patrick's Special Day is on March 17th, but why the Irish People wear a piece of Shamrock on that day is Another Story.

ST. DANIEL

Once upon a time there was a very young monk called Daniel and he lived in an Abbey in Syria.

One day the Abbot of the Abbey—(what is an Abbot? What is an Abbess?)—the Abbot of the Abbey sent for Daniel and said:

"Brother Daniel, I have to go on a journey to Antioch, and I shall take you with me."

"Thank you, Father Abbot," said Daniel politely, and he waited to see what next.

"You are very Young, Brother Daniel," said the Abbot, "and it will do you good to see a little more of the World before you settle down. We will start to-morrow."

"Thank you, Father Abbot," said Daniel politely, and went away, shutting the door carefully and quietly. But when he was in the corridor he couldn't help giving a little skip sometimes as he hurried back to his work because he was so Delighted.

One day when they were in Antioch Daniel was waiting for the Abbot who was talking Business with the Bishop. He stood outside the door and looked at the people passing by.

"Where are so many of them going?" he asked a man who was waiting for someone else.

"They are going to see Simon," said the man.

"Who is Simon?" said Daniel.

"Don't you *know*?" said the man.

"No," said Daniel.

"Well," said the man, "he is a very holy man who

lives on the top of a Pillar and prays. At least he stands there all day. I believe he sleeps in a little hut at the bottom."

" But why does he do that? " asked Daniel.

" I'm not quite sure," said the man. Just then the person he was waiting for came out and they went away.

Daniel thought what an Extraordinary Thing it was to live on a Pillar and pray. All the monks prayed at the Abbey, but no one had thought of standing on a Pillar.

When the Abbot came out from seeing the Bishop, Daniel told him about Simon.

" Oh yes," said the Abbot. " I've often heard of him. I'd forgotten that he lived here."

" But why does he stand on a Pillar? " asked Daniel.

" Well," said the Abbot, " I believe that at first Simon was a monk. Then he became a Hermit. God was very Good to him and when sometimes he asked for things for the people living near by He gave them to him. So more and more people came to see Simon and soon there was always a crowd round him and nobody can be a Hermit in the middle of a crowd.

" So then," said the Abbot, " Simon went to a little hill and he built a stone wall round the top, not a high wall, and he built it right round himself and made a tiny little hut in the middle. He thought that the crowd would stay outside the wall and talk to him over it. So they did, at first. Then the people got over the wall and made such a jostling crowd that poor Simon was always being trampled and squashed so that when he preached he used to climb on to the little roof of his hut, so that people could see and hear him. But the people used to grab his feet to make him listen to them and so he made a high Pillar and climbed up there so as to be out of the way. So he could still be a Hermit."

" Oh I *see*," said Daniel. " Thank you, Father Abbot, for telling me." Then he said, " Oh, *please,* Father Abbot, before we go home *could* we go and see Simon? I should so love to see him."

" I don't see why not," said the Abbot. " We will go this evening."

So they went. And there was Simon standing on the top of a Pillar with crowds and crowds of people all jostling and pushing round. He was just finishing his evening Sermon when the Abbot and Daniel came.

" Who is that young monk I see coming up the hill? " said Simon.

" It is Brother Daniel, the youngest monk in our Abbey," said the Abbot.

" Come up to me, Brother Daniel," said Simon.

" May I, Father Abbot? " said Daniel.

" Yes, go on," said the Abbot.

So Daniel climbed up a ladder to the top of the pillar and all the people stared.

There wasn't much room on top, but Simon told Daniel to kneel down and then he blessed him specially.

Daniel was *very* pleased and when he came down and they were going down the hill he told the Abbot how wise and good Simon looked when you saw him close, and what a splendid view there was from the top of the Pillar.

When they reached home again Daniel settled down in the Abbey and was a good and humble monk for years, and he often thought about Simon.

After years and years the Abbot died and Daniel was chosen to be the next Abbot.

" Oh no, *please!* " he said. " The Abbot said I could be a Hermit, and I would be a very bad Abbot." Well, they found that it was quite true and that the Abbot *had* said so, and Daniel set out.

First he spent a fortnight with Simon and learnt how Hermits lived and prayed and taught. Then he went to visit all the Holy Places in Palestine before settling down. He went to Bethlehem and Nazareth and Jerusalem and the Sea of Galilee and the Mount of Olives and all those places and he looked at them very often and very carefully so that he would be able to make Sermons about them when he became a Hermit.

Then he found a lonely cave near Jerusalem and began his Hermit's life. But it was very Disturbing and Noisy there. Owls hooted and swooped about in the night, and bats flew round his lamp, and jackals howled outside, and he had to block up his door with big stones to keep out the wolves in the cold weather.

" Really," he thought, " I might just as well live in a Noisy Street." But he did his best to put up with it all because if you only have your own way, you very often miss God's way. So Daniel lived in his Noisy cave for nine years and then he said to God:

" Please, dear God, do you think I might move to a Quieter Place now? Not, of course, if you want me to stay here."

And God, who liked Daniel very much because he had tried not to mind the Noise for such a long time, said:

" In a little while, Daniel, you will see that it will be time to go."

And sure enough, in a few days a man called Sergius came walking by and stopped to ask Daniel how far he had got.

" Where did you come from? " said Daniel.

" I was the servant and disciple of Simon who stood on a Pillar," said Sergius, " but he died a little time ago. This is his Cloak, would you like it? "

" Oh I *would*," said Daniel. " I always thought Simon

was a very Holy Man. I'd love to have something of his to remind me of him."

" Shall I stay with you and be your Disciple? " said Sergius. " I could do the Shopping and so forth."

So that is what they did. But the more that Daniel wore Simon's cloak the more he wanted to live on a pillar too. So Sergius helped him to find one in some nearby Ruins. It was quite short, but it was easier to get used to a short one.

But the people who came to hear him preach didn't like the Ruins at all. They slipped about on the broken stones and twisted their ankles and grumbled to Sergius.

" It was much easier for us when he was in the Cave," they said.

" But it was too Noisy," said Sergius.

At last a Rich Man built a new tall Pillar in an easy place for the pilgrims and Daniel stood there from Dawn to Dusk and he slept in a little hut at the bottom, just like Simon did. More and more people came to see Daniel and to listen to him, and God made him cure ill people as soon as he touched them. There was a little kind of Lift that the Ill people went in to the Top of the Pillar, and when Daniel blessed them they were better at once.

One winter Daniel was very ill himself with a Terrible cough and cold and couldn't stand on the pillar for a day or two.

" Why? What happened? Is he ill? Is he dead? Where is he? " asked all the people who came to see him.

" Well," said Sergius, " in that Snowstorm we had last week Daniel had to stay up on his pillar for two whole nights and days. He couldn't come down because of the Ice. He hadn't an extra rug or anything."

" But this is Shocking! " said the Emperor. " A Holy Man like that catching his Death of Cold! I'll see to it."

And he had an enormously fat Pillar built by a Famous Builder, and he made a tiny little hut on top in case Daniel got Snow Bound again.

Daniel was very pleased with his smart new Pillar, but he hadn't lived on it for long when there was a Terrific Thunderstorm. The pillar shook and trembled and a crack came all down one side of it!

The Emperor was Furious!

"Where's that Builder?" he shouted. "I *will* not have Shoddy work, especially now that bricks and cement are so Expensive! He has Cheated me, I'll have his blood!"

"Wait!" said Daniel. "It wasn't the Builder's fault! God sent the Storm and no one can make anything so strong that God can't break it if he wants to. Perhaps I am Too Vain with my smart new Pillar!" And he came down to pray about it in case it was so.

So the Emperor got on his horse and rode away from Daniel, but on the way down his horse tripped and fell and the Emperor was flung to the ground so hard that all the Pearls were jerked out of his Crown.

His groom who was riding behind him was so terrified when he saw the Emperor sitting in the Road, that he turned round and hurried back to Daniel.

"I am sure His Majesty will blame *me*!" he said. "He will say that the horse's shoe was loose or Something."

So Daniel hid him in the little house on the top of the Pillar and went to help the people who were picking up the Emperor, who wasn't really hurt and rode off saying that now he would have the Groom's blood!

The Groom stayed with Daniel for a while and was baptised after he had learned about being a Christian. Then Daniel sent him back to the Palace with a letter for the Emperor which said:

" Your Majesty,

" I am sending you back your Groom. Do not blame him for your accident, it was not his fault and he is a good friend of mine. God bless you.

"From
"Daniel."

The Emperor read it and then he looked at the Groom. " What's all the fuss about? " he said. " I'm not blaming *you*. It was probably my own fault for Riding Away Grandly from such a Holy Man instead of Walking Away Humbly."

Daniel lived on his Pillar until he was Eighty, and hundreds and hundreds of Pagans became Christians after they had listened to his Sermons and his teaching.

St. Daniel's Special Day is on December 11th, and people all over the world are called after him.

ST. ALAN

O nce upon a time there was a man called Alan
and he lived in Rome. One day, when he was out
and about, he heard that England wasn't all Christian,
but only in patches.

"It seems to me," said Alan, "that the only thing
to do about it is to go to one of the Pagan Patches and
start a Christian Patch in the middle of it and wait
till it spreads."

So he went home, and while they were all having
supper he told his family that they were all going to
England to start a Christian Patch.

Alan's wife was rather fussed over the packing, and
in the end they thought it would be best to have a Whole
Boat to themselves and put all their things in it like
in a Removal Van.

So they took their clothes and their furniture and a
lot of food and a cooking stove, and the Children and
the dogs and their servants, and twelve cows and some
hay and turnips for them, and Alan's Tame Deer,
and they all sailed away to England.

After some weeks they landed on the Island of Anglesey off Wales. It took Rather a long time to get all
their things off the boat, what with the cows and all, but
luckily it was flat and sandy and no cliffs, and at last
they were all Safely Ashore.

Alan looked all Round and About.

"Well, my dear," he said to his wife, "there doesn't
seem to be anybody here at all. Perhaps you wouldn't
mind seeing to Supper while we build a House."

" Certainly, dear," said Alan's wife, and she got her cooking apron out of her trunk and began to make some supper.

Meanwhile Alan and the children and the servants all raced about with axes and hammers and spades and saws and I don't know what all, and in Next to no Time, strange as it may seem, they had a nice new house, all ready to go to bed in! It was built of grey stones mostly, because the trees were so Far and Few because of the wind.

Next day Alan and his people built a stable for the cows and a little small loose-box at the end for the Tame Deer.

" Now for the Church! " said Alan, rubbing his hands and beaming at all his Household.

" The *Church*! " they all said in Surprised Voices. When they had all finished shaking little fingers because of saying the same thing at the same time Alan said:

" Yes, because we came here to make a Christian Patch, did you forget? "

They all said no, of course they hadn't forgotten, but what with unpacking and building and all that it had just Slipped their Minds.

So they built a good big Church, so that there would be room for all the new Christians there were going to be. They had just finished it, and Alan's wife was giving the brasses a final Polish Up with her yellow duster when someone shouted:

" Hey! "

" Who said that? " said Alan looking round at his Household.

" It wasn't me," they all said, and they shook little fingers again.

" Hey! " said the voice.

Alan went round to the back of the Church, and

there he saw two strange men staring at the House and Stables and Church and everything.

" What *is* all this? " said one of the men.

" It's where we live," said Alan.

" Who said you could? " said the Other Man.

" Nobody," said Alan, " but there hasn't been a soul near the place since we came a month ago, so no one can use it much."

All Alan's Household edged a bit closer to hear what was going on.

" All the same," said the First Man, " our King, whose name is Cadwallon, will be very displeased."

" *Cadwallon?* " said Alan. " Is that really his name? "

" Yes, it is, and what's wrong with it? " said the Other Man.

" Oh, nothing, nothing," said Alan, and he waved his hand behind his back at all his Household, who were giggling and saying " Cadwallon! " to each other.

" Well, we will go and see what he has to say about it! " said the men, and they went away.

Now King Cadwallon was really Very Displeased with Alan for making a Church without asking, and he said so very Loud and Clear. So all the British people decided that *they* wouldn't like Alan either, and they used to throw stones and steal the vegetables and things to annoy Alan's wife. But one day somebody stole two cows and their calves, and Alan thought that was a Bit Too Much, and he went to King Cadwallon and said:

" Please may I have my cows back? "

" What cows? " said Cadwallon, and he winked at one of his Nobles, and Alan saw him do it.

" The cows your people stole from me," said Alan.

" How do I know you ever had any cows? " said Cadwallon.

"Well, the others are still there and you can see their footmarks on the stones where they landed," said Alan.

"Well, anyway, you can't have them back," said King Cadwallon, "because you are Christians, and I don't like your God."

"Don't like him?" said Alan. "What a Horrible and Stupid thing to say!"

"He isn't any Good," said King Cadwallon.

Alan said to God:

"Please show him how strong you are, dear God, he will never believe me if I try and explain."

And God said very quietly to Alan:

"It is quite all right, this will be the beginning of your Christian Patch." And he made Cadwallon and his nobles Blind! and Alan went home.

In a little while some messengers came from King Cadwallon to Alan and this was their polite message:

"Please Alan will you very kindly come and visit me at my Palace?

"With kind regards,

"from

"Cadwallon (King)."

So Alan went, and there was King Cadwallon sitting sadly in his chair by the fire.

"Is that you, Alan?" he said, when the door opened.

"Yes," said Alan.

"If you will only make me Un-Blind again I will give you Ten Extra Cows," said King Cadwallon.

"But *I* didn't make you Blind!" said Alan; "it wasn't because of Cows."

"Well, why am I?" said King Cadwallon.

" God made you Blind because you said he was No Good," said Alan.

" Well, could you ask him to make me better? " said King Cadwallon; " and I will give you Anything in my Kingdom! "

" Promise? " said Alan.

" I promise," said King Cadwallon.

So Alan prayed for King Cadwallon and God made him and all his nobles as Good as New.

" Now what do you want for a Reward? " said King Cadwallon to Alan.

" As much ground as my Tame Deer will graze over in one day," said Alan.

" What for? " said King Cadwallon.

" To make a Christian Village which will spread into a Christian Patch among the Pagans," said Alan.

" All right," said King Cadwallon.

So the next day Alan let the Tame Deer out of the stable and she started to eat the grass round about. As the day went on she wandered further and further away until she had covered a Tidy Piece of Ground. But a Miserable Thing happened. While everyone was at Tea somebody's Greyhound killed the Deer! Alan was dreadfully upset, and his wife was even sadder, and all the Children cried and King Cadwallon was so sorry for them that he made a New Rule. And this was the New Rule:

That nobody in Anglesey was ever to have a Greyhound again, until the End of the World.

And he gave Alan the Tidy Piece of Ground, and some of the Nobles who had been blinded became Christians, and were the first people to live in the new Christian Village, and in time it spread quite a long way.

An interesting thing is that at the place where Alan

ST. ALAN

landed from his ship you can find stones with the hoof-marks of his ten cows just like he said to King Cadwallon, but I don't know if people still keep the Rule about the Greyhounds.

St. Alan's Special Day is January 12th. Llanelian in Anglesey is called after him, and King Cadwallon is buried in Bangor Cathedral.

ST. BENEDICT

Once upon a time there was a boy called Benedict, and he lived in Italy, and when he was Ten years old he went to School in Rome. His old Nurse that had looked after him when he was Little, went to Rome with him to mend his things, and cook, and So on, and So forth. But after five years of living in Rome, he saw so many Thieves and Pickpockets and Robbers and things that he said to his Nurse:

"You know, Nanny, the World must be a very Bad place."

"Not so bad when you know it better, Benedict," said the Old Nurse.

"It seems too Bad to live in until I *do* know it better, though," said Benedict.

"What will you do, then, Benedict?" asked the Old Nurse.

"I shall be a Hermit, Nanny," said Benedict, "and I shall live all by myself in a Wood or something and grow my own food and get to know God better, instead of the World."

"I shall go too, Benedict," said the Old Nurse.

"But you *can't*, Nanny!" said Benedict. "Hermits *never* have Nurses!"

"Well, you'll be the Only One then, Benedict," said the Old Nurse, "because I'm going with you to mend your things and cook and All That."

"Perhaps there won't be anything to cook, Nanny," said Benedict.

"Then I'll beg for you, Benedict," said the Old Nurse, and so it was settled.

ST. BENEDICT

One day Benedict's Nurse was carrying a Sieve with some bread in it, when she tripped on a Stone and dropped it. The sieve was Smashed beyond Repair, and she was Distracted! Because the sieve wasn't hers, but a borrowed one.

So she sat on the ground and cried and tried to stick it together, but it was too badly broken.

"What *is* the matter, Nanny?" asked Benedict, coming back with some Crab Apples that he had found.

"I've broken the sieve and I can't mend it, Benedict!" said the Old Nurse.

"Well, give it to me a minute, Nanny," said Benedict. And he took it away and said:

"Please God, we are very Poor, so as to try to be Good and Pleasing to you. So we can't Afford to buy a new sieve for the lady that Nanny borrowed it from. So what shall we do? Would you please Mend it for us?"

And at once the sieve was as Good as New!

Now, of course, the Old Nurse couldn't keep such a marvellous thing to herself! Her Benedict that she had looked after all his life, and Bathed, and Dressed, and Brushed his hair, and Fed with porridge when he was Little. And now, when he was Big, she still looked after him. So, next time she went out to beg for food she told all the people that she met! And when she got home there was already a Crowd all standing round and Staring at poor Benedict, and asking him to do Miracles for them, and to let them live with him, and to Bless things, and I don't know What All.

"Nanny, what *have* you been saying?" he asked, as she came up with her bag of Beggings.

"I only told some people how wonderfully you mended the sieve, Benedict," said the Old Nurse.

"Is that all?" asked Benedict.

"I said maybe you were a Saint, Benedict," said the Old Nurse, "and so you are, my dear."

"But I'm *not!*" said poor Benedict, "and I can't Bless all these people, I'm not a Priest, I'm only a Boy! Tell them to go away, Nanny, they make me feel Shy."

So the Old Nurse sent the people away, and that evening, when they were having Supper, Benedict said:

"You know, Nanny, we can't stay here any more. All those people will come back to-morrow."

"What shall we do, then, Benedict?" asked the Old Nurse.

"Well, I'll go on somewhere and be a Proper Hermit by myself," said Benedict, "and you, Nanny, can go back to the Family and tell them that I'm quite all right and All That."

So that is what they did. And Benedict went and lived in a Cave by himself for years and years, and he learned a lot about God, and God loved him and came and talked to him and told him things.

Now there was a Raven (which is a big black Bird rather like a Rook and rather like a Crow) and it lived near Benedict's Cave, and it used to come and eat Crumbs and things, and it got quite Tame.

Well, as time went on, people began to hear about Benedict and how good and kind he was, and one day some Monks came to see him, and they asked him if he would go and be their Abbot (which is the Head Monk), because their Abbot had just died.

"But I'm a Hermit, not a Monk," said Benedict; "I'd never thought of being an Abbot."

"Well, but," said one of the Monks, "we *need* some-one like you to be Head Monk because you know such a Lot."

In the end Benedict said that he would, and off they went at once, and Benedict took the Raven with him in case it got lonely.

But after a few days Benedict was so Shocked at the Monks' lazy ways that he said:

"It's no use at all you being Monks if you don't behave like Proper Monks. You all Eat too much and Sleep too much and Talk too much. You quarrel, and tell lies, and pretend to be very Holy, but you forget God. What sort of Monks do you suppose you are? Come now, let's Pull ourselves Together and live in the way that God means us to!"

But the Monks were Furious! They had been having a very good time in their Monastery, pretending to be good and holy. It was too much Work, they said, to be a Proper Monk.

At last some of them got together and had an Idea. And this was the Idea.

Just before Dinner they put some POISON in Benedict's cup. Then they went round and filled up all the cups so that it wouldn't show. Then one of them Rang the Gong, and all the Other Monks and Benedict came in to Dinner. They all went and sat in their places, and the Wicked ones waited for Benedict to drink the Poison and fall down Dead. But, as he picked up his cup, Benedict made the Sign of the Cross over it, and what do you suppose happened?

The cup smashed into a Thousand Pieces and the Poison trickled over the table and dripped down on to the floor!

The Monks stared at it in Horror and Fright! What would Benedict do to them? What excuses could they make?

Benedict looked at them:

"May God forgive you, Brothers," he said, and he

went out of the dining-room, leaving the Monks still Staring at the broken cup!

Benedict took his Raven and went back to his Cave. But he was so Famous that a lot of other Hermits came and lived near him, and soon they asked him to teach them more about God.

So Benedict and the Hermits built a Monastery with a Church in the Middle, and Benedict made up some Rules, and they lived very Strictly. They did all their own work and grew their own things to eat, and they said the Office and had Mass every day. They got up in the Night to pray in the Church, and so they soon learned a lot about God, and they were very Happy.

Then Benedict went to Rome to ask the Pope if he and his Hermits (who weren't Hermits any more, now) could please be a New Order. An Order is a lot of Monks or Friars or Nuns who live together with Special Rules. Like the Dominicans, who live by the Rule of St. Dominic, and the Franciscans who live by the Rules that St. Francis made up, and the Carmelites who have St. Simon Stock's Rule.

"Yes, Benedict," said the Pope, "you may certainly start a New Order because I have heard about how well you pray and how hard you work. Teach your Monks to do the same, won't you? What sort of Habit would you like?"

"All Black, please, your Holiness," said Benedict in a Pleased voice, "all Black, habit and cloak and all, like my Raven."

"Very well," said the Pope. And so it was. And so it is.

While Benedict was in Rome seeing about his new Order, he met some friends of his who were going on a Journey with their wives.

"But what," they said to Benedict, "can we do with our Little Boys?"

"I'll take them back to the Monastery with me, if you like," said Benedict, "and we'll look after them for you." And he did. And soon other people brought their little boys to St. Benedict's Monastery to be brought up and taught their Lessons. And that is why so many Benedictine Monasteries are Schools as well. I expect, when you are Older, that some of you will be going to Ampleforth or Belmont or Fort Augustus or Downside or somewhere, and when you do you can remember about Benedict and his friends' little boys who had nowhere to go to when their Families went travelling.

Well, Benedict started Twelve other Monasteries of Monks in their Black Habits, and I can't possibly tell

you all the Interesting things that happened to him.
But I will tell you some of them.

Once, Attila, who was the King of some people called
Huns, wanted to find out if God really told things to
Benedict like people said that he did. So he made
up a Trick. And this was the Trick.

He got one of his Courtiers and dressed him up in
all his Royal clothes and Crown and things and sent
him to Benedict and told him to pretend to be Attila-
King-of-the-Huns. Attila himself went with him and
hid a little way from the Monastery.

When the Courtier-dressed-like-Attila got to the
Monastery he knocked at the door.

One of the Brothers opened it.

" Good morning! " he said politely, like Benedictines
always do.

" Good morning! " said the Courtier. " May I speak
to Benedict? "

" What name shall I say? " asked the Monk.

" Say that Attila-King-of-the-Huns would like to see
him," said the Courtier.

" Certainly, your Majesty," said the Monk, " please
come in." And he went away to tell Benedict.

" Please, Father Abbot," he said, " his Majesty Attila-
King-of-the-Huns would like to see you."

" Would he? " said Benedict. " You know, Brother,
he is a very Wicked man by all I've heard tell. I've
never seen him, have you? "

" Only just now, Father Abbot," said the Monk,
" never before."

" Well, show him here, please, Brother," said Benedict. (And in case you may not know, Monks and things
always call each other Brother because of all being
the Children of God.)

So the Monk went out and fetched the Courtier

(who was pretending to be Attila-King-of-the-Huns).
He opened Benedict's door and said:

"His Majesty Attila-King-of-the-Huns, Father Abbot!"

Benedict looked up.

"Where?" he asked.

"Here," said the Courtier, "*I* am King Attila!"

"No you are not," said Benedict, "Attila is still outside, send him in to me!"

The Courtier was so Taken Aback that he hurried out at once without saying a word! He quickly found King Attila and told him what had happened.

"And he wants you, your Majesty," he said. "You'd better go at once!"

Attila-King-of-the-Huns hurried up to the Monastery, and the Monk who had taken up the Courtier took him up to Benedict's room.

Attila went in very quietly without opening the door very wide and then he stood just inside the door. He was Afraid of Benedict.

"So there you are!" said Benedict; "now, you Silly Man, just listen to me! You are fifty years old; you have never done a single Kind thing in your life; you have killed Hundreds of people and told Hundreds of lies. You have cheated and stolen from your Subjects. *And you have just Ten Years more to Live!* So what are you going to do about it?"

Attila was Astonished that Benedict knew so much about him, and he was Afraid as well.

"Only Ten more years?" he said.

"Yes," said Benedict; "you'd better hurry up!"

"How do you mean, hurry up?" asked Attila.

"Well," said Benedict, "you have been Impossibly Wicked for fifty years and you've only got ten years to Make Up for it."

" Oh, I see! " said Attila-King-of-the-Huns. " It isn't much time when you think of it like that, is it? What shall I do? "

" Go back to the Huns and lead an Exemplary life," said Benedict; " I'll help you! " (Exemplary is when someone sets a good Example.)

So Attila did, and he was very Honoured and Respected after that.

Then there was a Wicked Priest called Florentius who was very Jealous of Benedict because he was so Good and Wise, and so he wanted to get rid of him. So he got into the Monastery one night and went into the Dining-Room. Now the Monks used to get up so early in the morning that they used to set Breakfast ready before they went to bed. So Florentius put a piece of Poisoned bread in Benedict's place and took away the nice piece. Then he got out of the window again and hurried away.

When all the Monks came in to Breakfast, God said to Benedict:

" Benedict, your piece of bread is poisoned."

" Is it? " asked Benedict; " thank you *very* much for telling me."

He picked up the piece of Bread and gave it to the Raven who was hopping about the floor waiting for his Breakfast.

" Here," he said, " fly away with it and put it out of Harm's Way."

But the Raven knew that it was Poisoned and he daren't touch it. He hopped round and round it and cawed and croaked and flapped his wings.

" Go on! " said Benedict, " it won't hurt you, I promise! "

So the Raven picked up the piece of bread in his Beak and flew away with it for three whole days and put it out of Harm's Way. Where he put it we don't know, because no one ever found it. Then he flew back again for three whole days, and there he was, as usual, in time for Breakfast on the Seventh Day.

One day Benedict had been out very Late, and the Next Top Monk said to one of the young ones:

" Will you wait up for the Father Abbot, Brother, and get him some supper and hold his Candle for him when he gets back? "

The Young Monk said that he would, and all the Others went to bed. So the young Monk Waited Up, and when Benedict came in he gave him some Bread and Cheese and an Apple and a cup of Water. But while he was holding the Candle so that Benedict could see what he was doing, he thought this thought:

" Why should *I* have to Wait Up for this Old Man? *My* father was a Noble Lord, this man's father was quite ordinary. Really, a gentleman like me shouldn't have to Wait on people! " And he made a Disgusted Face.

" Never mind, Brother! " said Benedict, who knew what he was thinking, " go and rest! I thought that you wanted to be like Our Lord, who washed his disciples' feet, and got their Breakfasts ready for them. But you needn't! "

" But I *want* to be like Our Lord! " said the Young Monk, who hadn't thought about Our Lord Waiting On people.

" No, " said Benedict, " go and rest. " And the Young Monk went away very sorry that he had missed his chance of being like Our Lord.

Once a Rich friend sent Benedict two bottles of Rare

Wine for a present. But the servant who took them
to the Monastery thought to himself:

"Why should Benedict have *two* bottles of Rare
Wind, and me none? He'll never know, if I keep one
of them." So he hid one of the bottles under a Tree
Root and went on to the Monastery. When he got there
he said to Benedict:

"Please, Father Abbot, my master has sent you this
bottle of Rare Wine for a Present. And he hopes that
you will enjoy it."

"Please thank your master for me!" said Benedict,
and the servant went to the door, delighted that Benedict
hadn't Found Out. As he got to the door Benedict
said:

"Good Sir, be careful not to drink anything out of
that bottle you hid under the Tree Root. You don't
know what is in it!"

The servant was very much Ashamed, and he hurried
away. When he got to the Tree Root he took out the
bottle.

"I wonder what Benedict meant?" he said to himself; "surely it must be Rare Wine!" But he took
out the stopper very carefully and Tipped the bottle.
Out crawled a Snake!

Well, Benedict did heaps and heaps of other things.
It would fill a Whole Book if I told you them all. But
I'll tell you One More Thing.

It is about the Raven.

Often in England you will see Inns called the
"Raven," especially in Shropshire. And that is almost
always where there used to be Benedictine Monasteries.
When Henry VIII spoiled the Monasteries, the people
who lived round them called the Inns after Benedict's
Raven, in memory of the Kind Benedictines who had
helped and looked after them.

ST. BENEDICT

St. Benedict's Special Day is on March 21st, and lots of people have Benedict for their Second name. And even if they haven't, they can have St. Benedict for their Special Saint if their Birthday happens to be on March 21st.

ST. KENNETH

O nce upon a time there were a Welsh Prince and a Village Woman and they had a baby son. But when the Prince came to think about it he didn't like the idea of having a Common son instead of a Royal one and so he did a very Heartless thing. He told the Village Woman to throw away the baby and say nothing about it.

"Throw it away!" said the Village Woman. "Do you mean really Throw it Away like rubbish?"

"Throw it on the Rubbish Heap or throw it in the Sea," said the Welsh Prince. "I don't mind which you do, but I never want to see or hear of it again. Here is some money for you." And he went away.

The poor Village Woman was in a Great Way, because, after all, it was her baby, and she liked it. But she was afraid of what the Welsh Prince might do to her if she disobeyed him, and so this is what she did:

First she took the baby to the Church to be Baptised, and his name was Kenneth. Then she took him home and put a label on a string round his neck with " My name is Kenneth " written on it. Then she wrapped him up in a warm woolly shawl and thought to herself:

" I *couldn't* put him on the Rubbish Heap, poor little Kenneth, so I'll have to throw him in the Sea," and she picked him up and she carried him down to the Beach, and all the time she cried and cried it was so Sad.

Just as she was going to put him into the cold Sea she saw a round Fisherman's Boat called a Coracle, like Ailein sailed in to see St. Columba, and she dragged it down to the water and put Kenneth in it.

"Never mind whose it is," she thought to herself, "they wouldn't mind if they knew why I took it."

And she pushed the coracle farther and farther out to Sea until the water was too Deep for her to go another step. Then she shut her eyes and gave it one last push and turned back to the beach. When she was standing on the sand she turned round and saw the coracle bobbing away out to Sea, but she couldn't see Kenneth, because he was lying in the bottom of it. She sniffed sadly, and walked home to change her wet things.

Kenneth, in his coracle, floated away down the Coast until he reached the Gower Peninsula, and there he was washed ashore. Even now the Gower Coast is very wild and lonely, so it must have been even lonelier in those days. He hadn't been lying there very long when a Most Unusual thing happened, and this is what it was.

A whole flock of Seagulls came, and each of them took a little piece of the woolly shawl in its beak. Then they all flew up together and carried Kenneth to a wide ledge like a Grassy Shelf high up on the Cliff. And what is more they flew down and brought up the coracle as well. Then they all sat in a ring round the edge of the coracle and they each pulled out a few feathers, and soon there was a lovely warm nest for Kenneth. They lifted him in, and then flew away screaming and crying, in the way that Seagulls always do.

Not long after this a Deer came along the top of the Cliff with her calf. Suddenly she pricked up her ears and stopped dead. The calf stopped so suddenly that he skidded on all four feet and bumped into her. She stared over the edge of the cliff and there, just below her, was Kenneth in his coracle. Now the Deer didn't know about People because of the Gower Coast being so Wild and Lonely, but she did know that this was a Baby Something, and she was a mother Deer with a Baby of her own.

" Poor little thing," she thought, " I have quite enough milk for two, but how shall I get it to the other Baby? "

Just then a still More Unusual thing happened, and an Angel came along the cliff carrying a Silver Bell. He put the Silver Bell upside down in the coracle and went away.

" The very thing! " thought the Deer, and she put some milk in the Bell and Kenneth turned over and saw it. He took hold of it and the milk tipped over his face, and so he learned to drink! Every day the Deer came and gave him some milk, and he began to grow and get strong.

One day a Good Shepherd came walking along the cliff edge looking for Sheep that had fallen over and might want helping back again. From far away he saw something moving, and he thought:

" There is one of my Sheep! It does not look as though it could get back over the Top very easily. I'd better go along and help it."

But when he got there he saw a fine Fat Baby crawling about in the sun! He stared and stared!

" Well, upon my Sam! " he said. " Whoever saw the like of that? "

He climbed over the edge of the cliff and tried to pick up Kenneth. But he was a real little Wild Baby, because he had never seen a person before that he could remember, and so he crawled away into a little cave where he sheltered in Bad Weather. However, the Shepherd fished him out with his Crook (like Bishops have because of Feed My Sheep and because of Our Lord being the Good Shepherd) and he put him on his

shoulder like a Lamb and climbed back to the top of the cliff.

When he got home he wrapped up Kenneth in his cloak and went indoors.

"Guess what I have here, Wife!" he said to his wife.

She looked at the Wriggling Bundle.

"I should think that it is a Cosset Lamb for me to bring up, same as usual," she said. (A Cosset Lamb is a Lamb whose mother is dead, so that it has to be looked after and have a Baby's Bottle and all that. Some people call them Pet Lambs, but there is no difference.)

"No, it isn't," said the Shepherd.

"Well, it's *something* small and wriggling," said his wife, "and I suppose that it is for me, or you wouldn't have brought it in. Extraordinary thing, it makes noises just like a Baby!"

"That's right!" said the Shepherd, and he Roared with Laughter.

"What's right?" said his wife, and she took hold of the cloak and out rolled wriggling little Kenneth!

"Goodness gracious me!" said the Shepherd's wife, all Astonished. "Whose is he?"

And the Shepherd told her all about how he had found Kenneth, and about how they had better keep him and bring him up Properly.

"Good!" said the Shepherd's wife. "I've always wanted a Baby, and now I've got one. Look! his name's Kenneth, it says so on the label."

So she washed and fed Kenneth, and wrapped him up, and put him outside the Cottage door to go to sleep.

But the Seagulls saw him! They all swooped down and lifted him up to take him back to the Cliff, because they were used to seeing him there. But a Very Dangerous Thing happened. Kenneth was much older and heavier than he was the last time, and he kicked and wriggled, and the Seagulls dropped him! Kenneth lay at the end of the Garden and screamed and screamed.

The Shepherd's wife came running out, and when she picked him up she found that he had a Broken Leg! Now there were no good Doctors in those days, and so forever afterwards Kenneth had a Lame Leg, and he Limped.

The Shepherd and his wife brought up Kenneth just as if he were their own child, and he went to School, and he learned his Catechism and all that, but when he grew up he was a Hermit, and he lived on the same ledge with the little Cave that he had had when he was a Baby. He taught the people all about God in Nature, because of the Seagulls and the Deer that had been so kind to him, and because of the beautiful View that he could see from his Cave, and every Sunday he used to go to the Parish Church and help the Priest there by doing all the Catechism Classes for him. And all the people loved the kind old man with a Lame Leg who lived all alone on the Cliff.

St. Kenneth's Special Day is on August 1st, and there are a lot of Kenneths in England.

ST. COLUMBA

This is a Story for People who live in Scotland, but especially those who live on the West side of Scotland, so you know who it will be about, don't you? (Well, yes, it *could* be about St. Brigid, I know, but she *really* belongs to Ireland now.) Well? Who? St. Columba, of course! Or Colum-cille as he is often called.

I am not going to tell you about how he was the first person to tell the people in Scotland about being Christians, because you know that. Or about how he chose the little island called Iona to build a Monastery for monks there, because you know that, too. But this is about when Columba was living on Iona with his monks, and the Fame of him was soon over the water to all the other Islands, and everybody wanted to see him, he was so Kind and so Different.

One day, a little Boy called Ailein was sitting on a skerry on the Island of Rhum and was looking at the Boats going out. (They were the little round boats made of wicker and covered with skins, called Coracles.) And the little Boy thought this thought:

" If only I could get across to Iona to see Columcille, perhaps he might bless me. But I haven't a Coracle."

Just as he was thinking, there came a Gentleman who said:

" What would you give to a man, Ailein, who would sail you across to Iona and back? "

" I would be his Gillie for ever and ever," said Ailein. (In case People who don't live in Scotland don't know

158

what a Gillie is, he is sometimes a son and sometimes a servant, like we say Boy.)

He had only just said it when there they were in a Coracle, sailing so fast to Iona that the Wind could hardly keep up with them to keep the sails full!

When they had landed on Iona the Gentleman said:

" Now hurry up and see Columba, and I will wait for you."

Ailein ran up the Beach and soon found an Old and Beautiful Man who Looked like a King, and who Dressed like a Monk. He was mending the broken wing of a Sea Gull, and the Sea Gull wasn't minding it a bit.

" Well, Ailein," said the old man, " so you managed to come after all! Kneel down, and I will Bless you. Then I will Tell you Something and Give you Something."

So Ailein knelt down and Colum-cille blessed him.

" Now," he said, going on with the Sea Gull's wing. " I'll Tell you something about the Gentleman who brought you here." And he told him something.

" Now, I'll Give you something." And he gave him a Candle.

Ailein ran back to the Gentleman and they sailed back to Rhum.

" Praise be to the Good Being! " said Ailein (that was his name for God). " Now I have seen Colum-cille and had his Blessing."

" Yes," said the Gentleman, " and now you must remember your Promise, and be my Gillie for Ever and Ever."

And, as he was speaking, Ailein saw that it was really

Satan pretending to be a Gentleman! But he wasn't a bit frightened because of what Columba had told him.

He pulled out his Candle that had been Blessed by Columba, and he lit it and he said:

"Please, Gentleman, before I am your Gillie, may I be the Gillie of Jesus, like Colum-cille, just until my Candle burns out?"

"No, it is too long," said Satan.

Ailein lit the other end too, and, holding it sideways so that it wouldn't go out, he said:

"Until it burns out now?"

"Yes, it is not a very Important Thing to want. You can be Jesus' Gillie until the Candle is burnt out."

Then Ailein blew out the Candle and said:

"Please, Gentleman, it will never *burn* out as long as I live, because I will never light it again, and *you can't*!" And he popped it into a bowl of Holy Water, which, as you know, the Devil can't touch!

"*Well*!" said Satan as he went away, "I must say, that what with Columba and Ailein, Jesus does have Gillies with Good Ideas."

After that, Ailein was often called Gillosa, which means Jesus' Gillie, and he went and lived with Columba (whose Good Idea it was about the Candle) for the rest of his life.

St. Columba's Special Day is on June 9th, but very few People that aren't Scottish are called after him. (And I'll tell you another thing, because this Story has such a lot about Gillies in it, and that is that most names that begin with Gill-something mean Servant- or Son- of someone. Like Gilchrist, Servant of Christ; or Gillespie, Servant of the Bishop; or Gillander, Son of Andrew. So perhaps someone will be called by one of these names instead of Columba, and, if they are, then they can have this story for their Special one.)

ST. MUNGO

Once upon a time there was a Monastery at Culross, in Fifeshire, in Scotland, and it was a Boy's School, and it was near the sea.

Very early one morning one of the monks (whose name was Servan) was saying his Office when God said to him:

"Servan, go down to the sea and you will find something."

So Servan got up and put his Breviary away, and then he went outside. It was so very early in the morning that it was still nearly dark, but he found the path that led to the sea, and was soon on the Beach. There he saw a Dark Bundle. He peered at it, and found that it was a Girl wrapped up in a dark cloak with a tiny, brand-new Baby! They were sopping wet, and the girl was Very Ill with a Temperature.

"Poor things!" thought kind old Brother Servan, "they must have been wrecked or something!" and he lifted up the girl and her baby and carried them back to the Monastery. He called the other Monks, and they gave the girl a Hot Tot to try and warm her up, but it was so sad because she soon died. She had caught her Death of Cold.

So there were the Monks in the Abbey at Culross with a tiny little boy of one day old in their School!

They Baptised him Kentigern, but he was such a nice baby that everybody called him Mungo, which means Dearest.

When Mungo was old enough he went to the school

with the other boys, but they didn't like him because he belonged to the Monks, and the Abbey was his home.

"That Mungo gets all the Tit Bits when we're not looking," they said, "and I expect he Tells Tales about us to Brother Servan." Mungo didn't do any of those things, but the Other Boys used to do everything that they could to make his life Miserable.

There were no matches in those days, and so the kitchen Fire had to be kept burning Day In and Day Out, because it was such a bother to relight it. So it was the job of the boys to take it in turns to get up in the Middle of the Night to make up the fire. Once, when it was Mungo's turn to get up, he found that the Other Boys had poured some water on it, and that it was dead out. Poor Mungo was Distracted! He wasn't quite sure how to light it again (one of the monks always did it), and if he left it then none of them would be able to have any Breakfast! Now whenever anything happened Mungo used to tell the Holy Spirit, and so, before he thought what he was doing he started to say the Prayer to the Holy Spirit to comfort himself. And what do you suppose happened? When he got to "Enkindle in them the Fire of thy love," all the dead wet ashes blazed up, and there was a lovely Hot Fire! When the Other Boys came down in the morning they were all whispering and Nudging one another while they were waiting for Breakfast. "Now," they said to each other, "that horrid little Mungo will get into trouble, because there won't *be* any Breakfast!"

But when the servery door opened, instead of an Angry Brother Cook, there was their nice Hot Breakfast just the same as usual! So they thought of a worse thing to do and this was the Worse Thing.

Old Brother Servan had a tame Robin that used to come into his room and pick up crumbs and sit on

the back of his chair and all that. (I expect that you
have often seen Robins in the house. There is one that
nearly lives in my Kitchen!) Servan was very fond
of his Robin, and he was always hoping that one day it
would get tame enough to sit on his finger, but it hadn't
yet.

One day, while Brother Servan was teaching in the
school, some of the boys caught the Robin and killed it
and put it in Mungo's pocket with a few feathers sticking
out so that it would show. They put the coat in Servan's
room so that when he came in and saw the coat he would
think that it was Mungo who had done it. But luckily
it was Mungo who came in first, and he saw the
Robin.

"Oh, *poor* little thing!" said Mungo. "What a
shame! What will poor old Brother Servan do when
he knows?" And he began to cry, it was so sad. And
he began to say his favourite Prayer to the Holy Spirit.
While he was saying, " they shall be Created " the Robin
shook out its crumpled little feathers and flew to Brother
Servan's desk! There it sat, tidying itself up, and Mungo
couldn't thank God enough for saving Brother Servan
from being so sad.

But at last Mungo was so Miserable because of the
Other Boys that he ran away! Brother Servan followed him.

"Now, Mungo," he said, "never you mind those
silly boys! We all know that you are all right, and that
you don't do all these Fearful Things," and he patted
Mungo's shoulder kindly.

"I know, Brother," said Mungo sniffing sadly, and
rubbing his nose, "but I couldn't go back, really I
couldn't. Besides, I do want to be a Hermit for a little
while, and then I want to be a Priest."

"All right, then," said Servan, "but come and see

us whenever you like, we shall always be pleased to see you."

"Yes, I will," said Mungo, "because you are all my Fathers, and the Abbey is my Home."

Mungo found a cave near Glasgow, on the banks of the Clyde, and he did just what he had said. First he was a Hermit, and then he was a Priest, and in time he was made the Bishop of Glasgow. He spent a lot of time teaching people about God, and once he went to Wales. (In our next story you will read how David had a Meeting and a lot of Bishops and suchlike went to it. Well, Mungo, was one of the Bishops.)

Now when Mungo was the Bishop of Glasgow the King's name was King Roderick, and they were great friends. King Roderick's wife was a Young and Giddy Queen, and once she did a very Young and Giddy thing. She gave her Engagement Ring, that King Roderick had given to her before they were married, to a Knight that she liked very much.

"You can wear it as a Favour," she said to him. (When you read the story of St. Walter you will know what a Favour is.) And the Knight put it on his finger and thought that no one would notice.

One day King Roderick and the Knight went hunting together, and they got very hot and tired, so the King said:

"Let's stop and have our lunch under these trees by the stream. We can get cool, and we might have Forty Winks."

So they had a lovely Cold Lunch that the Queen had packed for them. They had Chicken Patties and New Bread and New Butter and Cheese and Wild Strawberries and Whisky. Then they put the plates and things back in the basket and settled down for their Forty Winks.

But King Roderick wasn't so sleepy as the Knight, and he lay on his back and stared at the leaves against the sky, and thought about his Young and Giddy Queen. Then he rolled over and looked at the Knight who was asleep, and there, on his finger, he saw the Queen's Engagement Ring!

He was Simply Furious. He leaned over and very carefully pulled off the ring without waking the Knight and Threw it in the Stream.

ST. MUNGO

When they got home he asked the Young and Giddy Queen where her Ring was. "You ought to wear it always with your Wedding Ring," he said.

"I've lost it," said the Queen, feeling Rather Nervous.

"Well, why did you take it off, then?" said King Roderick.

"It must have Fallen Off," said the Queen. "I'm thinner than I was," she said in a Pathetic voice.

"Then you must find it," said King Roderick in a Stern voice. "If you don't find it by to-morrow lunch time I shall know that you have been Giddier than usual and you will have to be Executed. Queens can't afford to be Giddy." And he Stamped out of the room.

The poor Queen was very Frightened, and she sent a quick message to her Favourite Knight, and this was the quick message:

"Send back my Ring Quickly, because if you don't I will be Executed to-morrow at Lunch Time."

But the Knight sent back a quick message, and this was his quick message:

"I can't, because it was lost when I was out hunting with the King."

The Queen was in a Frenzy of Despair, and she sent for the Bishop of Glasgow, who was Mungo, and she went to Confession, and told him all about everything. So Mungo gave her Absolution and a Penance, and he was sorry for her, because she was so Young and Giddy, and so he went to the Church and he prayed and prayed that she wouldn't have to be Executed.

"Because, dear Lord," he said to God, "she really is sorry she was so Silly, and it does seem a shame to Execute her when she is so Young."

When he got back to his Bishop's Palace, in Glasgow, he found a Mysterious Parcel waiting for him. It was Long and Heavy and Rather Damp.

167

" Well now," said Mungo to himself, " who could be sending me a present at this time of night? I do believe it smells of Fish! "

And he unpacked his Parcel, and there inside it was a fresh-caught Salmon from the River Clyde!

" How very kind of Who-ever-it-is," said Mungo. " I'll invite some Poor-and-Raggy people to dinner to-morrow, and we'll have my Fine Fat Salmon! " And he took it to the kitchen.

Early in the morning, on his way back from Mass, his servant met him.

" Look, my Lord," he said. " Look what the cook found inside the Salmon! " And there was the Queen's Ring!

Mungo quickly took it to the Queen, and when King Roderick went to see her after breakfast she said:

" Here is my Ring, Roderick. Will you please forgive me? "

And Roderick was so Surprised that he said that he would if she promised not to be so Giddy again. And she did.

Anybody who lives in Glasgow will know that in the crypt of the Cathedral is St. Mungo's Tomb (which is where he was buried when he died) and I expect lots of people have seen it. Have you?

St. Mungo's Special Day is on January 13th, but not many people out of Scotland are called after him. I really made this story for somebody called Cora, because she hasn't got a Special Saint, and so she is always called Mungo.

ST. DAVID

Once upon a time there was a Welshman and his name was David, and he lived in Wales, and he was very Good at Farming and Gardening and Fishing and all that. As time went on he used to look at the Mountains and the Rivers and he thought to himself:

"How Grand and Lovely all these things are, and how Clever of God to have thought of them. I have to carry water to water my plants, but God puts His plants in a Valley and makes the River run down the Mountain to water them, or else He makes it Rain on them. I have to put my plants in a greenhouse to keep them warm, but God makes the Sun shine on His."

And more and more he used to sit and stare at all the things of Nature, and think how Marvellous it all was!

"Fancy thinking of making little coloured feathered things that fly!" he thought; "and fancy making them sing and build nests!" And he listened to the birds singing, and thought how wonderful God was to Invent all these things.

At last David built himself a tiny little House with one room in it, and lived there all alone thinking and thinking about God. He would look at a Mountain and he would think this thought:

"How strong and big God is, like a Mountain. He never changes whatever happens, and He is always there."

And he would look at the River and he would think this thought:

169

" How clean and cool God is, and He is always ready
to run to help us; nothing will stop Him. He is like a
River, and we live in Him like the little brown trout
live in the water."

And when it Rained he would think this thought:

" The Rain comes and Freshens the earth and waters
the growing things and makes them live. God is like
the Rain, and He freshens our minds when we are Cross
and Tired. We couldn't live without Him."

And in the Sunshine he thought:

" The Sun is warm and comforting and gives us light
to see by. It is like the Warm and Comforting Love of
God shining on everybody and everything that He has
made."

And he thought like this of all Nature, like the Wind
and the Sky and the Green Grass and the Sea, until he
suddenly had a Good Idea.

" I know! " he said. " We can't *see* God Himself, but
He lets all the things that He has made remind us of
Him and all these things must be Good because He made
them."

And he was quite right, because you couldn't have a
Bad Sweet Pea, now could you? Or a Wicked Rabbit,
or a Jealous Cloud, or a Proud Hay field, or an Angry
Tree? It is only people who do these things, which is
so sad, because God made us too. (Why did God Make
us?)

So there was David in his little house peacefully
thinking about God in Nature (like Owen thought of
God being Beautifulness) and the more he thought about
God the more he learned about Him.

But one day his peacefulness came to an end.

Do you remember the Pelagians who were the people
who liked Morgan the Welshman's Idea? They were
the ones who said: Everything that you *can't* do you

needn't do. Well, in Wales this idea had spread and spread until hundreds and hundreds of people used it. Things got so bad that people stopped going to Mass and they never went to Confession (because they said that it wasn't their Fault that they were Bad) and they didn't let their babies be Baptised because they said that there wasn't any Original Sin. At last all the Bishops and Princes and Abbots and that sort of Person had a Meeting with all the Pelagians at a place in Wales called Brefi (St. Mungo was one of the Bishops who went there, from Glasgow). They argued and they argued, and first one side secmed to be winning and then the other, but they *couldn't* get it settled. At last one of them said:

" What about sending for David? He is a very Wise Hermit, and perhaps he could make these Pelagian People see sense."

So they sent two men called Daniel and Devereux to David's cell, and there was David making deep little holes and planting Leeks in his garden.

" But I don't want to go and do a lot of Arguing," said David, when Daniel and Devereux had told him what they wanted. " It is nice and Peaceful here and God is Good."

" But it isn't Peaceful there for all of us with those Pelagians all over the place," said Daniel; " they're turning Wales into a Perfect Bedlam! If you will come and if you happen to Win the Argument then we can *all* be Peaceful, not only you! "

" Well," said David, and he planted the last leek of the row, " if you put it like that I suppose that I ought to go with you." So he put away his Trowel, and he shut his Front Door, and went away with Daniel and Devereux.

When they got to Brefi the Bishops and all were

still Arguing, and the Pelagians were still Shouting, and everything was in a Pandemonium. (Which means that it sounded as if there were Devils all over the place, and perhaps there were.)

David stepped up on to a little knob of ground and clapped his hands and shouted "Hey!"

That made all the people stop talking and look at him, which was what he wanted, and he started telling the Pelagians, not how Stupid their devil's Idea was, but Why it was stupid. And because he knew such a lot about God he told them about Him, too. And because he wasn't Calling them Names but just Explaining, the people listened, and as they listened a Most Extraordinary thing happened.

The Knob of Ground where David was standing grew bigger and bigger, and taller, and taller, until it turned into a High Hill, and his voice got louder and louder so that in Spite of his standing on the top of the High Hill the people could still hear him talking!

What with all that and David's most Excellent Speech, the Pelagians stopped being so Tiresome and went to Church again. But of course there were still lots of them all over the world, and there are still a few about to this very day, and I expect you have seen some, but you didn't Know it!

The Bishops and Princes and Abbots and all were so pleased with David because God had done this surprising thing for him, that they made him the Head Bishop in Wales. And the New High Hill that wasn't there before was called Llandevi Brefi (which means David's Hill at Brefi) and there it is still.

Now that David was an Important Bishop he started building Monasteries, specially for Monks who would teach all the Pelagians to be Christians again. He built Twelve, and the one that he lived in himself was at a place called Mynyw (or Menevia for people who can't Spell in Welsh).

All these Monks of David's Farmed and Gardened and all that as well as doing their Teaching and they all kept Bees for Honey for the Ill people with Coughs.

One of the Monks, who was a Brother Beekeeper was called Modemnoc, and the Bees loved him, and they would never sting him, and they used to follow him about the garden.

One day David said to Modemnoc:

" Brother, I want you to sail to Ireland with a message and give it to an Abbot who is a friend of mine."

" Certainly," said Modemnoc politely, " but what about the Bees? "

" We'll look after them until you get back, they'll be all right," said David kindly.

" Well, don't forget to give them Syrup when the weather gets cold," said Modemnoc.

" No, we won't," said David.

So Modemnoc went down to the ship, and just as he was Going Aboard all the Bees came buzzing round in a Swarm, so that the sailors ran away in a fright.

" They won't hurt you! " said Modemnoc. " They only came to see me because I am going away from them," and he tried to shoo them back home, but they wouldn't go. So he turned and walked back to the Monastery, and all the Bees flew along with him, and when he got to the Garden they went gathering Honey in the flowers as though nothing had happened! Very Quietly Modemnoc slipped out of the garden and hurried back to the ship.

" They didn't see me go! " he said to himself, but just as he was Going Aboard all the Bees came buzzing round in a swarm so that the sailors ran away in a fright! The sailors were very Angry because they were frightened, and although Modemnoc kept on saying how Sorry he was they said that if it happened again they would sail without him!

So Modemnoc went back again to the Monastery, and the Bees went too. He went to David, who said:

" Haven't you gone yet, Brother? "

" It's those Bees," said Modemnoc.

" What about them? I told you they would be all right," said David.

" Well," said Modemnoc in an Apologising voice, " they will keep coming after me, and the sailors are getting Furious."

" How Trying of them," said David. " What are you going to do about them? "

" I wondered if you would let me take them with me, please," said Modemnoc. " They wouldn't be any Trouble, really they wouldn't. I could take them in a Skep." (A Skep is one of those round Beehive things made of straw.)

" All right, if you think you can Manage them," said David, " but there's to be no Coming Out and Stinging the Sailors, mind! "

" No, they'll keep quite Quiet, if you will please Bless them," said Modemnoc, and he smiled an Enormous Smile because he was so pleased.

So David blessed Modemnoc and the Bees, and the Bees went into the Skep and the sailors never even knew that they were there! When they got to Ireland they started making Honey in the Skep, and the Irish people were All Astonished, because it was the first time they had ever seen Tame Bees in a Beehive.

Lots of other things happened to David, and I'll tell you One More.

ST. DAVID

When the Monks at Glastonbury, in England, had finished building their Famously Beautiful Chapel in their Monastery by St. Joseph's Thorn Tree they wrote and asked David to come and Dedicate it for them. Now you know all about Dedicating because I remember telling you about it before (I think it was in the Westminster Story, wasn't it?) but in case you have forgotten I will tell you again. When a Church is built it is given to Our Lord or to Our Lady or to a Saint so that it can be their Special Church to look after. That is why Churches are called St. Edmund's Church or St. James's Church or the Church of the Sacred Heart. (What is the name of the Church that you go to, do you know?) And it is always the Bishop who comes and Dedicates the Church. The Monks, of course, wanted their Church to be Dedicated to St. Joseph of Arimathaea, and David was very pleased, because he loved Dedicating, and he said that he would come and do it to-morrow as he was in the Neighbourhood. That night Our Lord came to him when he was asleep and He said:

" You needn't Dedicate the Church to-morrow, David, because I have Dedicated it Myself."

David was so glad that Our Lord had come to see him that he quite forgot to be disappointed about not doing the Dedicating himself, but Our Kind Lord never forgets anything like that, and He said:

"I do know, David, that you love Dedicating, and the Monks have not built a Lady Chapel yet for their Beautiful Church. Will you build one on to the end of the Church and Dedicate it yourself to My Dear Mother? "

David was Delighted, and he spent a long time at Glastonbury building the Lady Chapel. And when it was finished he Dedicated it to Our Lady to be her Special Chapel. But I am afraid that you will never see it, because Cromwell's soldiers pulled it down and Smashed it up, together with the Famously Beautiful Church, because they said that beautiful things are Wicked. (But you know better than that.)

St. David's Special Day is on March 1st, and Thousands of people are called after him, not only in Wales.

ST. GREGORY

Once upon a time there was an Abbot called Gregory. (An Abbot is the Head Monk in a Monastery, and a Monastery is the house that the Monks live in.) Gregory was quite a nice Abbot and he was very clever at books and writings and things, and all the Monks that he was head of liked him. A long time after this story happened Gregory was the Pope and he was the one who sent St. Augustine to England to tell us about being Christians.

One day after breakfast, Gregory was writing in his Cell (a Cell is a Monk's bedroom), when somebody knocked at the door.

Rat! Tat! Tat!

"Come in!" said Gregory, busily writing. After a minute, when he had finished the word he was writing, he turned round, and there was a Sailor! Now, a Sailor is Rather Unusual to find in a Monastery. He was quite an ordinary-looking Sailor with wide trousers and a square collar and a Round Hat with *H.M.S. Raphael* written on it.

Gregory was very Surprised, but he was very polite, too, so he said:

"Good morning, what can I do for *you* to-day?"

"Oh, Father," said the Sailor, "I fell out of my ship and got Washed Ashore and my purse is in my Hammock and a Thousand Miles away, and the Captain he is sleeping there below and he never even *noticed* that I wasn't there!"

"I'm very sorry indeed to hear that, my poor sailor,"

177

said Gregory kindly, " and what are you proposing to
do about money, now that you have no purse? "

" Well, Father," said the Sailor, " I *thought* perhaps
you might give me a penny or so, I have always heard
that you were such a Kind man."

" And so I will," said Gregory. " Just ring that Gong,
will you, and someone will come."

" Yes, Father," said the Sailor, and he picked up
the Gong Stick and hit the Big Black Gong, Bom! Bom!
Bom!

In a minute he heard a Clappety noise coming down
the stone passage. Clippety Clap! Clippety Clappety!
He was wondering what it would be when round the
Corner came running the Youngest Monk of All, and,
as he ran, his sandals went Clippety Clap! Clippety
Clappety! because they were both unfastened!

" Before we proceed, Brother," said Abbot Gregory
(Monks often call each other Brother because they are
all Sons of God, so they must be brothers), " Before
we proceed, Brother, why do your sandals have to be
that way? "

" I'm very sorry, Father, indeed, Father," said the
Youngest Monk of All, who was Out of Breath with
Running, " but I was just drying my feet, they got
Rather Wet while I was feeding the Chickens, when
the Gong went, and I hadn't time to do up my Sandals
because the Buckles are Rather Difficult. I must ask
your Pardon."

" Granted," said Gregory kindly, " and now will
you go and find Sixpence out of my purse in the
Study, please, Brother, and give it to this Unfortunate
Sailor? "

" Yes, Father," said the Youngest Monk of All.

" Thank you, Father," said the Sailor, and they went
away.

After Lunch Gregory was writing in his Cell (you know what a Cell is now), when somebody knocked at the door.

Rat! Tat! Tat!

"Come in!" said Gregory, busily writing. After a minute, when he had thought how to spell "Antediluvian" he turned round and there was the Sailor again!

Gregory was Very Surprised, but he was Very Polite, too, so he said:

"Good afternoon, what can I do for you this time?"

"Oh, Father," said the Sailor, "I've lost the Sixpence!"

"I'm very sorry indeed to hear that, my poor sailor," said Gregory kindly, "and what are you proposing to do, now that you have lost your Sixpence?"

"Well, Father," said the Sailor, "I *thought* perhaps *you* might give me a penny or so, I always heard that you were such a Generous man."

"And so I will," said Gregory. "Just ring that Gong, will you, and someone will come."

"Yes, Father," said the Sailor, and he picked up the Gong Stick and hit the Big Black Gong, Bom! Bom! Bom! Bom!

After a minute he heard a Clappety noise coming along the stone passage, Clippety Clap! Clippety Clappety! and round the Corner came running the Youngest Monk of All, and, as he ran, his Sandals went Clippety Clap! Clippety Clappety! because they were both unfastened.

"Before we proceed, Brother," said Gregory (because they were both Sons of God), "Before we proceed, why do your Sandals have to be that way?"

"I'm very Sorry, Father, indeed, Father," said the Youngest Monk of All, who was Out of Breath with

Running, "but it was the Ducks, this time. I must ask your Pardon."

"Granted," said Gregory kindly. "But now, Brother, go and find Sixpence out of my purse in the Study and give it to this Unfortunate Sailor."

"Yes, Father," said the Youngest Monk of All.

"Thank you, Father," said the Sailor, and they went away.

After Tea Gregory was writing in his Cell (do you know what a Cell is?) when somebody knocked at the door.

Rat! Tat! Tat!

"Come in!" said Gregory, busily writing. After a minute, when he had Blotted his page, he turned round and there was the Sailor again.

Gregory was Very Surprised, but he was Very Polite, too.

"Good evening, what can I do for you *now*?"

"Oh, Father," said the Sailor, wiping his eyes with a Blue Pocket Handkerchief to match his Sailor's Suit, "I've lost the Sixpence again!"

"I'm very sorry indeed to hear that, my poor sailor," said Gregory kindly, "and what are you proposing to do for money, now that you have lost your Sixpence *again*?"

"Well, Father," said the Sailor, "I *thought* that perhaps *you* might give me a penny or so, I always heard that you were such a Forbearing man." (Forbearing is when you are all for bearing with people's importunities and you do not get impatient.)

"And so I will," said Gregory, "just ring that Gong, will you, and someone will come."

"Yes, Father," said the Sailor, and he picked up the Gong Stick and hit the Big Black Gong, Bom! Bom! Bom! Bom! Bom!

After a minute he heard a Clappety noise coming down the stone passage, Clippety Clap! Clippety Clappety! and round the corner came running the Youngest Monk of All, and, as he ran, his sandals went Clippety Clap! Clippety Clappety! because they were both unfastened.

" Before we proceed, Brother," said Gregory (because of both being Sons of God), " Before we proceed, why do your sandals have to be that way? "

" I'm very sorry, Father, indeed, Father," said the Youngest Monk of All, who was Out of Breath with Running. " It's those Turkeys, their field is wet. I must ask your Pardon."

" Granted," said Gregory kindly, " and now, Brother, go and find Sixpence out of my purse in the Study and give it to this unfortunate Sailor."

" Yes, Father," said the Youngest Monk of All.

" Thank you, Father," said the Sailor, and they went away. But in a few Minutes they came back, again; and the Youngest Monk of All said:

" There isn't any more money, Father, there is only the Silver Dish that your Mother sends you your Porridge in."

" Well, give that to the unfortunate Sailor, then," said Gregory, " perhaps he won't lose it so easily because it is bigger than a Sixpence."

" Yes, Father," said the Youngest Monk of All.

" Thank you, Father," said the Sailor, and they went away.

After Supper Gregory was writing in his Cell (what is a Cell?) when there came a knock at the door.

Rat! Tat! Tat!

" Come in! " said Gregory, writing busily. After a minute, when he found the stamps, he turned round and there was . . . who? No! *not* the Sailor! Surely

182

you have had enough of him by this time? No, there was a Very Beautiful Angel!

Gregory was very Surprised, but he was very Polite, too, so he knelt down and said:

"Good evening! May I do something for you?"

"Good evening, you have already done something for me Three Times to-day," said the Very Beautiful Angel. "I am the Archangel Raphael, and I was Pretending to be a Sailor so as to see how Kind and Generous and Forbearing you were! And you *were*! Very! And God says that you can have your two Sixpences and your Silver Porridge Dish back again, if you like, and that He is very pleased with you."

"Good," said Gregory. "Wasn't it lucky that I was Forbearing and everything just when you happened to come?"

"Yes," said the Archangel Raphael, "it was, rather."

Now, of course, there are Two Special Days belonging to this story. One belongs to St. Gregory whose Story this is, and his Day is on March 12th. And the other Day belongs to St. Raphael-who-was-pretending-to-be-a-Sailor, and that is on October 24th.

St. Gregory

I like St. Gregory because
He wasn't impatient, whatever he was.
And I like St. Raphael, don't you?
He acted so well—Angels do.
But I like the Youngest Monk the best,
So I'll be him, and you be the rest.

SSB-M

ST. OWEN

Once upon a time there was a Prime Minister whose name was Owen, and he was Prime Minister for Queen Audrey, who was a Royal Nun. Now Queen Audrey was having a Holiday from being a Nun, so that she could build an Abbey and Cathedral on the Island of Ely, which belonged to her, and while she was doing all that Owen did the Ruling in the Island for her.

Queen Audrey, as I expect you know, was building her Abbey and Cathedral on one of the Hard Places in the Fens that are called Islands, but they are not near the sea at all, and they are only Islands when the Floods come and make all the Soft Places into swamps and lakes and that sort of thing. Well, what with seeing to the Building and Draining her Island as much as she could she left more and more of her Governing work to Owen, and once every week or so he used to go and see her on Business or something.

One day he went to Ely to see the Queen on Matters of State, and found her choosing patterns for the Carving inside the Cathedral.

" Good morning, Your Majesty," said Owen, bowing Politely.

" Good morning, Prime Minister," said Queen Audrey, " which do you like best, This or That? "

" This, I think, Your Majesty," said Owen, " it looks more Dignified, don't you think? "

" I believe you are right," said Queen Audrey, " you usually are."

" Well, Your Majesty," said Owen, " I really came

184

to say that your people would like to see a bit more of you now that you are out of your Convent for a while, and they sent me to ask if you would go and do some Reigning for a little while."

"But I am just in the middle of building my Cathedral," said Queen Audrey. "I couldn't go now, possibly."

"Perhaps I could stay and look after it for you," said Owen. "I could always ask you if I wasn't Sure."

So that is what they did, and Queen Audrey went back to her Palace, and all the people Cheered.

Now Prime Minister Owen got more and more Interested in the Cathedral, and soon he could think of nothing else.

"How much more Satisfactory," he thought to himself, "it is to work for God than it is to work for a Queen, however Good and Noble she may be; I *do* like building Cathedrals!"

As time went on he thought more and more about making the Cathedral more and more Beautiful because of God being the most Beautiful of All. (Beauty is one of the Divine Attributes, but I wonder if you know about that yet.)

"That is not beautiful enough," he would say to the Carving Men, or:

"Make it more beautiful than that," he would say to the Painting Men. At last the workmen began to get Irritated.

"We are making the most beautiful things that we have ever made," they said, "and you are not Satisfied. What is the matter with you?"

"What *is* the matter with me?" said the Prime Minister Owen to himself. "Nothing seems Perfect, and I want it to be Perfect as God Himself is Perfect."

He went into the Cathedral and stared at the lovely Carvings and things.

"Perfect," he said, "perfect. I know what I want! I want God, not His Cathedral! I'll go away and be a Monk and belong to God, who is the most Beautiful of All."

He called all the Workmen and said to them:

"Listen, everybody! I've just had a very Good Idea, and I want you to make a Stone Cross and put it just here where I had the Idea, to remind people of the Beauty of God. And I want it to be Perfectly Plain."

"What!" said the Head Carver. "No carving?"

"What!" said the Head Painter. "No painting?"

"No," said the Prime Minister Owen, "just a Plain Cross. If you carve it it would be like carving Patterns on a Flower, and if you paint it it would be like painting colours on a Butterfly. Just Plain, I want it."

So they made a Plain Stone Cross, and they put it where Owen had had his Good Idea, and then he went and told Queen Audrey that he was Leaving.

"But, my dear Prime Minister!" said Queen Audrey, "I can't run the Kingdom without you. But I must say, being a Monk is a Far, far Better Thing."

"You'll get along without me very well, Your Majesty," said Owen, "of course you will." And he went up to his room. He took off all his Rich and Rare Prime Minister's clothes and put on very Plain ones. Then he went out and got a Spade and an Axe from the potting shed and went to say Good-bye to the Queen.

"Why on Earth are you taking those with you?" asked Queen Audrey as she stood at the Front Door to see him off.

"It's part of my Idea. Good-bye, Your Majesty," said Owen, and he walked away down the drive and out through the front gate and turned to the left down the long road.

ST. OWEN

He went to a Monastery at Lastingham, near Whitby, that he knew of, where the Abbot's name was Chad. (He was St. Chad, actually.) When he got there he knocked at the door and waited.

"Good evening!" said the Brother Porter as he opened the door, "what may I do for you?"

"May I please see the Abbot?" asked Owen.

"Please step this way," said the Brother Porter politely, and Owen, with his Axe and his Spade, followed him along the long stone passage until they came to a door. The Brother Porter knocked and someone said, "Come in!"

"Somebody to see you, Father Abbot," and Owen went in.

"Good evening," said the Abbot whose name was Chad, "what may I do for you?"

"Please may I be a Monk in your Monastery?" said Owen.

"Why?" said the Abbot whose name was Chad.

"Because the only thing that I *really* want is God," said Owen.

"Well, that is as good a Beginning as any," said the Abbot whose name was Chad, "but why the Axe and the Spade, if you don't mind my asking?"

"Not at all," said Owen. "I brought them because I can't Sing in Tune, so I thought I could perhaps work with my Hands to the Glory of God instead of with my Voice."

"Well, that is as good a reason as any," said the Abbot whose name was Chad. "Would you mind being the Brother Gardener - who - also - looks - after - the - Chickens?"

"Thank you, Father Abbot," said Brother Owen, who wasn't a Prime Minister any more, "that is exactly what I should like to be!"

So Owen worked outside all day. He grew the most beautiful flowers he could for the Chapel, and when he took them to the Brother Sacristan who looked after the Altar he used to stop by the Blessed Sacrament and say to God:

" Here, dear Lord, are some of your flowers for you. I know that you made them yourself but nothing that I could make would be so beautifully made as these. All I can do is to dig the soil and sow the seed and water it when it is dry and wait for you to make it grow."

He grew vegetables and fruit for the Monks to eat, and soon he knew all about Trenching and Double Digging and Pruning and Stopping and Mulching and all That.

He kept the Chickens and the Hens, and the Brothers all said that they had never had so many Eggs before, and how *did* Brother Owen manage it.

One day all the Monks were in the Chapel singing Compline, and Owen was outside tying Black Cotton round about the Crocuses to keep the Sparrows from spoiling them. The Abbot was in his study, and all of a sudden he heard the sound of singing very far away. He stopped reading and listened.

" It must be a Procession!" he thought. " I wonder where it can be coming from? "

He looked out of the window, but he could only see Owen cottoning his crocuses. The singing came nearer and nearer, until at last it was in the Abbot's study, but still he couldn't see anything! He listened to the singing, and got more and more interested in what he heard, so that before he could think about it it was half an hour later, and the singing Procession was going away again. When it had gone the Abbot looked out of the window again, but all that he could see was Owen still kneeling by his crocuses and threading the cotton between them.

ST. OWEN

The Abbot clapped his hands, and Owen looked up.

" Come up here a minute, Brother Owen," said the Abbot.

Owen stood up and brushed his knees with his hands and rubbed his hands on his Sacking Apron.

" Certainly, Father Abbot," he said, and he went up to the Abbot's study.

" Did you hear anything, Brother Owen? " said the Abbot.

" No, Father Abbot," said Owen.

" Well, some people were singing," said the Abbot.

" I know," said Owen.

" How do you know? " asked the Abbot.

" I saw them," said Owen.

" Did you indeed? " said the Abbot, all Astonished. " Who were they? "

" Angels," said Owen.

" *Well!* " said the Abbot. " You saw them and I heard them, but I thought that they were in here."

" They were," said Owen. " The room was full of them. I saw them through the window. They passed me on their way in."

" They told me that I would die in Seven Days," said the Abbot. " It is very kind of them to let me know so that I have time to get ready to see God. They told me lots of other things, too, but I can't tell you, because they said that they were a Secret! " The Abbot whose name was Chad looked very Wise and Solemn. " Well, Brother Owen, aren't you Rather Sorry that I can't tell you the Secrets? "

" No, Father Abbot," said Owen.

" Why not? " said the Abbot. " After all anyone might reasonably feel a little Jealous if he wasn't allowed to hear a Secret like that."

" Because they *showed* me something," said Owen.

" *Did* they now? " said the Abbot, opening his eyes very wide. " What did they show you? "

" They said that was a Secret, too," said Owen, and bowing politely to the Abbot he went away. When the Abbot looked out of the window there he was kneeling by his crocuses with a reel of Black Cotton in his hand and a look of Great Happiness on his face.

The Abbot did die in seven days, and he had plenty of time to put his affairs in order, but no one ever knew what it was that the Angels had shown to Owen.

St. Owen's Special Day is on March 4th, and there are a lot of people called after him. The Plain Stone Cross that he put in Queen Audrey's Cathedral at Ely is still there, perhaps you will see it one day, and remember Owen's Good Idea.

ST. CUTHBERT AND ST. HERBERT

Once upon a time there was a little boy called Cuthbert, and he lived in Northumbria, near Melrose Abbey, and he was Eight years old.

He lived with an Aunt and he looked after her Sheep so as to Earn his Keep.

Every day, after breakfast, he used to go out with his parcel of Lunch and take the Sheep up the hills round about the Abbey. And there he used to wander about and watch the Sheep and watch the Monks at the Abbey. He watched them Gardening and Fishing and Farming and Praying and in time he got to know quite a lot about them, and then he used to play at being a Monk himself.

Now what with walking Miles with the Sheep up Hill and down Dale, Cuthbert got very strong. And when he ran races with the other boys he nearly always won. And he won at jumping, too.

One day, when he was playing with all the others, he knocked over a little boy of Three quite by mistake. Cuthbert picked him up and dusted him and said:

" Did you Hurt yourself? "

" No," said the little boy, crying very hard.

" Well," said Cuthbert, " what are you crying for then? Cheer up! I'm sorry I knocked you over."

" I'm crying because you are wasting so much Time," said the little boy.

" What *do* you mean? " said Cuthbert, all astonished.

" A priest like you ought to be Teaching and not Running Races," said the little boy.

Cuthbert was quite Taken Aback.

"*I'm* not a priest!" he said. "Who told you to say that?"

"I don't know," said the little boy, and he Sniffed, and Cuthbert blew his Nose for him very Kindly.

Cuthbert thought for a long time about this. The little boy was too little to know very much about what he was saying, and Cuthbert came to the Conclusion that the Holy Ghost must have told him what to say.

Then he thought this thought:

"If it was the Holy Ghost then I must be going to be a Priest when I grow up."

So he went to Melrose Abbey and saw one of the Monks, and he told him about what the little boy of Three had said. Then he said:

"Can I come here and be a Monk?"

"Well," said the Priest, "you are not really Old enough, you know."

"But couldn't I just live here and see how you do things?" asked Cuthbert.

"I don't see why not," said the Priest, "seeing that you are an Orphan. I don't suppose anyone would mind."

And no one did, and so Cuthbert went to live at Melrose Abbey, and when he was Old enough he was a Monk there.

After he had been a Monk for some time the Abbot sent for him and said:

"Good morning, Brother Cuthbert."

"Good morning, Father Abbot," said Cuthbert.

"I've got a Surprise for you, Brother," said the Abbot.

"Thank you, Father Abbot," said Cuthbert.

"You must leave Melrose Abbey now," said the Abbot, "you have been here ever since you were a little boy, you know. I am sending you to Ripon in Yorkshire, where we have another Monastery. You will be the Guestmaster there." (Ripon was the Monastery that St. Robert made, you remember.)

Now the Guestmaster is the Monk who looks after the Visitors in a Monastery. Sometimes people go to a Monastery for a holiday, or for a retreat, or if they are sad, or if they are getting better from being Very-ill-in-bed. So you see, the Guestmaster sees quite a lot of Life.

The Abbot at Melrose was very Sensible to send Cuthbert to Ripon. You see, ever since he was eight or nine he had lived in the same place and in the same house. He had lived like a Monk, only seeing all the other Monks, and so by the time he was Grownup he knew nothing about the World. So the Abbot sent him to be the Guestmaster for a time to Broaden his Mind.

So Cuthbert looked after the Visitors and the Travellers at Ripon. He gave them clean Sheets and Towels, and Breakfast in Bed if they were ill or tired. He cleaned their Shoes and washed their Clothes and saw to their Meals and so on and so forth.

One snowy morning in the winter Cuthbert was tidying round after some Guests who had just gone away, when an Elderly Gentleman came to the door.

" Good morning, Sir! " said Cuthbert. (Benedictines are Renowned for their Politeness.)

" Good morning, Brother," said the Elderly Gentleman.

" Come in! " said Cuthbert, opening the door Wider.

The Elderly Gentleman walked in and sat down on a chair. Cuthbert took off his wet shoes for him and brought him some slippers to wear while they were being dried. Then he brought some water to wash his hands, and a clean Towel.

"Now," he said, "you must have some Breakfast.
I'll just go and get you some, if you'll wait here a
minute."

"No, thank you, Brother," said the Elderly Gentleman, "I don't want anything to eat."

"Oh, but," said Cuthbert, "*please* have something!
You've had a long walk, by the looks of things, and I
suppose you'll be walking all day. Do wait for a little
while. Honestly, I won't be a minute! "

"All right," said the Elderly Gentleman, "and
thank you very much."

So Cuthbert quickly set the table. He put on Milk
and Apples and Pears and Butter and a Bread knife.

"Where's the Bread? " he thought, "those last Guests
must have finished it all. I'll just go to the Kitchen,"
he said, "I won't be long! "

He hurried away to the kitchen.

"Please, Brother Cook," he said, "may I have some
more bread? There's an Elderly Gentleman in the
Guest House and I've only got Fruit for him to eat."

The Brother Cook looked very Worried.

"I'm terribly sorry, Brother," he said, "but I've
just been Baking and the bread is still in the Oven.
There isn't any Stale! "

"Well," said Cuthbert, "Milk and Apples and Pears
are not very Filling for breakfast on a cold day, I must
say! What about Potatoes? "

"Here! " said the Brother Cook, "take these! I
was just going to the Infirmary with them. They are
all Piping Hot! "

"Thank you, Brother! " said Cuthbert, "you *are* a
Comfort to me! " And he hurried away with the dish
of Hot Potatoes.

But when he got there the Elderly Gentleman had
gone!

ST. CUTHBERT AND ST. HERBERT

"There now!" fussed Cuthbert, "he's had no Breakfast! Which way did he go, I wonder?"

He went to the door and opened it. There was the Snow, white and smooth with never a Footprint upon it! Cuthbert stared. He went out and walked a few steps. Then he turned round and looked at the snow. There were his footmarks, clear as clear.

"He *must* be in the house somewhere," thought Cuthbert as he went back indoors. But the Elderly Gentleman was nowhere to be found! Cuthbert sighed and went to clear the table again, and there in a row, were three Hot Loaves of Bread.

"Brother Cook must have brought them, how Kind!" thought Cuthbert, and he went to the Kitchen.

"Thank you for the Loaves, Brother," he said, "but I'm afraid they were too late. The Elderly Gentleman had gone when I got back with the Potatoes!"

"But it wasn't me!" said the Brother Cook; "my loaves are still in the Oven only half-baked!"

So the only thing to think was that the Elderly Gentleman had been an Angel in Disguise. Which was an exciting thing to happen to anyone, wasn't it? I wonder how many Poor-and-Raggies that we see are People in Disguise. Our Lord sometimes does it, and so do Saints, as well as Guardian Angels and things. I wonder if I've ever seen one. I wonder if *you* have?

After a time Cuthbert left Ripon and went to be Prior at Lindisfarne, which is an Island near Berwick (a Prior is the Next Head Monk under the Abbot). This Island belonged to the Monks, and was often called Holy Island. Nowadays it is never called anything else.

Now Cuthbert had a Great friend called Herbert who lived on a tiny little Island (just big enough for one) in the middle of Lake Derwentwater, in

Cumberland, and Herbert was a Saint too. Once a year St. Herbert, who was a priest and a Hermit, used to get into his little Boat and row to the shore near Keswick. There he landed to see people and to buy a few Stores and to go to Confession and things. And when he came Ashore Cuthbert always went to see him. Sometimes they met at Carlisle instead.

One day after seeing Herbert, Cuthbert was sitting in his own Cell, looking out to sea.

"I've had a very busy time, being Prior here for Twelve Years," he thought, "I wish I could live like Herbert and have more time to pray."

Then he had an Idea, and this was the Idea:

"What about the Rocky little Island called Farne Island? We can easily see it from here, and so I can come here for Stores when I want to, if I need them. I'll go and be a Hermit there."

So he was. And although it was Little, Bare and Rocky, and not like Herbert's Island, which was Little, Wooded and Green, he managed to grow corn enough for himself, and he was very happy, and had heaps of time to spend with God, which is what he had always wanted. And every year he used to sail ashore and go to meet Herbert for a little Chat.

But he hadn't been there long when he had to stop living on his Island because he had to be a Bishop, and so he was one until he died on the very same day as Herbert did. Which was very nice for them, because they could go on being Friends in Heaven without having to wait for each other.

In the end Cuthbert was buried in Durham. And people built a great Abbey and Cathedral at the very Place. Durham Cathedral is one of the nicest Cathedrals in England, and to whom do you suppose it is Dedicated? To St. Cuthbert, of course! (If you don't know what Dedicated means, it shows that you haven't read the Third Story in this book, so you'd better read it and see!)

St. Cuthbert's Special Day is on March 20th. A good many people are called after him, but nearly all of them are English.

Now this story is a bit about St. Herbert too, so I'll tell you a little about him in case anyone reading this book is called after him. I can only tell you a very little because he was the sort of Hermit who likes to be Forgotten by people so as to be Remembered by God.

"The less company and Interesting things I have," he said, "the more I hope that God will be my company, and that he will tell me Interesting things."

And so it must have been, because now we know very little about him, and when he died he was Completely Forgotten. But a very long time afterwards (not so long ago, in fact) people remembered him again, and they used to go every year to his Island in Lake Derwentwater in boats with Priests and Incense and Banners and things, and they used to say Mass in the remains of his Chapel. But after the Reformation, Mass wasn't allowed, and so soon Herbert was Forgotten again!

Nowadays the only thing left is the Name of the Island and a few stones that were once a Chapel. The Island is called St. Herbert's Isle, but if you ask the people living round about *why* it is called that they don't know! So now no one remembers much about St. Herbert except God, which is what he wanted. I wonder how long it will be before *you* forget him?

His Special Day is March 20th, but not many people are called after him, because so few people even remember his name.

ST. WILFRID

Once upon a time there was a boy called Wilfrid, and he had a Wicked Stepmother. Now, as lots of people know, most Stepmothers are nearly the same as Mothers, but a few of them are Shocking. Wilfrid's was one of the Shocking ones.

Well, one day, when he was thirteen years old, he simply couldn't Stand it any longer. So he went to his father, who was a Noble Lord.

"Daddy," he said, "it doesn't seem to be any Good my staying at home, does it?"

"Well," said the Noble Lord, "now that you mention it, it doesn't. You certainly don't have much of a time, but what can one do?"

"I *thought*," said Wilfrid, "that perhaps you would let me have some Armour, and then I could learn more about Fighting and things. Then I could go to the King's Court."

"But your Stepmother would never let you go," said the Noble Lord, "she'd miss having someone to Scold."

"I know, Daddy," said Wilfrid, "but she won't know that I'm going. You'll see. That is," said Wilfrid in an Asking kind of voice, "if *you* don't mind?"

"Very well," said the Noble Lord, "on your own Head be it" (which means if anything happens, don't blame me).

So Wilfrid had a new Horse, and some Armour and a Sword and a Lance and a Retinue to follow him about and Look Grand.

" What *is* all this about? " said the Stepmother, when she saw all the Goings On. " Fancy giving a child of that age a Retinue! "

" Well, my dear," said the Noble Lord, " he's got to learn some time, and I suppose the Sooner the Better."

So Wilfrid went out every day with his Armour and Horse and Retinue and things, and some of the Retinue, who were real Soldiers, taught him how to be a Swordsman and a Leader and a Chivalrous Knight and all that. And the Wicked Stepmother got quite used to seeing them start off every morning.

But one day, when they had gone about a Mile away from the house Wilfrid said to them:

" To-day we are going to the King's Court."

" Aren't we going home? " asked one of the Retinue.

" No," said Wilfrid, " I am Escaping. If there are any of you who don't want to come, go home at the Usual Time and say nothing about it."

Two of the Retinue thought that they'd rather not go to the King's Court, but all the Others cheered, they were so pleased. And they started off at once.

The King's name was King Oswy, and he was quite pleased to see Wilfrid and the Retinue, and gave them some rooms in the Palace to live in. Everything was Grand for a few weeks, until one day Wilfrid thought this thought.

" I do believe I'm getting rather Tired of just marching round with my Retinue. I wonder how long I'll have to go on doing it? "

After another few weeks he thought:

" I *know* I'm getting Rather Tired of just marching round with my Retinue. I *wonder* how long I'll have to go on doing it? "

After another few weeks he thought:

"I'm *very* Tired of just marching round with my Retinue. I hope I can soon stop."

The next day the King sent for him.

" Good morning, Wilfrid," he said.

" Good morning, Your Majesty," said Wilfrid.

" I've been thinking," said King Oswy, " do you still like just marching round with your Retinue? "

" Well," said Wilfrid, " as a matter of Fact I'm sick of it. Only I thought that you wanted me to."

" Not at all," said King Oswy, " *I* thought that *you* wanted to! "

" I did at first," said Wilfrid, " but there doesn't seem to be anything *in* it, does there? I can't go on marching about with my Retinue All my Life, can I? "

" Would you like to go to School with the Monks at Lindisfarne? " said King Oswy.

" Yes, please," said Wilfrid, and so there he went.

He was there for a good many years, and when he grew up he went on a Pilgrimage to Rome to see the Pope, and he walked all the way. After lots of Adventures he got to Rome and there (when he had seen the Pope and the Books and the Churches and things) he was made a Priest. Then he came home to England to tell people all about the Wonderful Things that he had seen.

" You know," he said, " we seem to have got Out of Things here. More people ought to go to Rome. They do things differently. They have better Churches and *lovely* Music."

So a friend of his called Alfred gave him some land at Stamford, in Lincolnshire, to build a Monastery.

" Then," said Alfred, " you can do it like they do in Rome, and then we can all see."

So Wilfrid made a Benedictine Monastery, because

no one in England had seen one before, and all the People were very Impressed.

And Wilfrid built some more Monasteries, and people got quite Keen on Benedictines and the Roman way of Doing Things.

Well, when Wilfrid was about Thirty he had to be a Bishop. Now you know, only a Bishop or an Archbishop or a Cardinal or the Pope can make a Bishop, and Wilfrid rather wanted the same Bishop who had Ordained him to do it. (*Ordained* is making someone into a Priest by giving him the Sacrament of Holy *Orders*.) But it was a French Bishop who lived in Paris, which was Rather Awkward.

However, Wilfrid liked the French Bishop very much, and so he decided to Sail to France. All went very well, and he was made a Bishop, and then he set Sail for England again with some other priests who were coming home too. It was a big ship, with a Hundred and Twenty people in it counting the Sailors. They hadn't gone far when a Terrible Storm came up. The wind was so strong that it blew the ship right away off its course, no matter how everyone Worked. At last they were blown up on to the Beach of a different part of England belonging to the Saxons who were Pagans.

Then the Tide went down and left them High and not very Dry on the sand! And most of the Sailors got out of the Boat and walked about, or sat and rested on the Sand. The Saxons thought that this was great Good Luck, and they came hurrying down to the Sea to steal things from the Wreck and to take the people Prisoner and to Rob them.

Now there were heaps more than a Hundred and Twenty Saxons, so Wilfrid thought that they had better try and Bargain. So he told the Others to get back into the ship and Stay there. Then he stood up in the bows and said (very loud):

"Listen and I'll tell you something! It won't do you any Good if you come and Rob us because we are only Priests and Sailors and we haven't got any Valuables. But if you help us to get Afloat again, when we get to our part of England we will send you a Lot of Money for Ransom."

Now the Saxons were just beginning to listen when a Tiresome Thing happened.

While he was talking the Pagan Priest belonging to the Saxons came down to see the Wreck. When he saw that they were Christians and Priests he climbed up on to a Rock on the Beach and began to Curse them because Pagans don't Hold with Christians (Cursing is *Un*blessing).

Wilfrid saw him out of the Corner of his Eye, but he went on talking to the people as if he hadn't seen him at all. But one of the Sailors, who was behind Wilfrid, took a stone out of his pocket that he had picked up on the Beach (when he was looking for Shells) and he threw it at the Pagan Priest. It hit him bang on the forehead and Killed him Dead!

Well, that settled it. The Saxons were Furious, of course, and they Rushed at the Wreck and there was a Fierce Battle. Five of the Sailors were killed, but they were Winning when Wilfrid shouted:

"Keep in the Ship! *Don't* chase them, but go on fighting."

He had seen the Tide. It had been Creeping up behind them, and just as the Sailors were almost too Tired to go on any longer the ship floated up off the Sand! Wilfrid and the Priests set the Sail while the Sailors kept off the Saxons, and they sailed away safely.

" Well," said Wilfrid, as they sat down to Supper, " I never thought that being a Bishop would be so Strenuous! " (Strenuous is having to use a lot of Strength.)

When they got to their own part of England Wilfrid was sent to be the Bishop of York. Now York hadn't had a Bishop for some time, because there weren't enough Bishops to go Round, and when Wilfrid saw his Cathedral he was Horrified! No one had bothered to look after it at all. " It isn't *my* Job! " everyone had said, " it's the Bishop's job, and we haven't got a Bishop!" (York Cathedral is called York *Minster*. Lots of Cathedrals that are, or used to be. Monasteries as well are called Minsters. Like Beverley Minster and Southwark Minster and Newminster and Westminster, it is just a Short way of saying Monastery.)

Well, York Minster was in a sad way, the Foundations had sunk a bit with the Wet and had made the walls Crack. The Rain had got through the cracks and Moss grew in them. The windows had no Glass left. Birds' nests were very untidily everywhere. Everything was Wet and Green and Slippery! Wilfrid went up to the Altar. It was Dirty, and the vestments and the altar cloths were Moth-eaten and shabby and the silver chalices and things were Tarnished.

Wilfrid was very Angry! He called the people together and he said:

" Now, all of you! You have let the Minster get into a Disgraceful State! You ought to be thoroughly ashamed of yourselves. What are your own houses like? Are they damp and dirty? No, you take good care of that. But what about God's House? How *dare* you ask God to come to a place like this? Aren't you afraid? Would you treat the King like that? And you priests that live in York. You are the Worst of All.

You know more than the Others, and yet you actually *ask* God, when you say Mass, to come to this Disgusting Place! Now, all of you, for a *Privilege* (that none of you deserve) and not as a *Penance* (which you do deserve) you must work hard, and make the Minster a lovely place. I shall not allow Mass to be said here until we have made the most beautiful place that it is possible to make. And even then, remember, it wouldn't be good enough for God. But He will know that it is at least our Best, and He will come."

All the People trooped up and looked at the Minster. They had got so used to it being Shabby that they almost didn't notice it, on Sundays. But now that Wilfrid had been so Angry about it they had a Good Look Round.

They began to be very Ashamed and then they began to Work. They cleaned and mended and scrubbed. They put Glass in the windows and they Threw Away the moth-eaten vestments and things. Their wives stitched and embroidered new Altar Cloths and washed and ironed the albs and cottas. Artists came and painted beautiful Patterns, and carvers came and Carved wood and stone until at last they had a Really Beautiful Minster.

The Sunday after it was finished they had Solemn High Mass there, and everybody came and sang the Te Deum, which is what we always sing on Special Occasions.

But some people were very Dissatisfied.

" Why do you spend so much money on the Church? " they said, "when so many people are so Poor? You ought to give it to the Poor-and-Raggies. Think how Sad it is for them to come from their cold little cottages to the Rich Church. It must make them feel very Jealous! "

"Not at all," said Wilfrid. "Think how nice it is for them to have somewhere where they can come at any time of day. Somewhere to sit and rest and think about God and talk to him without being Bothered by the Household. There are lovely things to look at and plenty of room. There are Lights and Incense and Flowers and Music. And it is all Free. They don't pay for it, and they have just as much right here as Kings and Queens with Crowns on. They can sit in the very Front if they want to. They can learn to sing and be in the Choir and serve Mass. In fact God's Home is their Home, and that is as it should be."

"Even so," said the Dissatisfied people, "it is still a Waste of Money."

"Did you never hear a Story," said Wilfrid, "about Our Lord and the Precious Ointment? "

"No," said the Dissatisfied ones.

"Well, go home and read it then," said Wilfrid. And they did, and they didn't say any more about Waste.

Well, this is turning into a very long Story, and if we don't stop there won't be Room in the book for all the Other People. Wilfrid did so very many things that I can't possibly tell you even One Quarter of them. But I expect someone else will.

St. Wilfrid's Special Day is on October 12th, and many and many a person is called after him. Perhaps you are.

ST. JOHN OF BEVERLEY

Once upon a time there was a boy called John and he lived in a village called Cherry Burton in Yorkshire. (In case anyone doesn't know what a Burton is, it is a Yorkshire word for a Piece of Land, or a Field. So that places called Bishop's Burton and Burton Agnes and Burton Constable and Burton-on-Trent really mean the Bishop's Field, and the Lamb Field and the Constable's Field and the Field beside the River Trent, and all that.)

So John lived in a place called Cherry Burton which sounds like a very nice place, doesn't it?

Well, when John grew up he learned to be a priest at St. Hilda's Abbey in Whitby, and then he came back and he made an Abbey at Beverley which was the nearest Town to his home. And there he worked and taught. And he used to go to all the Villages called Something Burton and Burton Something and all the other Villages round about and Teach and Baptize and Marry and Bury and Generally Look After all the people in them. And he used to go to them on Horseback, and thereby Hangs a Tale. (Which means that there is a Story about it.)

John used to have Boys' Clubs and things in Beverley, and when he rode round the Villages lots of the Bigger Boys used to ride with him. One of the boys was called Herebald and he was the one that John liked best, although he really liked them all.

One day John said to all his Beverley Boys:

"I'm going to ride to Waghen to-day, is anybody coming?"

(Waghen was one of his Villages. And it rhymes with Pawn. I know it isn't one of the Burtons, but it's got a field called Cherry Paddock in it, and that's nearly as good.)

" Can I come? " asked Herebald.

" Can I ? " said one of the Others.

" Can I? Can I? Can I? " said all the Rest.

They loved going to Waghen because they had to cross a River that hadn't got a Bridge and they had to go on a Ferry Boat that pulled across by Chains, which was Most Exciting what with the Horses and all.

So they started out and John had a Bay Horse and Herebald had a very Fiery Chestnut that Pulled. Just out of Beverley they came to a long narrow straight road called Long Lane, and all the Boys said:

" Here is a lovely place to Gallop. Let's have Races with the Horses! "

" It's bad for the Horses to gallop on the road," said John, " wait until we get over the Ferry and then you can Gallop along the Grass at the side of the road."

" But this is so *straight*, Father," said the Boys, " *please* let us Gallop! "

Well, they kept on about it so, that at last John said:

" Oh well, but be careful of Loose Stones," and then he said to Herebald, " Not you, Herebald, because your Horse is so Fiery. He might kick the others and you aren't strong enough to hold him."

Herebald was very disgusted when he had to stay by John, and when the others all galloped off down the road he made a Sulky face and wouldn't speak.

Presently the others all came Galloping back.

" Just once more! " they shouted, and they turned their Horses round. As they clattered off Herebald felt he could bear it no longer. He kicked his heels and was off too! John shouted after him:

"Herebald! don't let him have his Head or you'll never stop him!" But Herebald didn't care! He gave the horse his Head and simply Flew along the road after the others. (And anyway, the Horse Pulled so hard that he couldn't have stopped even if he had tried.) He soon raced the others and was galloping in front when they came to the end of Long Lane and the road turned a very sharp corner round a Ditch and over a little Bridge. The Horse saw it just in time and made a huge Leap over the ditch but Herebald wasn't good at Jumping. He had never jumped without a Leading Rein and so, of course, he Fell Off. And, of course, there was a Stone just where his head landed, and, of course, he cracked his Skull. He broke his Thumb, too, because he hadn't been holding the Reins properly and so he got it caught when he fell.

Herebald lay on his back beside the ditch and stared at the sky. He *was* so Angry! Not because he'd hurt himself, or even because he'd Fallen Off (which is always Ignominious. Ask someone else!) but because now John could say I Told You So, and he would be quite right!

Then all the Others came trotting up with John, and some of them kindly caught Herebald's Horse and some of them tried to stop their own horses from Shying at Herebald lying on the ground, and then the other horses Shied because the Others were, and there was a Stamping and a Jingling and a Creaking and a Snorting, and people Patting necks and saying "Steady lass!" and All That and Herebald felt Giddy because of his Cracked Skull.

Then John came and knelt beside him and said:

"That's all right, Herebald, you're not Killed," and

he tied a scarf round Herebald's head to keep the Cracks together. Then some of the Beverley Boys carried him to a cottage by the Ferry where they left him for the Time Being.

" We'll stop and see you on the way back," they said, and they led the Horses to the River Bank. At the place where the Ferry Boat came there was a thing called a Hard. It was really a little steep road made of Cobbles so that people could walk down and get on to the Boat without climbing down the grassy and muddy Bank. The Ferry Boat was a Raft with a railing at each side and with nothing at each End. You just Walked On, then pulled it along by a chain fixed on to a post on the other Bank, and when it got to the Other Side you just Walked Off on to another Hard and then on to the road.

Now this time the Ferry Boat was on the Other Side (it always was), where the Ferry Man's house was. And so they all shouted and whistled with two fingers in their mouths for him to bring the boat across. But the Ferry Man was milking his Cows and couldn't come, so they waited for Ages, and meanwhile they watched the Ferry Man's geese swimming about in the River. At last they saw him coming slowly along and down to the Boat. He made a Clanking noise with the Chain and pulled it Hand over Hand until it landed with a bump on the Hard where John was waiting with the Beverley boys. It took some time to get all the Horses and Boys sorted out tidily, especially as they all wanted to help with the Chain, and that meant that someone else had to hold the Horses. However, they all got to the Other Side quite safely without anyone Falling In. Which was Good Luck because the Ferry Man said that when Cows or Hounds had to cross they often fell in and had to Swim, and the geese hated it.

In a very short time they got to Waghen, and all
the people came out to see John, and they said:

" Please, Father, will you Baptize my Baby? " or
" Please, Father, will you Marry Annie and me? "
or " Please, Father, will you look at my Bad Leg? "
When he had done all these things a man called Alfred
came with his mother. Alfred was Deaf and Dumb
and, although it wasn't really anything to do with it,
he was Bald. *Quite* bald.

" Can you please cure my Son, Father? " said Alfred's
mother.

" No, but God can," said John, and he said to God:
" Please Lord would you be so very Kind as to make
Alfred Talk? It is so difficult for him when he can't
say anything at all, ever."

And because John was one of God's Special People
and because he always did everything that God wanted
him to do however much he sometimes didn't want
to, and because he really did love God, God said to
him:

" Yes, John, I will make Alfred better. But you will
have to teach him to speak."

So John went up to Alfred and said:

" Alfred, say ' Yes '."

" Yes," said Alfred, and all the people Cheered.

" Say ' No '," said John.

" No," said Alfred.

" Say ' A '," said John.

" A," said Alfred.

" Say ' B '," said John.

" B," said Alfred.

" Say ' C '," said John.

" C," said Alfred.

Now you know your Letters as well as I do, and
so I needn't go right through the Alphabet like

John did with Alfred. When they had done Z, John said:

" Say ' God '."

" God," said Alfred.

" Say ' God made me '," said John.

" God made me," said Alfred.

And so they went on until, by the end of the day, Alfred could talk quite well. Everyone was so delighted that they got ready a Huge Party to Celebrate, and they asked John and the Beverley Boys to come to it. But they couldn't stay because of seeing Herebald and getting home in time for Supper.

Just as they were starting home, Alfred ran after John.

" Please, Father! " he said.

" What do you want? " said John.

" What about me being Bald? " said Alfred.

" What about it ?" said John.

" Well, will you Cure that, too? " said Alfred.

" Good gracious me! " said John, " go and see the Doctor, *I* can't cure you! " And he rode on.

" Some people," said John to the Beverley Boys, " some people are never Satisfied."

They went back over the Ferry and stopped to see Herebald and his Cracked Skull. He wasn't feeling very well, so John sent the Beverley Boys home alone and said that he would stay the Night with Herebald. So the kind man in the cottage very kindly found some more Bedclothes and made a bed on the Floor for John. He would have given him a bed, but there wasn't another one.

In the night John and Herebald got talking of This and That and saying where they had been at school and who Confirmed them and where their homes were and all that.

" Who baptized you, Father? " asked Herebald.

" The Parish Priest at Cherry Burton," said John, " who baptized *you*? "

" Father Ethelbert," said Herebald.

" Do you mean Father Ethelbert who used to live at Leven? " asked John.

" Yes," said Herebald, " why? "

" He is a very Wicked man," said John; " so Wicked that he isn't allowed to give any of the Sacraments or say Mass or anything at all. He hasn't been allowed to since long before you were born. But you can pray for him; ask God to give him the Grace to be sorry for having been wicked and disobedient to his Bishop, and ask his Pardon. His Bishop will then allow him to say Mass and give the Sacraments once more.

" Of course I expect you know that people who are not Baptized never see God. They don't go to Heaven. But, of course, if they are good people (and most people *are* good), they don't go to Hell. That wouldn't be Fair, and God is the Fairest person there is. So they go to a place called Limbo, where they are very happy, but not so happy as if they could see God. It is the same place that people went to before Our Lord opened Heaven for us. So it is very sad if people die before they are Baptized, and that is why we Baptize them when they are only a Few days Old, so as to be in Time."

After a while John had to go and be Archbishop of York, but when he got old he gave up his place to a Bishop called Wilfrid, and he came back to Beverley, where he stayed until he died, and was buried at his own Monastery.

Then the people built a beautiful Minster there to belong to the Monastery. You remember that Minster is short for Monastery, don't you? And when Monastery Churches are Cathedrals as well they are called Minsters.

ST. JOHN

Like York Minster, and Westminster and Southminster and Newminster and just plain Minster.

St. John's Special Day is on October 25th, and hundreds and thousands of people are called John. But anyone called John whose Birthday is on October 25th can have St. John of Beverley for his Very Special Saint.

ST. GILES

Once upon a time there was a priest who wanted to be a hermit and his name was Giles. So he asked his Bishop if he might, and the Bishop said, " Yes, but if I were you I should start off by living with an old hermit who will tell you all about how to be one."

" Thank you, my Lord," said Giles. " Now I come to think of it I don't really know *how* to be a hermit, I just want to *be* one."

" Yes," said the Bishop, " that's what I thought. Now go in peace and God bless you."

So Giles went to live in a desert with an old Hermit who taught him how Hermits live. Giles stayed with him for Three Years. But after that, because he had learned to Know and Love God so well, God made miracles for him and that Attracted Attention.

Now you know that a Desert is very poor and sandy and dusty and nothing much grows, and it very rarely Rains? Well, after the Three Years, Giles said to the old Hermit:

" If you like, Father, I will do the Gardening for you. I am younger than you and it is Heavy work."

" Thank you, my Son," said the old Hermit, " it is lucky indeed, in this Waste Place, if anything at all will grow."

So Giles began Digging and Raking and Sowing and Praying and in a few days there was a Rainstorm.

" Thank you, God," said Giles. " Now I can get started properly."

The extraordinary thing is that it rained at least every week, and trees and flowers and grass grew up and in a month or so there was no Desert at all just in that place. Well, people soon heard of it and came to see Giles, and ask him to do Miracles for them, or sometimes they just came to Stare and Point.

"I'm sorry, Father," said Giles, "that this isn't a Lonely Place for you any more. I will go away because I might get Vain. I hope I won't because it wasn't *my* doing, but God's. But sometimes we forget that."

"You are quite right," said the Hermit. "Good-bye, my Son."

So Giles went away, but that bit of the Desert still stayed like a garden and it is still there, so far as I know.

One day, when he was travelling through a Forest he found a cave, and in front of the cave were thick thorny blackberries growing. There was a little track behind the brambles to get into the cave, so he went to look. It was an airy light cave and at the back of it was a little well with a spring of very cold fresh water.

"What a lovely place," said Giles. "I can live here beautifully and the door of the cave is almost Invisible behind the blackberries." He went out of the cave and looked round about until, not far away, he found a flat open space in the woods that was exactly right for a Vegetable Plot and he lost no time in planting some of the packets of Seeds he had brought with him. Hermits generally made gardens and grew their own food.

In the evening he was lying in the cave, just ready to go to sleep, when he heard a Pitter-pattering noise, and a Rustling noise round about the Blackberry Bushes. The pattering noise came round the back of the brambles, along the little narrow path and into the Cave. Giles had been rather nervously wondering what it could possibly be, and he kept as Still as a Stone. The pattering stopped just inside the cave and there stood a little deer! She lifted up her head and sniffed, and stared into the dark cave. Giles didn't move. The deer thought it seemed quite safe so she trotted to the back of the cave, drank some water from the Spring and lay down near the doorway and went to sleep. So did Giles.

When he woke up in the morning the deer was gone and he wondered if perhaps it had been a dream. But the same thing happened the next night and every night.

"It must have been the deer who made the little path round the Blackberry Bushes," said Giles to himself. "So really it is her cave and not mine!"

After some time the deer and Giles got so used to each other that the deer wasn't frightened any more and became Tame and friendly. She followed Giles about and poked in his pockets for pieces of bread. Giles found it very difficult to teach her that although she could eat all the grass she liked, she Must Not touch his vegetables.

One day, Giles was walking up and down in front of the cave when the Deer galloped up through the woods, round the bushes and into the cave in such a tearing hurry that Giles quickly went in after her to see what was the matter. The deer was hot and tired and panting and was lying near the pool.

Giles went out to the doorway and just then heard hunting Horns and hounds and Galloping Horses. He stayed behind the bushes and watched the Hounds come right up to bark and howl round about.

"Please, dear Lord," he said, "don't let them hurt the Deer. She has run to me to save her, just as I would run to you. She trusts me, as I trust you."

The hounds poked their faces into the brambles, but

the thorns were so thick and the branches so close that they wouldn't risk the Scratches.

The King's Huntsman tried to get the hounds to go in but they wouldn't, and as it was now getting dark they all went home. Giles went and stroked the Deer and soothed her down and thanked God for the Blackberry Bushes.

But the King wanted to know why the Huntsmen had brought nothing home with them, and so they told him about the Deer they had seen.

"It absolutely Disappeared, Your Majesty," said one of them. "It galloped up to some Blackberry Bushes and Vanished."

"Are you *sure* you didn't imagine the whole thing?" said the King.

"No, because the hounds saw the deer, too," said the Huntsman.

"Well," said the King, "we'll go out again to-morrow. I'll go with you and you shall show me the place."

So the next day the King and his Huntsmen all rode into the Forest to see if they could find the Vanishing Deer.

By the time they got to the place the Brambles had grown so thick that they couldn't have found the little path even if they had looked for it.

"Are you *sure* this is the Right Place?" said the King.

They all said it was, so they tried again to make the hounds go into the Brambles and drive out the Deer. Then one of the Huntsmen shot an arrow into the Bushes to frighten the deer out, but nothing happened.

"There's something Odd about this," said the King. "I don't know what it is, but I feel it in my Bones."

So he told the Huntsmen to cut down the Brambles with their Hunting Knives. So they did. Soon of course they saw the opening into the cave, and when they had cleared a way through the thorns they called up the Hounds, to send them into the Cave.

" No, don't," said the King, and he held up his hand to stop them. " Don't do that. I'll go in myself and see what is there."

" Do be careful, Your Majesty," said the Head Huntsman. " Something might Jump Out at you! "

" It would have Jumped by now," said the King, and he walked into the Cave.

There he saw an Old Man with an arrow through his shoulder, and with his other arm round a Deer. Neither of them moved. The King stared.

Then he took off his hat.

" I'm sorry, Father," he said. " I'd no Idea anyone lived here. And look at your shoulder! Let me help you."

" Thank you," said Giles, " but first will you promise that no one will hurt my Deer? She lives here with me and is my friend."

The King sent away the Huntsmen and the Hounds and then asked Giles to come back to the Palace to see a Doctor about his wounded Shoulder.

" Thank you, but no," said Giles. " I have lived here as a Hermit too long to go back to towns and things. It will get better."

But the King went home and told the Bishop all that had happened and the Bishop went to see Giles.

" You must have a Doctor, Father," he said. " You help us all with your prayers here alone, and you must not stop us when we want to do you a kindness."

So the King's Doctor went and bandaged Giles's Shoulder and he lived in the cave for years more, and the Blackberries soon grew again.

Afterwards Giles had to stop being a Hermit and

be a Bishop and some more very Interesting things happened to him, that you must not forget to read about one day.

St. Giles's Special Day is September 1st, and a fair number of people are called after him especially in Scotland because he is the Patron Saint of Edinburgh.

ST. EDMUND

Once upon a time there was a King called King Edmund, and he lived in Norfolk. He was Twenty-Eight years old, which is fairly old, but not for a King. King Edmund was a Specially Good King, like Alfred the Great and King Arthur and Edward I and our own King George and all the people loved him.

One day some Fishermen were mending their nets on the beach when they saw sailing towards them a little boat with a man in it.

"That's funny!" said one of the Fishermen, "that isn't an English boat! We don't make sails that Shape!"

"It's Danish," said another Fisherman. (The Danes were great Enemies of ours at that time.)

"It can't be, *surely*," said another Fisherman; "one Dane wouldn't be so stupid as to come to his Enemies' country all alone!" And they all stared out to Sea.

When the little boat came ashore the Fishermen ran down the beach and found that the man *was* a Dane. So they took him Prisoner.

They took the Dane straight to the King's Palace, and brought him to King Edmund.

"Who are you?" said King Edmund, "and why did you come here all alone?"

"My name is Prince Ragnar," said the Dane, "and I came here by Mistake."

"What happened?" said the King.

"Well," said Ragnar, "I took my Hawk out to catch some Gulls that were spoiling the Fishing. Most of the Gulls were too far to reach from the shore so I took my Boat and sailed out a little way to make it easier for my Hawk. Then there was a Storm of Wind and it blew me right out to Sea. I couldn't do much without any help, and after four or five days, I can't remember quite which, I got here. So I am your Prisoner now. I'm very Hungry and Thirsty, please!"

"You *have* had a Time!" said the King, "but if you will go with my servants they will give you a bath and clean clothes and food and anything else you may want. Perhaps you would be kind enough to have Supper with me?"

Ragnar was all Astonished. He thought that King Edmund would have put him in Prison or killed him, because he was an Enemy. Then he thought that perhaps the Supper was a Trick to make him think he was safe. But he was a brave man, so he said:

"Thank you, Sir. I will have Supper with you with great pleasure." And he bowed to the King and went away with some of the Palace Servants. They took him and gave him a bath and some of King Edmund's own clothes. He was surprised at the beautiful Palace and beautiful Things. Because in Denmark things were much more Rough and Ready even though he was a Prince. The Danes spent most of their time being Pirates, and the Ships and Towns they bothered most were the English ones. Which is why they were our Enemies.

At supper time King Edmund asked Prince Ragnar to sit beside him, and he gave him the best food, out of Silver Dishes, and the best Beer, out of a huge Drinking Horn made of a Horn bound with Silver, and Ragnar got more and more surprised.

At last he said to the King:

"It is very good of you to treat me so well, and to give me Supper first. When am I going to be killed?"

"You're not going to be," said King Edmund; "you are my Guest, not my Prisoner. You didn't come here on purpose, and so you don't count as an Enemy. If you will, I would like you to Stay the Night. Or better still, stay for Some Time. I would be glad of your company."

"But *why*?" asked Ragnar. "I'm sure, if *you* had been Washed Ashore in Denmark my father would have killed you!"

"That is because he doesn't know about being Kind to Strangers," said King Edmund, "because Danes aren't Christians. Besides I like you. Why should I kill you? You haven't done me any harm."

"You ought to kill me *because* I'm a Dane," said

223

Ragnar; "you aren't a very good Enemy, if you don't mind my saying so."

"But I never kill Danes because they are Danes," said the King; "I kill them when they come and kill my poor Fishermen, or when they Rob my Ships, or Burn my Villages."

"We kill the English because they are English," said Prince Ragnar; "my father always says that is a very good Reason."

"Well, some English people kill Danes because they are Danes," said the King, "but I don't, because Danes are very nice people when they are not being Enemies. We grow the same Roses after all."

"So we do!" said Ragnar, "and we Hunt and Fish and sit by the Fire, and feel Cold in winter and Hot in summer, just like you do! How funny! I never thought of that!"

Next day they went Hunting, and King Edmund, who was a Strong and Clever hunter, found that the Prince was an even Greater and Stronger one. And he was pleased, and they became very good friends. And Ragnar stayed in England for a very long time.

But one of the King's Courtiers was very Dissatisfied.

"What *is* the King thinking about?" he said. "He has an Enemy to stay with him and he treats him like a Friend. And Ragnar isn't even a Christian! He's sure to be a Spy!"

But it wasn't all that that he minded. He was Jealous because Ragnar beat everyone hollow at Hunting and Shooting and Fishing, which are all very English things to do.

So one day, when all the Court was Hunting, he waited until no one could see him, and he shot Prince Ragnar and killed him dead! Then, because he knew how terribly angry the King would be if he found out, he hid Ragnar's body in some bushes and rode on and joined the others.

At the end of the day when they all got home King Edmund said:

" Where is Prince Ragnar? Hasn't he come home? "

" Perhaps he has run away! " said the Wicked Courtier.

" Why should he? " asked the King in a Surprised Voice.

" Because he is a Spy," said the Wicked Courtier.

" Nonsense! " said King Edmund, " he is my Friend! "

But Prince Ragnar never came back, and no one could think what had become of him. (But *you* know!)

But it was all Found Out in the End, and this is how:

When he first arrived in his little Boat, King Edmund very kindly gave Ragnar a Greyhound puppy. " In case you get Lonely, so far from home," he said. And when the puppy grew up he always followed Ragnar every-where, and slept in his room, and all that.

Now when Ragnar was lost, so was the Greyhound, because he saw what the Wicked Courtier had done and he waited by his Master's body until someone came to help. But no one did. And the poor Grey-hound got Hungrier and Hungrier until, at last, after some days, he thought he'd go to the Palace for some dinner and then come back. So he went into the big Dining hall and sat beside King Edmund. (Because, although it wasn't Allowed, the King always gave him Bits.)

" Hullo! " said King Edmund, " so you've come back? Where's Master? "

But the Greyhound only wagged his tail and looked at the King's plate.

" Good gracious! how Thin he's got! " said the King, and he told one of his servants to bring a Hot Dinner for the dog. As soon as he'd eaten it, he trotted out of the Hall towards the woods again.

" It's all very Queer! " said King Edmund, and he called some of his Courtiers.

" Follow the dog," he said, " and see where he goes. I can't understand it at all."

So the Courtiers did, and of course they found the body of Prince Ragnar. When they came back and told the King he was Very Angry and Very Sad.

" Ragnar was my Friend and my Guest," he said, " Who dared to be so Treacherous? " After a whole lot of Asking, some people who were out Hunting on the day that Ragnar was killed remembered that the Wicked Courtier had stayed behind with him and then followed on alone, and so he was found out.

So the King called his Counsellors and they all decided what to do with the Wicked Courtier. And when everything was settled they sent for him.

" This is your punishment," said King Edmund. " You must get into the little Boat that Prince Ragnar came in, and you must be towed right out to Sea and left there. If God wants you to be punished he will arrange it. If not, he will save you."

So the Wicked Courtier was towed out to Sea in Ragnar's little Boat and left there.

And now a very Interesting thing happened. In Denmark Ragnar's father was Hawking for Sea birds on the beach with Ragnar's brother. Suddenly they saw a little boat sailing towards them with one man in it!

" Look! " said Ragnar's father, " Ragnar's boat! He's come home at last! "

" I wonder where he's been all this time," said the brother; " we were sure he must be Drowned. I *am* glad he's safe! "

And they ran down to the edge of the Sea to meet Ragnar. (But you know who it really was, don't you?)

When the boat landed they saw that it wasn't Ragnar at all, but the Wicked Courtier!

"Wicked Christian Englishman!" said Ragnar's father, "you have killed my son!"

"No, no!" said the Wicked Courtier in a Fright.

"Well, how did you get his Boat then?" said the brother. "Where is he?"

"Well," said the Wicked Courtier, "don't take me Prisoner and I'll tell you. Our Wicked King Edmund killed him! He sailed to England by Accident and, instead of helping him and letting him rest, the King killed him because he was a Dane. Now he is sitting at home in his Palace. He is Absolutely Delighted that Prince Ragnar is dead!"

Now *you* know that none of all that was true. The Wicked Courtier wanted to be Revenged on Edmund for punishing him. (Revenge is paying someone Back and paying him Out.)

But of course, Ragnar's father and brother believed it all. And they said:

"WE WILL KILL KING EDMUND AND ALL HIS SUBJECTS!"

And then they said to the Wicked Courtier: "And first we will kill *you* because you are one of the Subjects and an Englishman!" And they did, and it served him right, didn't it?

Then the Danes got together a great Army and put them in a fleet of Ships and they sailed across the Sea to England. And they landed and they burnt all the Houses and all the Corn and they killed all the People and all the Cattle, and they went further and further inland looking for King Edmund, who was far away from the Sea, seeing to some Business or other.

Then they burnt the big Monastery at Peterborough and sent this Message to the King:

" Give us half of your Kingdom for our own and yourself as a Prisoner and we will go away! "

Now King Edmund wasn't Ready when the Danes came, and he was busy collecting his Army when the Messenger came. So he asked his great friend Hubert, who was a Bishop, what he ought to do.

" Well," said Hubert, " I think you'll have to Run Away, Your Majesty. I don't know what all your people will say if you are taken Prisoner by the Danes."

" They can have another King," said Edmund.

" But," said Hubert, " they'll never love one as much as they love you. You are their Best King."

" Well, I'll stay and fight with them, I think," said King Edmund. " I would hate to be a Prisoner in a Pagan Country. There'd be no Sacraments. I don't know what I should do."

" The People would much rather you ran away," said Hubert, " then when the Danes have gone away, you can come back safely."

" Oh no," said the King, " whatever I do, I won't do that. But I am afraid that if I don't give in to the Danes so many more of my people will be Killed."

" They'd rather That than the Other," said the Bishop.

So King Edmund said to the Messenger:

" Go back to your Master and say that I would rather Die with my own People in my own Land and in my own Faith than give them up to the Rule of Pagans."

So, with his Army, King Edmund marched to meet the Danes. They met at Thetford, and there was a Terrible Battle. At last the Danes won and King Edmund was taken Prisoner!

ST. EDMUND

The Danes were delighted to have caught the King! "Come on!" they said, "let's Poke him Up a bit before we take him to Denmark!" Then they said to the King:

"Now we'll have fun with you, you Horrible Christian!"

"I am glad," said King Edmund. "The Roman soldiers had what they called Fun with Our Lord before they killed him. It is very kind of Him to let me be the Same."

"*That's* a good Idea!" said one of the Danish soldiers. "Let's be like the Roman Soldiers! They Scourged their Prisoner first!" All the Danes thought that this was a Grand Idea, and they tied King Edmund to a tree outside a Church and scourged him. Then they had a Shooting Competition with their Arrows, with the King for a Target. He was glad he was so near the Church because the Blessed Sacrament helped him to be Brave. Just when he felt he couldn't be brave any longer the Danes Cut off his Head.

"There!" said God to Edmund, "you were quite right not to give Half your Christian Kingdom to Pagans."

"I'm glad I was," said Edmund, "but all Pagans are not Wicked are they?"

"No, of course not," said God.

"Ragnar wasn't was he?" said Edmund. "Ragnar was my Best Friend. I am sorry he wasn't a Christian, because now he'll be in Limbo instead of here. I *did* pray for him, too."

"Yes," said God, "you did. Would you like to see him?"

"Yes, I would," said Edmund.

"There he is," said God. "He has got a lot to tell you."

Edmund went up to Ragnar.

" How *did* you get here when you are not a Christian? "

" I *am* a Christian though," said Ragnar with a big smile.

" But you weren't Baptized, were you? " said Edmund, all surprised.

" I had the Baptism of Desire," said Ragnar. " I wanted to be a Christian after I had lived in your Palace for a time, but I was Rather Shy of asking you. I was just going to Do Something about it when I was killed. So Our Lord very kindly let me be a Christian and come to Heaven."

" Good! " said Edmund. " I *am* glad to see you again." And they went away together to find some other friends.

When the Danes had Beheaded King Edmund they hid his head so that the English people couldn't find it to bury it, and then they sailed away.

But one day some Shepherds saw a Great Wolf sitting by something and looking after it. And it was King Edmund's head.

So they thanked the Wolf and buried the King's head with his body, and they built a great Church and Benedictine Abbey at the place where he was buried. The Town was called Bury St. Edmunds, and it still is.

St. Edmund's Special Day is November 20th. And lots of people are called after him, mostly in England.

ST. HAROLD

Once upon a time there was a King of Denmark and his name was King Harold. And because there had been other King Harolds in Denmark this one had a funny nickname as well. (Instead of being Harold the Second or Third or whatever he was.) First I will tell you why he was called it, and then I'll tell you what it was that he was called.

Once when he was a little boy Harold was playing on the floor with his brother. All of a sudden Harold tripped over his brother's legs and fell on his face on the floor. He cut his lip and he bit his tongue and he gave his front teeth such a knock that they were loose for days and days. None of them Actually Came Out but one of them was bruised inside and it looked quite blue. But after he was better and his teeth were tight in again the tooth was as blue as ever and was blue to the end of his life. So he was always called Harold Bluetooth so as not to be mixed up with the other Harolds. (Once there was a King of Norway who was called Harold Greycloak. I wonder why?)

Now Harold Bluetooth was not a Christian and neither were his friends and relations, but he was not like a good many other Pagan Kings. He did not martyr the priests and imprison his people for being Christians, and this is the reason why.

"You see," he said, "the Christians don't make so much Trouble as the others. Their God tells them to be good neighbours and to look after each other. He likes them to be farmers and to garden in their gardens

231

and all that is Useful for the country. He likes them to look after ill people and so they build Hospitals and *that* is Useful for the Country. He likes them to use their brains (because that is what they say that he gave them brains for) and so they build Schools and that is Useful for the Country, too. Another thing is that the Christians' God does not like them to be lazy. He gave them hands for use not for idleness. So the Christians Make Things. They make shoes and ploughs and blankets and bread and furniture. So," said King Harold, " of *course* I don't mind having the Christians in Denmark! " And they all laughed to think what a lot they were getting from the people who were silly enough to be Christians.

King Harold and his friends and relations were not often at home because their favourite thing to be was to be Sea Robbers and Pirates. They sailed about in their ships and fought any other ships that they met and Robbed them. They were excellent fighters and nearly always won. If there did not seem to be many ships out that day they would sail into someone else's Harbour and steal from their houses and shops and take away their strongest-looking people to work for them. When their ships were full of Robbings they would sail home and divide out the Goods and spend the money in Feasts and Junketings. (What is Junket?) Then, when they felt a little poor again, out they would sail to see what they could find.

Well, one time King Harold Bluetooth had had a very lucky outing. He brought back enough valuable goods to last for some time and any amount of Gold and Jewels and Money. The Junketings and Goings On at the Palace were simply terrific and after a week everyone was sitting back quite exhausted and full of food and drink.

Just as they were all having a good forty winks to rest themselves, someone came in and whispered to the King.

"Your Majesty, one of the Christian priests wants to see you."

"What for?" said King Harold, and he opened one eye, then he quickly shut it again.

"I don't know. He didn't say," said the King's servant.

"Well, go and ask him then," said the King. "Oh, I *have* got a headache! Mind you don't stamp your feet as you go out, and shut the door *quietly* for goodness' sake!"

The messenger went out on tiptoe and shut the door very carefully. Soon he came back with the priest and King Harold opened one eye again. (If he opened both eyes at once it let in too much light and that made his headache bang about in his head.)

"What do you want?" he asked. "Excuse me lying here with one eye shut but I have *the* most awful headache."

"It's all those Junketings, I shouldn't wonder," said the priest; "it might be better to have the curtains drawn, Your Majesty, the light will be Dimmer." And he went across the room and drew the curtains without rattling the rings.

"Thanks, old chap," said King Harold; "that is a good deal better. What did you want to see me about?"

"Well," said the priest, "perhaps I'd better come back when your headache has gone, because it is quite a long thing that I want to see you about."

"Oh no," said the King, "I can listen all right so long as I don't have to move and so long as you keep still."

"All right," said the priest, "it's like this, Your Majesty. As I expect you know, there are more and

more Christians in Denmark every year, because you
don't imprison us and all that. And now quite three
quarters of the Danish people are Christians."

" Are they, by Jove? " said King Harold; " I had no
idea that they had spread so much. But I don't mind,
my dear chap, you're useful people and do no harm.
In fact you do quite a lot of good, taking it all round."

" But that wasn't all that I wanted to say, Your
Majesty," said the priest. " I really came with a Polite
Message from all your Christian subjects, and the
Message is this:

> Your Majesty. As most of your subjects are now
> Christian, and all your schools and hospitals are
> Christian, we think (if it is all the same to you) that
> we would rather have a Christian King and not a
> Pagan one."

" It is *not* all the same to me! " said King Harold and
he sat up suddenly and glared at the priest. Then he
groaned sadly and lay down with his eyes shut while
his headache went banging round inside his head. The
priest got up and dipped a clean handkerchief in some
cold water and put it on the King's forehead.

" Thanks, old chap," said the King and then he said,
" It is *not* all the same to me. What do they mean,
hey? "

" Oh, they don't mean that they want another King
instead of you," said the priest, " only that they'd like
you to be a Christian too."

" Oh, I see! " said King Harold, " but how can I do
that when I have no idea what it is all About? "

" Well, I could tell you," said the priest.

" All right, go on," said King Harold.

So the priest told King Harold all about God and

234

Heaven and Our Lord and the Holy Spirit and the Church and the Sacraments. And about the Masses that were offered in all the Churches all over Denmark. It took a very long time to say it all and the priest had to stay to supper it got so late.

" Well," said King Harold when he had finished his cup of soup, " it is extremely interesting but I couldn't *believe* all that, you know."

" Why not? " said the priest, " I do."

" Yes, I know," said King Harold, " you tell me all that, but how do I know that it is True? How do I know that you are not making it all up, or that you are not mistaken? Now if you could *prove* it by a miracle, or something like that, then I would believe it and you could Baptise me straightaway."

" But *I* can't do miracles! " said the priest; " I am not a very holy person."

" Ah, but that is where you are wrong! " said King Harold, " I thought that when miracles happened it wasn't the actual Person who did them, but that it was God doing them and that he was using the person as a kind of a Tool. After all, when I write a letter it isn't the pencil itself that writes, is it? "

" That is quite right," said the priest, " but I do not think that I am a good enough pencil! I'm too blunt or short or something."

" Anyway," said King Harold, " if you work a miracle for me I will be a Christian. That's a bargain! But it is so late that we will wait until to-morrow morning. Now you sleep here so that I'll know you won't go away and not come back. And in the morning we will all see what you can do. I've thought of something for you already."

" Oh, what? " said the poor priest, " what is it that I will have to do? "

"I won't tell you," said King Harold, "in case you do some jiggery pokery."

So they went to bed and the priest couldn't sleep for a long time. He prayed and prayed to God to do the miracle, whatever it might be.

"Because," he said to God, "if you don't, King Harold will not believe anything that I have told him about you, and he might lose his soul. Besides, he might be angry and kill the Christians. So *please* dear Lord, do show the King that you are a Strong and Mighty God and that your Church is True." But God did not say anything to the priest and he was very worried and at last he went to sleep.

In the morning, after breakfast, the priest went to find King Harold. He was very nervous because although he knew that God *could* do any kind of a miracle he was not sure whether he *would*. So all the time that he was walking to the King's room he asked God to prove to the King that the Church is True.

When he reached King Harold's room he found the King sitting beside a big fire with his feet on the fender and some of his courtiers with him.

"Good morning, Your Majesty," said the priest, and he saw that the poker was stuck in the fire, although it was a roaring hot one.

"Good morning," said the King, "do you suppose that God could let you walk right round the room and back to me with the Red Hot end of the poker in your hand without burning it at all?"

"Of course he could," said the priest.

"Ah, but *would* he?" said King Harold.

"Of course he would," said the priest.

"Good," said the King, and he took the poker out of the fire and he held the bright Red Hot end towards the priest. "Catch hold!" he said.

ST. HAROLD

The priest took hold of it at once with a firm grasp and walked quietly round the room and back to the King. While he walked all the people in the room stared at him to see if he was in any pain. They sniffed to see if they could smell burning hand.

But nothing unusual happened and when he got back to the King the priest held out the cool end of the poker to him and let it go when he took it. The King threw it down behind him and it burnt a hole in the carpet. The Courtiers all crowded round to see the priest's hand. There wasn't a scorch or even a dirty mark on it! (The priest had been thanking God all the time that he was walking round the room, because he didn't *know* even when he first took hold of the poker, that God would really do the miracle for him.)

Now he looked at the King and said:

"Your Majesty, now you see what a Strong and Mighty God our Lord Christ is! Kneel and worship him, Your Majesty! Kneel and thank him for the miracle!"

And King Harold and the Courtiers all knelt down with the priest and thanked God for his Goodness and his Truth.

After King Harold and the Courtiers were baptised the King sent messages all over Denmark to tell the people of the miracle and to tell them that he was now a Christian. And he made a new Law so that Idols were not allowed any more but that statues of Our Lord and Our Lady were to be put in their places.

By the time that he was old King Harold had done so much good and had learned to know and love and serve God so well in this world, that some Pagans killed him for it, and so now he is happy forever with him in the next and is called Saint Harold. But no one remembers the name of the priest, which is very sad, because God must love him dearly for his great Act of Faith in taking hold of the Red Hot poker.

St. Harold's Special Day is November 1st, and he must be proud to have All Saints Day for his. (Do you know which are the Saints belonging to All Saints Day? They are all the people who are Saints that we don't know about. But of course God does. Perhaps the priest with the poker is one. I hope he is.)

ST. GUY

Once upon a time there was a man called Guy and he lived near Brussels and he worked on a farm and he was a Belgian. (Which country do Belgians live in?) He worked very hard because the farmer was poor and rather mean and Guy was the only labourer that he had. Though I must say that he worked very hard himself, too.

Now Guy was afraid of Getting Rich. He prayed about it every day because, more than anything, he wanted to go to Heaven. Do you remember that Our Lord said that it was easier for a Camel to go through the eye of a needle than for a Rich Man to enter the Kingdom of Heaven? So Guy was glad that his wages were small and he hoped that they would stay small always so as to give him a better chance of going to Heaven.

Farming is very good work for people who love God because they very often work alone and so have plenty of time to talk to God, and Guy thought about God all the time and God loved him so dearly that he often did miracles for him, and I will tell you one of them.

Once when the weather had been very bad Guy had got behindhand with his work and he was very late in sowing the wheat. The farmer reminded him several times but every time that he started to sow the rain came and the ground was too soggy. Or sometimes one of the horses or cows was ill and he couldn't leave them.

At last the farmer was really angry and sent for Guy in the evening.

"Unless that wheat is sown to-morrow," he said, "it will be Too Late and we will have no flour next year and we will all go Hungry. I don't care *what* happens you must have it done to-morrow. All of it."

Guy went to bed very worried. Sowing all the wheat in one day was a tremendous work at the best of times and the weather was Simply Terrible. However, he got up early and did all the odd jobs quickly, but when he came to the stables he found that one of the horses, named Blossom, had Colic. (Colic is a very bad pain in the middle that horses get through eating the wrong things. Sometimes they die of it.) Guy couldn't leave Blossom and the farmer had gone to Brussels to market. So he sent a boy for the Vet. and he walked the horse up and down and up and down because that often makes them feel a little better.

By the time that the Vet. had gone and Blossom was quietly resting it was nearly tea time and there was the milking to do and the chickens to feed and a hundred and one other jobs, and so it was long past supper time when Guy had time even to think of the Sowing.

"Oh God, what shall I do?" he said, "I couldn't have left poor Blossom, could I? She might easily have died."

He hurried about getting supper ready for the Farmer and he worried and worried about the sowing.

Soon there was a clattering outside the back door and the farmer came stamping in from market.

"Well," he said, "done the sowing? It wasn't too bad after dinner, the sun nearly came out."

But when Guy began to tell him about Blossom and the Vet. and all, the farmer was too angry to listen.

"I'm sick of your Excuses!" he shouted, "I'll do it myself to-morrow!" and he slammed the door and went up to bed.

ST. GUY

Poor Guy was in a great way. Because, after all, the farmer did have an enormous amount of work of his own to do, without having some of Guy's as well. So he sadly went to bed.

In the morning the farmer got up very early and started off with sacks of wheat in a cart to sow the wheat crop. The fields that were to be sown were the furthest away of them all and all the way there the farmer grumbled and growled to himself about the Extra Work.

"But all the same," he thought, as the sun came up and made the wet hedges sparkle, "Guy is not such a bad chap. I'm lucky to have him because he is so honest and he works so hard."

You will never guess what the farmer found when he reached the fields. Yes, you may guess that God had sown it all and that it was coming up already, but I am sure that you did not guess that it was grown and fully ripe and ready to cut! And what is more there were Scarlet Poppies and Blue Cornflowers growing in among it.

The farmer couldn't believe it.

"I'm dreaming!" he said, "that's what it is," he said, "I'm still in bed and I'm dreaming that I got up early. I'll wake up soon."

But he was awake. And four other farmers came and saw it too.

After some years Guy got very Rheumaticky what with working in the rain so much, and he thought that he had better stop farm work and do something else. Not anything Enriching because of the Camel, but just some other job. So next Sunday, when he went to Church in a town called Laeken nearby he asked God to tell him what sort of work he ought to do. But nothing happened until, just as he was going out of the door to go home, he saw a friend of his who was the Sacristan.

" Hello," said Guy.

" Hello," said the Sacristan.

" I came to Laeken Church to-day," said Guy.

" So you did," said the Sacristan, " and I'm glad because this is the last Sunday that I shall be here."

" Why ? " asked Guy.

" I'm Retiring," said the Sacristan; " with a Pension," he said in a pompous voice.

" Who is coming instead? " asked Guy.

" We don't know yet," said the Sacristan. " The priest said that God would send somebody in his Own Good Time."

" Could that be me, do you suppose? " said Guy, " I came here to ask God what new job he thought that I should have."

" Well, it must be you then," said the Sacristan, " come and see the Priest."

So in next to no time Guy was the new Sacristan and he loved it. It was a dry indoor job for his rheumatism and he cleaned and polished all the day so that there shouldn't be one Speck of dust in God's house.

One day, when he was sorting out all the prayer-books and umbrellas and gloves and things that people had left behind them on Sunday, a Merchant came into the Church. After he had said a prayer to Our Lord who was waiting for him in the tabernacle, he got up and went to see what Guy was doing.

" I hope I didn't leave anything," he said.

" Is this yours? " said Guy.

" No," said the Merchant. Then he said, " Do you do this all day? "

" Only on Mondays," said Guy; " they leave the things behind on Sundays."

" Do you get any wages? " asked the Merchant.

" A little," said Guy. " I don't want to be Rich because of the Camel and the needle's Eye."

" Oh, I see," said the Merchant. " What do you do with it? "

" Keep it in my room," said Guy.

" Why? " said the Merchant.

" Well, I don't really need it much," said Guy. " I have somewhere to live and I have my meals with the Priest so I don't spend much."

" Couldn't you give it to the Poor? " said the Merchant.

" There isn't enough to be any good," said Guy.

" Well," said the Merchant, " I know how you could make more money and then it would be Worth giving away."

" Really? " said Guy in an interested voice. " How? "

" I've got a very good Ship," said the Merchant, " and in it I put all sorts of Goods and Merchandise (because I am a Merchant). And I sail along to a place that hasn't got any of it and I give it to them. In Exchange they give me things that they have Too Much of and I take it somewhere else and Exchange again. It is quite Enriching."

" What about me? " asked Guy.

" Well," said the Merchant, " if you let me have your Savings I will buy better Merchandise and so I will make more money. That would make you a Partner and you would have half the Winnings because it would be half your money."

" What a good idea! " said Guy, " but I think I'll stay poor."

" But you won't be Rich for yourself," said the Merchant, " you are going to give it to the Poor."

" So I am," said Guy, " all right then." And he went to fetch his purse.

"Here you are," he said to the Merchant; "you know more about it than I do!"

So the Merchant took the money and bought some Rich and Rare Merchandise with it and then he set sail for the Next Place and Guy went with him to help him to sail the boat and to Exchange the things. But a storm came up and the Ship and all the Merchandise was lost and the Merchant was drowned and Guy was washed up on a shore somewhere Far Away.

"It was my own fault," Guy said to God. "I always promised you that I wouldn't have much money and then I tried to make more and I lost it all. And there is another Sacristan at Laeken and so I am out of work as well."

"Why not go to Palestine?" said God to Guy. "Go and see Bethlehem and Nazareth and where we lived and where I was Crucified. Then you can come and live with me. You were always my very good friend."

So Guy started out and after months and months of walking he found Palestine and went and saw where Our Lord lived and died. And he saw the Mount of Olives and Jerusalem and all the Holy Places.

Then Guy thought, "Now that I have done what God told me to do, and I *have* loved the Holy Places, I will try to walk home because I am very old and rheumaticky and I want to make up to God in some way for trying to Get Rich Quick when I always said that I wouldn't because of the Camel."

So he started off back to Belgium. He wanted to see the Parish Priest at Laeken and tell him about the Ship and the Merchant and Bethlehem and Our Lord's Tomb and the Mount of Olives. But he was so tired and he had nowhere to sleep except the side of the road. At last God was sorry for his friend and one night, when he was asleep under a bush by the road and the wind was blowing round his rheumaticky old bones:

" Are you ready, Guy ? " said God.

" I'm always ready for you, Lord," said Guy. " I've been ready and waiting all my life." And he got up and went away with his very dear friend God. And there he is in Heaven, still happy and interested in farming because he is the Patron Saint of Farming.

St. Guy's Special Day is September 12th and people all over the world are called after him.

ST. HENRY

Once upon a time there was a man called Henry and he was a King. And all the time he was a Young King he kept on being very Tyrannical (which is a fierce and stern kind of King), and all his subjects were frightened of him because he chopped their heads off at the Slightest Provocation.

Well, when Henry grew to be an Old King, he began to be very sorry that he'd been so Tyrannical, and so he went to a Monastery and asked to see the Head Monk, and this is what he said:

"Couldn't I be a Monk, please, Father, instead of being a King, because I'm sorry about being Tyrannical and I want to make it up to God."

The Head Monk smiled to himself and said:

"Well, if you want to be a Monk, the first thing you have to learn is Obedience."

"All right," said Henry, "I will Obey."

"Well," said the Head Monk, "go back and go on being a King."

"Oh, but that isn't fair!" said King Henry Rather crossly.

"Oh yes it is, because you promised to Obey," said the Head Monk. "And if you come and be a Monk you are running away from the job that God gave you of being a King. And why *are* you running away? Well, because you have made a mess of things. So you go back and be a proper sort of King for the rest of your life, and that will make up to God for being so Tyrannical before."

ST. HENRY

"All right," said King Henry, and he went back to his Palace, where he stayed for a long time, being a Specially Good kind of King, and all his subjects stopped being Frightened of him.

Well, one day, when Henry was a Very Old King, there was a Hermit sitting in his little House saying his Office. (A Hermit is a Kind of Monk who lives all alone in a Desert Place or a Lonely Forest or something, and Office is a lot of prayers like Vespers and Compline and things that Priests say every day.) And the Hermit heard something like a Whistling Wind whizzing past his House and he went out to see what it was. He saw hundreds and hundreds of Demons, Rushing Along in a Tremendous Hurry. (Demons are the Angels who were on Lucifer's side against God when there was a Battle in Heaven, and Michael turned all the Bad Angels out to Hell.)

"Why are you all Rushing Along in a Tremendous Hurry?" said the Hermit to the Head Demon as he whizzed past.

"Oh!" said the Head Demon, stopping for a minute, "King Henry has just died and we are Rushing to grab his soul because he was so Tyrannical."

"Well, let me know what happens and whether you get it," said the Hermit, "stop and tell me on your way back."

"All right," said the Head Demon. "Come along, All You Others." And they all Rushed Away again.

The next day there was a whistling wind noise again outside the Hermit's little House, and when he opened the door there were all the Demons with Frenzied Faces, standing outside!

"Well?" said the Hermit, "did you get Henry's Soul?"

"No," said the Head Demon in a furious voice.

247

" Why, what happened? " asked the Hermit laughing in his Sleeve.

" Well," said the Head Demon, " we got there in Quite Good Time just when that Horrible Archangel Michael (who turned us Out of Heaven) was weighing all the things that King Henry had done. All the Good Deeds were on one side of the scales and all the Bad Deeds were on the other. Our side was miles heavier because of him being so Tyrannical and we were just Getting Ready to Carry him Off when St. Laurence-who-was-a-Martyr-by-being-Roasted came and put in the Good Deed side a big Golden Chalice that Henry had given to the Palace Chapel. It was so heavy that the Good Deed side simply banged down and we can't have King Henry after all! I don't know what Satan will say to us, I'm sure. He'll be simply Rampant."

" That must be very disappointing for you," said the Hermit kindly (he was always polite), " but really King Henry was Gooder than Bad. Are you sure you haven't made all this up? "

" Of course I haven't," said the Head Demon peevishly, " and to prove it I broke off one of the handles of the Chalice to show to Satan. Look! " And in his hand was a Lovely Golden Handle!

The people who went to King Henry's Funeral the next day noticed a Very Funny Thing. The Chalice that the Priest was using had had one of its Handles broken off! I wonder what Satan did with it.

St. Henry's Special Day is on July 14th, and there are Literally Thousands of people called after him. If anyone is called Henrietta, it counts.

SIXTY SAINTS FOR BOYS

King Henry

King Henry, King Henry,
Tyrannical King,
Did you go to Heaven?
That was an odd thing!

Little Girl, Little Girl,
Impertinent Child,
It's true in my youth
I was rather wild,

But I grew more gentle
As older I grew,
And that is the same
As a maiden should do!

King Henry, King Henry,
Now thank you for this,
I'll get on your knee
And give you a kiss,

And when I am gentle
And loving and grown,
Perhaps I'll have babies
To sit on my own!

ST. EDWARD

O nce upon a time there was a King in England and his name was King Edward, and the Queen's name was Queen Edith, and they were very Kind and Good and they ruled the land very Wisely.

Now everything in the Palace would have been Calm and peaceful if it hadn't been for Queen Edith's father, who was called Godwin. Godwin lived in the Palace and he wanted to be the King himself. And he made Quarrels between the Royal Relations, and he told Tales about King Edward, and said to the Courtiers:

" Now if my son, Harold, who is the Queen's Brother, were King, it would be a much Better Thing for the Country than that old Edward who only thinks about Churches and things! " Now Edward knew all about what Godwin was doing, but he didn't say anything until one day at Dinner.

Everyone was sitting round the table, with King Edward at one end and Queen Edith at the other. And Godwin, the Queen's father, was there, and Harold the Queen's brother, and several other Royal Relations.

Suddenly one of the Servants who was carrying a heavy dish with a roasted lamb on it, kicked one of his feet against the other and nearly fell over. But with a great Effort he stood firm on one foot and put the other one down in its right place again and just managed to save himself without tipping the heavy dish.

Then Godwin said:

" Our feet are like two Brothers, aren't they? If one gets into trouble the other helps him and so they both Recover."

" Yes," said King Edward, " my brother Alfred would

have been a great help to me if Godwin hadn't had
him so cruelly Blinded that he died when he was young!"

"Your Majesty!" said Godwin, feeling very Frightened
because he thought that the King didn't know who had
blinded Alfred. "Your Majesty! Surely you don't think
that *I* had anything to do with your Brother's death?"

"Hadn't you?" asked King Edward.

"I pray God that this piece of Bread will Choke
me if I had anything to do with it!" said Godwin.

"All right, eat it then, and let us see," said King
Edward. And Queen Edith and Prince Harold and
all the Royal Relations stopped eating their Dinner to
see what would happen.

Godwin popped the piece of Bread into his mouth
and looked at the King:

"There you see!" he said with his Mouth Full, "I
was right and you were wrong!" and he laughed, and the
Bread stuck in his throat and choked him and he died!

"Well," said King Edward, to Queen Edith, "I'm
sorry your Father is dead, my dear, but God only did
what He was asked to do!" And so Queen Edith dried
her tears on a silk handkerchief with a crown worked
on it and said:

"Yes, dear."

King Edward was very kind to Burglars and things
because, he said, people don't usually steal things
unless they are Poor or Hungry and so, if you give
them some food or money instead of putting them in
Prison, they won't steal any more.

One day the King was Very-Ill-in-Bed with a bad
Cold. In his bedroom there was a great chest full of
Gold and Silver Money.

Just after Dinner on this day the King's Door opened
very slowly and a Head poked round! It looked at
the King.

" He's asleep! " thought the Head, and it came further
round the Door until it was a Whole Man. The Man
(he was one of the Servants) walked on tiptoe across
the floor to the Treasure Chest. Then, very quietly,
so as not to make a Chinking Noise, he filled his pockets

with Golden Sovereigns and crept away! When he
got outside the door he ran as fast as his legs would
carry him to his own room; he hid the money under his
mattress and ran back to the King's door.

He poked his Head round and looked at the King!

" He's still asleep! " he thought, and he walked on
tiptoe across the floor to the Treasure Chest. Then,

very quietly, so as not to make a Chinking Noise, he filled
his pockets with Golden Sovereigns. He was just putting
the last ones in when a Voice behind him said:

" You are a Silly to come Twice! "

He jumped round feeling all Cold and Watery inside
with Fright! There was the King (who hadn't been
asleep at all) lying watching him!

" Why on Earth *did* you come twice? " said King
Edward. " You took all that you could possibly need
the first time! If the Treasurer finds out about it you'll
be Executed. So you'd better go quickly; take all the
money you've got, and leave the Palace! "

The man had only just gone when the Treasurer came
in. (The Treasurer is the Man who looks after the King's
money.)

After a few minutes the Treasurer looked very worried.

" What's the matter? " asked King Edward, who
knew all the time.

" I very much Regret to State, Your Majesty, that a
large Portion of Your Majesty's wealth has been Mislaid
or Purloined! "

(Which was the Treasurer's way of saying that some
of the money had been lost or stolen.)

" Never you mind," said King Edward, " very likely
he who has it needs it more than I do."

And so the Stealing Servant escaped.

King Edward's Special Person (after Our Lord)
was St. John. He loved St. John and did heaps of things
for him. And when anyone asked him to do anything
for St. John's sake he always used to do it at once.

Well, one day, the King and his Courtiers were riding
through Havering, in Essex, when they heard that
the New Church there was being Consecrated that
very day, and that it was being dedicated to St. John.
(Consecrating is when the Bishop comes and blesses

a New Church before Mass can be said in it. And Dedicating it is giving the Church to some Special Saint or to Our Lord. You know, all Churches have a Name. Like St. Peter's or St. Anne's or the Church of the Sacred Heart, or St. Michael and All Angels. Do you know the name of the Church that you go to?)

Now the New Church at Havering was going to be St. John's and the King said he'd stop and go inside because of St. John being his Special Saint.

Just inside the Church door a Poor-and-Raggy old man asked him for a Penny:

"Only a Penny for the sake of St. John!" begged the Poor-and-Raggy, holding out his hand to the King.

King Edward felt in his pockets :

"I haven't even got one Penny with me," he said. "You see I wasn't going to buy anything, so I didn't bring my purse!"

He looked at the Poor-and-Raggy sadly. He was so *very* Poor!

"Never mind," he said, "you can have my Ring if you like. It is worth quite a goodly sum really, much more than a Penny. Take it and God bless you!" He pulled a heavy golden ring off his finger and gave it to the Poor-and-Raggy.

"Thank you, Your Majesty," said the Old Man, and went away.

Now a very funny thing happened. Some years after the King had given away his Ring, two English Pilgrims (a Tall one and a Short one) went to Palestine to visit Bethlehem and Nazareth and Jerusalem and all those places. While they were there they got lost!

"I'm getting Frightened," said the Tall Pilgrim. "I'm sure there are a lot of wild animals here, and I daren't sleep outside!"

" I don't see what else we can do! " said the Short
Pilgrim.

" Look! " said the Tall Pilgrim, " what is that light? "

" Let's go and see! " said the Short Pilgrim.

" But let's be careful in case it's Robbers! " said the
Tall Pilgrim.

So they went towards the light and found that it was
a man walking along with a Lantern.

" Please, Sir," said the Shorter and Braver Pilgrim,
" can you tell us where we can go for the Night, because
we're lost? "

" Of course! " said the Man with a Lantern. " Come
with me! "

So the two Pilgrims went along with him, and very
soon they came to a small house.

" This is my House," said the Man with a Lantern,
" you can Stay the Night with me if you like. Supper
is all ready."

So the two Pilgrims had a good Supper of Cocoa
and Fish and Bread and Honey and then they all went
to Bed. The Man with a Lantern lent them Pyjamas
and Sponges and things.

Next day, after Breakfast, the man showed them the
way back to Jerusalem.

" Good-bye! " said the two Pilgrims, " will you please
tell us your name so that we can write to you when we
get home? "

" Well," said the man, " as a matter of fact I am
St. John. Will you take back a message from me to
your King Edward of England? "

The Tall Pilgrim said that he would be Only too
Pleased, but the Short Pilgrim said:

" How do we know that you are *really* St. John and
not just Pretending? "

" Here is a Ring! " said St. John. " Give it to King

Edward and ask him if he remembers my Church at Havering. And tell him from me that he will die in Six Months' time, and that I will come for him myself!"

When the two Pilgrims got back to England they told King Edward all about it. He was Delighted!

"Fancy St. John keeping my Ring all these years!" he said, "and I *am* glad that I know when I am going to die. Now I can get all Nice and Ready!"

One of the things that had to be decided was who was going to be King next, because he hadn't any sons.

"I don't want Harold," he said, "he is much too much like Godwin was. I think I'll ask my great friend William Duke of Normandy if he will come and be King of England after me." William Duke of Normandy said that he would be Only Too Pleased to oblige his old friend Edward, and so that was all settled.

But when the Six Months were up and King Edward went to Heaven with St. John (who didn't forget to call for him) Harold said:

"Now *I* shall be King! No one can stop me!" And he was, for a little time, until William Duke of Normandy came across the Channel with his Army and killed Harold in a Battle. And do you know what that Battle was? It was the Battle of Hastings—1066!

I expect you know St. Edward best by the name that his Subjects gave to him when he ruled in England all those years ago: Edward the Confessor. Because he was never afraid to say that he believed in God.

St. Edward's Special Day is on October 13th, and there are Hundreds and Thousands of people called after him. But if your Birthday is on that day and your name is Something Else you can have St. Edward for your Special Saint as well as your own one.

ST. WALTER

Once upon a time there was a Noble Knight and his name was Sir Walter, and he was a Crusader, and he fought the Saracens (who were Infidels) in the Holy Land (which was where Our Lord used to live). Infidels are not Christians but they believe in God.

Walter's favourite person of all was Our Lady, and he had a little Ivory Statue of Her. "Other people have a Master to work for," he used to say, "but I have a Mistress, and I am Her Servant."

One day Walter was going to fight in a Tournament, which is a pretence Battle. All the Knights dressed in their best armour and rode their best horses and they had coloured feathers in their Helmets and silk Cloaks to match, and Flags and all that. And they had a Battle Field with seats all round it, and all the Ladies used to go in their best clothes and watch. Then, at the end, the most Important Lady (sometimes it was the Queen), gave a prize to the knight who had fought Best of All. The Knights used to wear a Ribbon or a Handkerchief belonging to their Favourite Lady because they said that it brought them luck, and so the Ribbons and things were called Favours. Walter always wore a Blue Favour, because of Our Lady's favourite colour being Blue.

Well, on this day that I am telling you about, Walter and a lot of his friends were riding to the Tournament with their Colours, and their shining Horses clattering along the road, and they were all talking and laughing because they were going to have such a jolly day, and each hoped that he would be the one to win the Prize.

ST. WALTER

As they were riding along they passed a little Chapel ringing its bell for Mass. Walter stopped.

" I'll just hear Mass on the way," he said, " because it is one of the Feasts of Our Lady, and she is my Special Person."

Some of the Knights turned round and came back to see what was going on.

" But, Walter, you'll be late for the Tournament! " said one of the Knights, who wore a Scarlet Cloak.

" Yes, Walter, now do come along; you can go to Mass to-morrow instead! " said another Knight, in a Yellow Cloak.

" No," said Walter. " My Mistress comes first, but I will leave when we get to the Last Gospel, and I won't wait for the prayers at the end. I don't think I'll be very late! "

So all the other Knights went on to the Tournament and Walter tied up his horse to a nearby Tree and went in to Mass.

After the Last Gospel he came out and untied his horse and rode away to the pretence Battle Field. When he had nearly got there he met some Knights coming away from it all talking in Excited Voices.

" Good morning! " said Walter, " how is the Tournament going? "

" It is nearly over," said one of the Knights, who was wearing a Purple Cloak. " Sir Walter has carried away all the Honours! No Knight has ever fought so well before. He is a wonderful man! If you hurry you might just see him before he goes home." And they rode on.

Walter was All Astonished.

" What *did* they mean? " he said to himself. " I wasn't there at all! " And he went in to the Battle Field where the Tournament was.

The pretence Battle was just finished, and as he sat on his horse in his Sky Blue Cloak some Knights who were pretence Prisoners of the battle came to him and said:

" Be kind to your Prisoners, Sir Walter, we had no Idea that you could fight so well ! "

" But I wasn't there! " said Walter, and he made a Puzzled face. " You are not *my* Prisoners! "

And the prisoners all laughed, because they thought that Walter was making a Joke!

What do you suppose had really happened? Our Lady had sent an Angel, looking exactly like Sir Walter, Sky Blue cloak and all, to take his place in the pretence Battle while he was at Mass. Which was very kind of Her because he won the Prize.

Walter was so pleased and thankful to Our Lady for being so good to him that he thought that he would go and be a Cistercian Monk (like St. Bernard) so as to have more time for God. And so he went, and the only thing that he took with him was the little Ivory Statue of Our Lady. When he got there the head monk said:

" Well, Walter, you may certainly come and be a monk, but you can't be a priest, because you don't know any Latin."

" I know, Father," said Walter sadly, " but you see I was brought up to be a Knight and a Soldier, and so I only had to learn enough to be able to follow Mass and all that. I had to learn a lot about fighting and farming and landlording and all that."

" You will have to be a Lay Brother and look after the Vineyards then," said the Abbot, " that will be more in your line." And that is what Walter did, and very fine grapes he grew. You see, one of the ways that these monks Earned their Living was to grow a great many grapes, and they made a very good Wine out of them, and they sold it to all the people round about, and so they got the money to buy the things they needed.

Now in Monasteries and Convents they always Read Aloud at meal times so that the monks or nuns don't think too much about what they eat and perhaps get Greedy, and they nearly always read in Latin, because they all know it. If they read in English the French or German ones might not understand, and if they read in French or German then the English or the Italian ones might not understand. (That is one reason why Mass is in Latin, did you know? When you are bigger you will know and understand all the words, and then you can go to Mass in France and the words will all be in Latin, and you will know it even if you can't speak French, and that will be nice and homely for you, and the same in Germany or Poland. And the same for the Foreigners who come to us.)

Well, Walter hadn't learned much Latin, but at the Reading aloud at meal times sometimes he smiled and sometimes he nearly cried, and always he looked interested.

So the Abbot said:

" Brother Walter, why do you Smile or nearly cry when you can't understand what we are reading about ? Is it the book that amuses you ? "

" No, Father Abbot," said Walter, " I am not smiling at that book, but I have an Imaginary Picture Book (Imaginary is Pretence) and I imagine a picture of Our Lord when He was born, and then I turn over a page and I imagine Him in St. Joseph's Carpenter's shop, and then I turn over another page and I see a picture of Him being Crucified. I see pictures of all the things that happened to Him in my Imaginary Picture Book."

" Oh, I see! " said the Abbot. " Well, that is all right; I only wondered."

One day the Abbot said to Walter:

" Brother Walter, the grapes that you have grown have made a lot of very good Wine, and we are sending some of it to another Cistercian Monastery because their grapes did not do well this year. They had a drought or something. I want you to go in the ship with the load of wine and take it to the other Monastery."

" Yes, Father Abbot," said Walter in a Pleased voice. He thought it would make a nice change. But in the middle of the night in the Ship there was a Fierce Storm, and all the sailors were in a terrible fright, and they went to Walter and woke him up and asked him to pray for them. " Because," they said, " you are a monk, and God might, perhaps, listen to you more because you know Him better."

So Walter took his little Ivory Statue of Our Lady from under his pillow and he looked at it to gather his thoughts together and he said:

" Please, Our Lady, you have always been so kind to me, please will you ask God to remember us? I expect we are safe, really, but it is very Frightening for us to be in this Fierce Storm," and he went to sleep again, and while he was asleep God sent him a Dream, and this was the dream:

He thought that he saw a friend of his, called Brother Arnold, who was a monk at the Monastery, and who played the Harp. And Arnold was harping on his Harp and singing the Psalm about " Those who go down to the Sea in Ships."

Then Walter woke up, and he was very pleased, and he went to the sailors and said:

" It is all right, we won't be drowned, because my friend Arnold is harping on his Harp, and praying for us." And all the sailors cheered, and they sailed the ship safely into the harbour.

ST. WALTER

When Walter got back home he told the Abbot about his dream, and the Abbot sent for Arnold.

" Good morning, Brother Arnold," he said.

" Good morning, Father Abbot," said Arnold.

" What were you doing on Tuesday night? " said the Abbot.

" I couldn't go to sleep, and so I was praying for my friend, Brother Walter," said Arnold.

" But you were harping on your Harp," said the Abbot, " and you mustn't do that in the middle of the night, you might wake all the Others."

" But I don't *really* play my Harp, Father Abbot," said Arnold. " I just pretend to play it with my fingers in the Dark, and I listen to the Imaginary Music."

So Walter thanked Our Lady very much for letting him hear Arnold's Imaginary Music, too, because it did cheer the sailors up wonderfully, and helped them to Weather the Storm.

A lot of other things happened to Walter (one was about two little French boys), but you will read about them all one of these days.

St. Walter's Special Day is on January 22nd, and there are a few English people called after him, but mostly Dutch people are, because he lived in Holland.

SSB-R

ST. BERNARD

Once upon a time there was a little boy called Bernard and he lived in a Castle, and he was Seven years Old.

One Christmas Eve he was helping his Mummy to hang up the Holly and Mistletoe and they were talking about Our Lord being born at Bethlehem.

"*When* was he born, Mummy?" asked Bernard as he sorted out the Holly with the most Berries on it.

"In the Middle of the Night, darling," said his Mummy.

"But I mean what *Time* in the Middle of the Night?" asked Bernard.

"I don't know what Time, darling," said his Mummy, as she tried to reach a specially high corner, "why do you want to know?"

"Because it ought to be the most Important Time of Christmas," said Bernard. "Don't you think so, Mummy?"

"I never thought of it, darling," said his Mummy as she looked for the Scissors. "Where *did* you put the Scissors, Bernard?"

"Here they are," said Bernard, taking them out of his pocket. "I *wish* I knew what Time it was!"

All the evening Bernard kept thinking about the most Important Time of Christmas, and when he went to bed he asked Our Lady if she would please tell him. But she did not say anything, and soon Bernard went to sleep.

Suddenly he woke up. It was quite dark, and he began to think again about the Time that Our Lord was born. Then he had an Idea. He slipped out of bed; put on his Dressing-gown and Bedroom Slippers; gently opened the door and Crept downstairs! Very quietly he undid the Front Door and went outside. It was very cold, but he did not think of that as he hurried along the road to the Church.

" Perhaps if I stay in the Church until the Morning I might find out," he thought as he pushed open the Heavy Church Door.

It was Rather Frightening all alone in the Dark Church, and Bernard began to wish he hadn't come until he saw the little Light in front of the Altar, and he remembered that the Blessed Sacrament was there. He went and sat on the Altar Steps so as to be safely near to Our Lord and then he waited.

In those days there wasn't a Crib in Church at Christmas (it was St. Francis who invented those, and he didn't live until nearly Seventy Years after Bernard). So Bernard didn't have much to look at while he waited, and so he stared at the Altar Step just below his feet.

Suddenly he thought that he heard a Creaking Noise by the door! He got a Terrible Fright because he thought someone might have discovered that he wasn't in bed! He stared at the door, but nothing happened, so he looked back again at the Step, and there was Our Lord like a tiny little New Baby, fast asleep rolled up in a Shawl!

Bernard held his breath! He thought it might be a Dream, and he pinched himself so hard that he nearly Squeaked! It wasn't a dream though. Then he thought

that if the Baby moved it would roll off the Step and be hurt, so he put out his hand to hold it safe. Just then he heard someone say:

" Now you know what the Important Time of Christmas is, Bernard. Keep it for your own Special Secret! " And he looked round to see who was speaking, but he couldn't see anyone at all! When he turned back to the Baby it had gone, and the Church Clock was striking . . . what? Well, we don't know, because Bernard never told a single soul.

Bernard hurried home; crept upstairs and popped into bed. Nobody heard him, and the only thing that people Noticed was that he stopped asking everybody about the Special Time of Christmas as he always used to do before.

When he was Grown Up Bernard invented a new and Fiercer Kind of Benedictine Monk called Cistercians. (Because their first house was at a place called Citeaux.) And he could tell the people such wonderful things about God that he was called Golden Tongued.

One day Bernard, in his White Monk's Habit, was riding along the road to visit some friends of his when he came up with a man who was going the same way. This Man admired Bernard's Horse very much, and so they Got Talking of this and that.

"You know," said Bernard, "sometimes when I'm very tired I can't think Properly when I'm praying. Do *you* ever feel like that?"

"Never!" said the man, who didn't pray much anyway, and very Rarely went to Church. "No, I never feel like that. I can *always* pray Properly and I think what I'm saying, too. I must say I should have thought that a Monk like you ought to find Prayer easier than an Ordinary man like me."

Then Bernard said:

"Well, I daresay I'm not such a good Monk as I ought to be, but will you make a Bargain with me?"

"Yes," said the man, "what is it?"

"Will you go over there," said Bernard, "and say an Our Father without thinking of *anything* else? If you can do that I'll give you my Horse that you Admire so much. But if you *do* think of anything, you must promise to tell me because it wouldn't be Fair if you didn't."

"All right," said the man, "that's the easiest Bargain I ever made!"

So he went away a little way and knelt down and began the Our Father. He had got as far as " Thy Kingdom come," when he suddenly thought:

" By Jove! I was a Fool! I ought to have Bargained for the Saddle as well! What is the good of the Horse without it? "

And then he stopped! He *had* thought of something while he was saying the Our Father! He got up and went back to Bernard :

" It's no good," he said sadly, " I've lost the Bargain! I thought of having the Saddle too! "

Bernard laughed.

" Bad luck! " he said. " But, you see, praying without any Distractions isn't so easy as all that, unless you Concentrate."

After that Bernard and the man were great friends, and the man became a Monk in Bernard's Monastery.

Bernard did heaps and heaps of other things, and now he is a very Famous Saint Indeed.

One day when he was Preaching a Specially Good Sermon (you remember that he was called Golden Tongued?) the Devil said to him :

" You *are* a Clever Preacher! Look how everyone is listening to you! Think how they all Admire you! You really are a very Holy Man! "

And Bernard thought:

" I believe he is Quite Right! Perhaps I *am* very Holy."

Then the Devil said:

" Aha! Now I've caught you! I've made you Vainglorious. You'd better stop Preaching if it makes you Vain. That would never do! "

Then Bernard said:

" No. I didn't begin my Sermon because I was Vain, and I'm not going to end it because I am Vain! " and he went on with his Sermon. Which was an Awful Squash for the Devil, wasn't it?

St. Bernard's Special Day is on August 20th, and anyone whose Birthday is on that Day can have him for their Special Saint as well as all those people who are called after him.

ST. RONALD

O nce upon a time there was an Earl of Orkney. (The Orkneys are islands off the North of Scotland, where Scapa Flow and the Navy and all that are.) And this Earl of Orkney had a Favourite Granddaughter whose name was Gunnhild. Now lots of people wanted to marry Gunnhild, sometimes because she was an Earl's Granddaughter and sometimes because she was Very Pretty, but always the Earl said:

" No, m'dear, he's not good enough! "

" But," said poor Gunnhild, " if we go on like this I'll never get married at all! "

" That's all right, m'dear," said the Earl, " I'll find somebody Suitable, don't you worry," and he tweaked Gunnhild's ear and ambled off to the Stable to look at his Retriever Puppies.

Then one day a Norwegian ship came sailing into Kirkwall (which is the capital of Orkney) and out stepped a Very Handsome Man with Red Hair. He called on the Earl and said:

" Good day, your Lordship. I came to ask if I may have the honour to Marry your Granddaughter."

" Eh! What's that? " said the Earl. " But I don't know anything about you. Who *are* you? "

" I am a Norwegian Nobleman," said the handsome visitor.

" Got any money? " asked the Earl, pulling his moustache.

" Yes," said the Handsome Norwegian Nobleman.

" Got a decent place to live in? " asked the Earl, making a Fierce face.

" Yes," said the Handsome Norwegian Nobleman with Red Hair.

" I'll fetch the girl in to have a look at you, what? " said the Earl, and he trundled off to find Gunnhild.

When she saw the Handsome Norwegian Nobleman with Red Hair, Gunnhild thought that she'd never seen anybody that she'd rather have for a Husband, and so they were married at once, and they sailed back to Norway to her new home.

Soon they had a Son, and he was named Ronald, and he grew up in Norway, and was very Tall and Handsome, with Red Hair, just like his father's.

Ronald learned to Row and to Play the Harp, and to Play Darts, and to go on Snowshoes and to Ride a Horse and all sorts of other things. And he used to make up poetry about all the things that he could do. (That is how I know what he learned, because I've read some of the Poetry.)

One day, when he was Thirteen, Ronald sailed to Grimsby, in England, in a merchant ship, to see what it was like. They stayed there for Five Weeks, and poor Ronald thought that it was the most frightful place that he had ever seen. He wrote and told his Handsome Norwegian father that he waded in Mud, and that everything was dreadfully Dirty, and that he hoped he'd soon be sailing home on the clean grey Sea.

One Summer Holiday Ronald had an Adventure, and this was it: He went with a friend of his, whose name was Karl, to a Seaside place called Trondheim, and there was a little Island there. So Ronald and Karl thought that they would go over to the Island for a Picnic.

" Don't you go," said an old Sailor, who was sitting on a bollard and staring out to sea.

" Why? " asked Ronald.

" A Giant lives there," said the sailor; " has done for years. Really wicked, he is. Eats all the people that go to the Island and keeps their money. He must have got Hundreds and Thousands of pounds of Treasure."

Ronald looked at Karl, and Karl looked at Ronald.

" Shall we go and find the Treasure? " they both said at once. Then they shook little fingers because of saying the same thing at the same time.

So in spite of the old sailor's Warning they took some food and some water and rowed across to the Island. Very quietly they went up the beach and found the Giant's Cave.

" He must be out Fishing, or something," whispered Ronald.

" I'll get a rope from the boat in case of Accidents," said Karl, " and we'll Explore the cave."

So, carrying the rope, they went Carefully into the cave. They went on and on, and further and further, until it was nearly Pitch Dark. Then Ronald, who was in front, stopped so suddenly that Karl bumped into him.

" Don't do that! " said Ronald in a fright.

" I couldn't help it," said Karl, Rather Crossly.

" Well, look what you nearly made me do! " said Ronald, and there stretching out in front of them was a Deep Dark lake in the cave!

" Now what do we do? " said Karl.

" Swim across," said Ronald; "I expect the Treasure is on the other side, I haven't seen any this side."

" Neither have I," said Karl.

So they took out their Torches and stuck them on to their heads with little pats of clay, then they tied the rope between them. (They did that so that if one of them got Lost the other could find him.) Then they

272

waded out into the Lake and began to swim to the
Other Side. They swam on and on and on, and it got very
Cold, but at last they got to the Other Side!

"Now for the Treasure!" said Ronald.

"Come on," said Karl, and then he stopped. "This
is the End," he said.

"How do you mean, the End?" asked Ronald.

"The End," said Karl; "we can't get any further, it's the *End* of the Cave."

And so it was! So they looked and looked along the edge of the Lake for the treasure, but all they could find was a Very Nasty Smell. So they built a little heap of stones to show that they had been there and then they swam back again. They went very Quietly out of the cave on to the beach, because of the Giant, but they never saw a Sign of him!

"Well," said Ronald, "that was a Lucky Escape!"

"Yes," said Karl, "there was No Giant, but what a shame that there was No Treasure either!"

Now when Ronald was older, what with Fighting and Pirates and so forth, most of his relations in Orkney were dead, and so the Earl's Castle was his. But his Cousin Paul, who lived there, wouldn't give it up.

So Ronald's Handsome Norwegian Father sent six ships full of soldiers and sailors, with Ronald in the Front Ship, to fight Paul and win the Earl's Castle in Orkney. So Ronald sailed away, and first he went to Shetland to meet a friend of his who had Twelve ships. But what with Wind and Weather he missed the friend, and had to go and fight Cousin Paul with only Six ships. And who do you suppose Won? No, Paul did! And Ronald lost all the six ships, and by the time he got back home to Norway his Handsome Father was *Furious* because of the Waste of good ships, as well as the soldiers and sailors.

Now Ronald was Absolutely Determined that he would win Orkney from his Cousin Paul, and so the next year he got some more ships and some more soldiers and sailors. But this time, before he started, he went to Church and talked for a long time to his Favourite Saint, whose name was St. Magnus.

"You see," he said to St. Magnus, "my Cousin Paul

is a very Bad Ruler. He doesn't look after the people properly, he only thinks about making himself Rich. So I would be very Grateful if you could help me to take Orkney away from him, and then I can have it. After all, it is my own place!" And he made a Bargain with St. Magnus. (A Bargain is: If you do This, I'll do That.) And this was the Bargain that Ronald made with St. Magnus:

"If *you* help *me* to win the Battle with Cousin Paul, *I* will build a Stone Church (not just a brick one), in Kirkwall, which is the most Important town in Orkney, and the church will be Dedicated to *you*."

So then Ronald sailed away from Norway with his soldiers and sailors and fought with Cousin Paul, and this time he Won the Battle, and so he was the Earl of Orkney, the same as his Great-Grandfather used to be.

As soon as he had got settled in his new Palace Ronald called all the best Carvers and Builders and Carpenters and all that and said:

"Now all you Builders and things, now is the time to build that Stone Church that I promised to St. Magnus. So will you please start the First Thing to-morrow morning."

And the Stone Masons cut the stone and the Carpenters cut the wood and the Carvers carved it, and the Artists painted it, and there, in a very short time, was a lovely Stone Church in the town of Kirkwall, and it was Dedicated to St. Magnus. So if, one day, you go to Orkney, on Sunday morning you will go to Church in that very same church, and you will remember about Ronald and his Bargain.

Now Ronald did lots of other things, and one of them was Going to the Crusades. I expect you know what the Crusades were, but perhaps I had better remind you just in case:

All the places in Palestine where Our Lord lived are very Special because of His being Actually There. So Bethlehem is Special because He was Born there, and Nazareth is Special because the Holy Family lived there, and St. Joseph had his Shop there. (What sort of shop was it?) And the Sea of Galilee and Jerusalem and all those Places were Special. So of course all the Christians would want to have the Places for theirs, wouldn't they? But the Heathens and the Pagans (who don't believe that Our Lord was God, which of course He was) said:

"But *we* were there first, and we want to keep the Places, and you can't have Chapels and things because the places are not Special for us!" And they made Hotels and Market Places and things on the most Special Places of all, just to show what they thought about them.

So all the Christian Kings and Lords like the French King and the Spanish King and the English King and the Earl of Orkney and the German Princes collected their soldiers to Win Back the Holy Places from the Heathens and the Pagans. (Now this was at first a Very Good Thing, but in the end it turned into Anybody's Fight.)

So Ronald said to the Bishop of Orkney:

"I will go to the Crusades and help to save the Holy Places from the Pagans. Especially Bethlehem, because I can't bear Pagans spoiling the place where Our Lord was born."

And the Bishop said:

"Good. I will go with you."

But when Ronald wanted to collect Knights and Soldiers to go with him there weren't enough. (Because if he took *all* the soldiers Cousin Paul might come back and Capture Orkney again.) So he went to Norway, where his Handsome Father and Gunnhild, his Mother, lived, and he collected some Knights and Soldiers from there. When they got back to Orkney it was Winter, and much too cold to start, so they waited for the Spring. But the Norwegian soldiers were very Noisy and Tiresome, and the Bishop had to make a Speech to them and tell them to behave properly.

" Really," said the Bishop, " anyone would think that you were a Heathen Viking Expedition and not a Crusade at all! "

One man was especially Tiresome. His name was Thorbion Klerk, and he used to set haystacks on fire. When all the people Rushed Out to put out the fire, he used to Rush Into their houses and steal everything Valuable. He got so Rich that some wicked but not so brave men joined with him, and they were a Positive Menace. So Ronald sat on his Earl's Throne and sent for Thorbion Klerk.

When he came Ronald said:

" Thorbion Klerk, you are one of my Subjects, and you are no better than any other Subject, so why do you Steal and Burn and start Riots in my peaceful Orkney? "

But Thorbion Klerk was Stubborn, and he wouldn't answer.

" Very well," said Ronald, " then I won't have you for a Subject any longer. You will be a Public Enemy, and if *anyone* does *anything* to you I won't put them in Prison."

Thorbion Klerk was very Angry, but he couldn't say anything, and he had to go away and hide because of being an Outlaw.

Then Ronald and his Crusaders sailed away to the Holy Land, and Ronald fought very Bravely and very Hard for a time, but he spent more and more time

visiting all the places where Our Lord went so that
his Knights thought that they might just as well go
home, and some of them did. Ronald saw all the places
again and again, and by seeing them so often and by
thinking about Our Lord so much, he stopped wanting
to fight, and he wanted to go home and tell all his people
what all the places were like. So he sailed home, and
when he landed in Orkney crowds and crowds of his
people came to meet him, and they Clapped and Cheered
and Sang and the Band played, and Ronald climbed
up on a wall and told them all about the things that he
had seen. All the people were very Interested because
they had never seen anybody who had actually Been
to the Holy Land and Seen all the Holy Places. Then
Ronald got off the wall and started to walk up to the
Village to get a Horse to ride home to Kirkwall on,
and all the crowd went with him, cheering and bumping
up against him.

Suddenly a Terrible Thing happened. All in the
middle of the General Rejoicing Ronald fell down dead!
And this was why:

In all the crowd nobody saw the Wicked Thorbion
Klerk, and he got nearer and nearer to Ronald, until
at last he Stabbed him and Killed him because of being
an Outlaw.

So the happy crowd turned into a sad crowd, and
they picked up Ronald and put him into a ship all
decorated in Black and Purple, because they are such
Sad Colours, and they made a Procession of Ships and
Boats, and they sailed round to Kirkwall singing Sad
Songs and playing Sad Music. Now the people in
Kirkwall had heard that Earl Ronald had come home,
and they were all getting ready for a Glad Party to
welcome him, and when they saw the Sad Procession
of ships they couldn't think who it could be, and they

went down to the Sea to wait. When the ships landed all the people cried, and were as sad as sad, because they had liked Ronald very much, and he had only just come home. They took him and buried him in the Stone Church that he had built for St. Magnus, and it was a long time before they had a Ruler that they loved so much.

St. Ronald's Special Day is on August 20th, and hundreds of people can have him for their Special Saint, because there are hundreds of Ronalds.

SSB-S

ST. ROBERT

Once upon a time there was a boy called Robert and he lived in Yorkshire when Henry I was King. Robert was very Shy, and he liked reading by himself much better than playing with the Others, and so he was allowed to.

Now, in his Father's study Robert found a great, heavy Book made of Red Leather with Gold Writing and it had the most Gorgeous pictures in it. And Robert used to drag the Book out on to the floor and lie down on his tummy and put his feet in the air. And there he would lie for hours and hours, looking at the pictures in the Huge Book.

When he was older and could Read (I expect he was about Seven) Robert found that the Writing part of the book was all about Saints and what they did, and the one that he liked best was the Story of St. Benedict. The more that he read about St. Benedict the more he wanted to go and do the Same Things, and so, when he grew up, what do you suppose he was? A Benedictine Monk, of course! You guessed quite right. (Or perhaps you didn't!)

When Robert had been a Benedictine at York for some time, he thought this:

" I am not *really* like St. Benedict, like I wanted to be, because St. Benedict made his own Monastery and lived in a Home-made Hut while it was being built. But *I* just had this lovely Monastery all ready waiting for me! "

And when he had Talked it Over with the other Monks,

some of them said that this was just what *they* thought, too!

So after some Discussion and Arranging, Robert and Twelve Other Benedictines started out with Picks and Spades and things over their shoulders and Walked away from York to build their own Monastery and be More Like St. Benedict.

After they had been walking for some days they came to a River called the River Skeld that had a smooth, green field sloping down to it, and round the field were Beech woods. The field did not belong to anybody special and Robert said:

"Here's the place! Let's camp here and then collect Bricks and things to build our Monastery!" And they all sat down to rest.

The first thing that they had to do was to build themselves some Huts. They each had a little one to sleep in and then they had a bigger one for a Dining-room and Sitting-room. The biggest and best one they had for a Church.

None of the Monks had ever made Huts before, and they found it Pretty Hard Work. First they stuck big sticks in the ground and put smaller ones between and covered the Whole Thing with Leaves. But the leaves kept blowing off, and so that was no good.

"I know!" said Robert, and he got a spade and slid it along and cut out big flat Oblongs of Turf. One of the Others rolled them up as he cut them (so that they would be easier to lift), and Another one stacked them up. They looked just like Green and Brown Swiss Rolls.

When they had got enough they Roofed their Huts with Turf. It made them Rather Dark, but it kept the Weather out.

Robert and his Twelve Friends were delighted with

their new Home! There was the River for Washing and Fishing, and two Springs of Water for Drinking. The Beech Trees all round them kept the Wind off. And they were quite close to the Town of Ripon to do their Shopping.

"Really," said Robert, "I don't think we *could* have found a Better Place!"

Well, here they lived for a long time, trying to collect enough money to build a Beautiful Monastery.

"We *must* build the Church first!" said Robert. "It's all right for *us* being in these Huts, even if the Roofs do keep on slipping off, but I do wish that we had a Nicer Place for the Blessed Sacrament. I don't like to ask God to live in such a shabby, Tumbledown Church."

But they still stayed very poor indeed. Their Black Habits got older and raggier and the Monks got thinner and the Huts were always having to be built up again.

At last they all said to Robert:

"Listen, Robert, we know that it's just as Hard for you as it is for us, but what's the *use* of going on like this?"

"Well, we're being Poor now so as to be Rich in Heaven, for one thing," said Robert, "and as we're Benedictines we're trying to live like St. Benedict wanted us to, for Another Thing. And for yet Another Thing, which is more Important still, Our Lord was *very* Poor, so why should we, who aren't a bit Important, be any Better Off than he was?"

"Yes, Robert," said one of the Monks, "we quite see what you mean, and none of us *like* the Blessed Sacrament being in such a horrible Church we know. It isn't Polite to God."

"If God wants a Better Church," said Robert, "he'll see that we have something to build it with, never you

282

fear! But," he said, " if you like, we'll all pray together that Our Lord will please help us to make him a Nicer Church."

Everyone thought that this was an Excellent Plan, and they started praying at once, and then they all went to bed because it was nearly Dark and they couldn't afford Candles.

After Mass the next morning, while they were wondering if there was anything for Breakfast, they heard a Galloping Noise!

They all came out of their Huts to see, and there was a Rich-looking man, dressed in Fine Raiment, galloping along the River bank towards them!

The Rich-looking man galloped right up to the Huts and Dismounted. He took off his hat and said:

" Good morning! Please who is the Head Monk? "

" Good morning! " said the Monks, " Robert is! "

" Which is Robert? " asked the Rich-looking man, staring at all the Monks, one by one.

" He isn't here," said one of the Monks, " I think he is in the Church. It is that Bigger Hut over there."

So the Rich-looking man hooked his reins over the branch of a tree and went to the Church and met Robert coming out.

" Good morning! " said Robert, " can I do anything for you? "

" Good morning," said the Rich-looking man, " my name is Hugh, and I want to be a Benedictine with you, please! "

Robert looked at Hugh's Fine Raiment.

" You'll have to be Very Poor, you know," he said, " it won't be a bit like what you're Used to! "

" I know," said Hugh. " I want to be Poor, but can we use my Riches to build a Beautiful Church for the Blessed Sacrament instead of this Hut? "

" *Thank you,* God! " said Robert.

" I beg your pardon? " said Hugh.

So Robert told him about them all praying last night, and Hugh said in a Surprised Voice:

" Well, God must have sent me here *Specially* ! "

Well, they built a really lovely Church, and when they'd finished they found that there was plenty of money left to build a big Monastery as well, so that they could have heaps more Monks. When it was built they called it Fountains Abbey, because of the two Springs of Water in their field.

And it is still there. You can see it yourself if you ever go to Ripon. But Henry VIII robbed it, and Cromwell's soldiers kept horses in it and knocked a lot of it down.

One Easter Sunday Robert went in to Breakfast with the other Monks, but he had fasted all Lent without eating anything *at all* and when he saw his Breakfast he said:

" I'm sorry, but I don't think I *could* eat anything! I feel Rather Sick, even when I *look* at my Breakfast."

" Come along! " said one of the Others, " *try* and eat! It is a very nice fish! It is one of the ones I caught in the River yesterday."

" I'm quite Hungry," said Robert, " only Fish seems so Fill-upping just at first! "

" It won't be so bad once you start," said Hugh kindly, as he finished his own fish, " they are *very* nice. Especially after Lent! "

" What about some Bread and Honey? " asked one of the Other Monks, " perhaps that wouldn't be quite so Stodgy to start with."

" Yes! " said Robert, " that's just what I *would* like!"

And one of the monks hurried off to get him some.

But when it came Robert said:

" I don't think that I ought to be Spoiled like this. It isn't at all the Proper Thing for Monks. I'll try and eat my fish as a Sacrifice, and you take the Bread and Honey and see if there are any Poor-and-Raggies outside who would like it! "

So the Monk took the Bread and Honey outside, and there was a Poor-and-Raggy all ready waiting. He took it, plate and all, and went away.

At the next meal, when the Monks were all together again, that Very Same Plate suddenly appeared on the table! So that showed that God was pleased that Robert tried to eat his Fish when he didn't want it.

One day a very rich Baron came to visit Fountains Abbey, and he was so pleased with it that he built another Abbey and he called it Newminster. The Monks at Newminster were Cistercians, who have White Habits, not Black like Benedictines, and Robert became great friends with St. Bernard who was the one who invented Cistercians.

Afterwards Robert went to be the Abbot (or Head Monk) of Newminster and that is why, in some books, he is called St. Robert of Newminster.

St. Robert's Special Day is on June 7th, and lots of people are called after him, especially in England.

ST. GILBERT

Once upon a time there was a Knight called Sir Jocelin and he lived when William the Conqueror was King. (Who *doesn't* know the date of William the Conqueror?)

Sir Jocelin lived at Sempringham, in Lincolnshire, and he had a little boy called Gilbert. Now Gilbert was such a Mingy little boy that Sir Jocelin was Rather Ashamed of him.

"He'll never be Strong or a Soldier or Any Good at All," he sighed, "he is *so* Mingy!"

You see in those days men almost *had* to be Soldiers because of an Englishman's Home being his Castle and all that. So when Gilbert got Mingier and Mingier Sir Jocelin said he could have his meals in the Kitchen.

"I can't stand the sight of your Pasty little face any longer," he said, "it's just like a Bun."

So Gilbert lived down in the Kitchen and the Scullery and the Pantry, but the Cook and the Scullerymaid and the Butler and all the others were even Ruder than Sir Jocelin.

After a while Gilbert found that if he hid for most of the day no one bothered much about him. So he took all the books he could find (because Reading makes the day go quicker) and he hid in the Attic every day. He read Stories and History and Geography and all that kind of thing, and when he had finished them all he started on the Bible and the Psalms and Matins and Vespers and Lives of Saints and all *that* kind of thing. Until at last he had read every book in the Whole House from cover to cover.

ST. GILBERT

Then he summoned his Courage and went to Sir Jocelin.

" Please, Daddy," he said, " do you suppose I could go to School? "

" *School* ? " said Sir Jocelin, all astonished. "Why bless me, isn't it enough to know that you are a Weakling, without wanting to go to School? "

(Very few people except priests went to school in those days because of having to be Soldiers.)

" I would be more out of your sight if I was at School," said Gilbert.

" And a good job too," said Sir Jocelin; " I'll speak to your Mother about it. Now go away, do."

In the end Gilbert was sent away to a Monastery school in Paris, but Sir Jocelin was so disgusted with him that, although he was rich, he never paid the School Fees, and poor Gilbert had to work hard between times to earn enough money. At last, after years and years, and when he was grown up, Gilbert passed so many Examinations that he became a Schoolmaster and went home to Sempringham. He went into the house very quietly and there were Sir Jocelin and Gilbert's mother and some friends all having Dinner in the Hall.

Suddenly one of the servants saw Gilbert.

" Hey! " he said. " Get out! Sir Jocelin don't allow no Strangers here! Be off! " (Which was very Rude, especially if it really *had* been a Stranger.)

" What's all this? " roared Sir Jocelin. "How dare you make all that noise while I'm having Dinner! " He got up and stamped along to the door.

" Who are you? " he said to Gilbert. "Go away! "

" It's Gilbert," said Gilbert.

Sir Jocelin peered at him and screwed up his eyes.

" So it is! " he said, " pasty as ever. Come in, I suppose."

So Gilbert went in and said, How do you Do to his mother.

"Well, dear," she said, "and what have you been doing all this long time?"

"I've learned to be a Schoolmaster," said Gilbert.

"*Have* you?" said Sir Jocelin. "I wouldn't have thought it! *Have* you now?"

In those days Schoolmasters were very Important People. There were only a very few in England, and so Sir Jocelin was very Agreeably Surprised and Pleased. He gave Gilbert a lot of money to build a school and was quite nice to him. In fact, he was rather proud of having a Schoolmaster for a son. It made a nice change.

Gilbert soon had a good school, and then the Bishop heard of him.

"Come and live with me," he said, "and teach the children in my Parish!" So Gilbert went to the Bishop's Palace in Lincoln, and the Bishop made him a Priest.

"It is better for you to be a Priest as well," he said, "because then you can be a Parish Priest and Work your way Up."

"Work my way up Where?" asked Gilbert.

"Why, to be a Bishop, or even an Archbishop," said the Bishop. "You might even be a Cardinal!"

"Oh," said Gilbert, "I thought perhaps you meant Work my way up to Heaven."

"Of course," said the Bishop, getting Rather Red, "that *is* what I meant."

Now Gilbert, because he was a Schoolmaster and because he'd lived nearly all his life in schools, was very Keen on Obedience. Not the "do as you're told and don't Argue" kind, but the proper kind.

"Everybody *is* Obedient," he used to say, "even the people who think that they're not!"

" What *do* you mean? " people asked him.

" Well," said Gilbert, " suppose it is Sunday and it is time to get ready for Church. We all have to Obey the Rule about going to church on Sunday. Everyone has to, even Kings and Queens with Crowns on, and the Pope. But suppose you say: ' Why *should* I be Obedient? I *won't* be Obedient, so now! ' And you go off and read a book or play at something instead. ' There! ' you say, ' I'm not Obedient you see! ' But you are. You are obeying your own ideas out of your own rather silly mind instead of obeying God's ideas out of His very wise mind. You can't *help* obeying *something*," said Gilbert, " even if it is your own Self. And do you really think that *you* are worth Obeying? Soldiers have to obey Lieutenants and Lieutenants have to obey Captains and Captains have to obey Majors and Majors have to obey Colonels and Colonels have to obey Generals and Generals have to obey the Field-Marshal."

" Ah! " said the people who were listening to Gilbert, " now we've caught you! The Field-Marshal doesn't have to obey anyone because he is at the Top! "

" Not at all! " said Gilbert, " the King is Topper. And the King has to obey God."

Now you all know how to find out what God wants us to do. He doesn't go round to everyone and say:

" You do this," and " *You* do *that*."

" I'll tell the Church," says God, " and then, whenever you're not sure about anything, if you ask the Church it is Bound to be Right. "

It is just the same as if you are a Postman who has to obey the Postmaster at the little Post Office where he works, and *he* has to obey the Postmaster in London who has to obey the Postmaster-General, who has to obey the King, who has to obey the Church, who

has to obey God. Or the Priest who has to obey the
Bishop, who has to obey the Archbishop, who has to
obey the Cardinal, who has to obey the Pope, who has
to obey the Church, who has to obey God. Or the little
Girl who has to obey her Nanny, who has to obey the
Mummy, who has to obey the Daddy, who has to obey
the Head Man at the Office (or wherever he works),
who has to obey the Government, who has to obey the
King, who has to obey the Church, who has to obey God.

(Now I can't go *on* playing this " Who has to Obey "
game, but I wonder how many more you can think of?
I bet you can't find anyone who doesn't have to obey
something!)

" And so," said Gilbert, " nearly everybody has
somebody Over them, and somebody Under them.
So no one should be Stuck Up about giving Orders,
because, in the Long Run, he is only passing the message
down from the Next Step Up. God tells the Church
and the Church tells the Cardinal and the Cardinal
tells the Archbishop, and the Archbishop tells the
Bishop, and the Bishop tells the Priest, and the Priest
tells the Grownup People in the Sermon, and the
Grownup People come home and tell the People in
the Nursery that they must be Clean (why?) or not
Greedy (why?) and all that. And that is why," said
Gilbert, " we always ought to be Polite and Obedient
to the People in the Next Step Up because they generally know better than we do, and so are almost sure
to be right."

Well, to go on about what Gilbert did when he went
to live in the Bishop's Palace. He didn't much Care
for living there. It was too Rich and Rare.

" It doesn't seem proper," he said to the Bishop,
" to have all this Sumptuous Fare when so many people
are so Poor."

"But I'm an Important Bishop," said the Bishop. "I can't live like a Common Person."

"Well, Our Lord lived like a Common Person," said Gilbert, "and so I thought that perhaps we ought to, too."

"That's quite different," said the Bishop.

"Yes, my Lord," said Gilbert, obediently, because of the Bishop being the Next Step Up.

But the Bishop said that Gilbert could go away if he wanted to, and he did want to, so he did. He went back to Sempringham, and he built a Monastery. Now this was an Unusual sort of Monastery, because it had two Houses in it. One House had Nuns who did all the Washing and Cooking and Spinning and Baking and Sewing and Gardening. The other House had Monks who did all the Ploughing and Digging and Beekeeping and Shepherding and Fishing and Farming and Looking After the Cows and things. So you see, between them they had everything that they needed, and were Entirely Self-Supporting. The Pope liked this new English Order, and he made Gilbert the head, and gave them a Black Habit, and called them the Gilbertines. Well, soon there were lots of Monasteries of Gilbertines, and Gilbert went from one to another helping them and telling them specially about Obedience and the Next Step Up. The Bishop was so pleased that he gave some of the Nuns a little Island in the middle of the River Witham. It must have been a lovely place to live in, I wish I could live on an Island in a River.

Well, all was going very Well, when some of the Monks began Breaking Rules. They got so Out of Hand and Worldly that Gilbert went to their Monastery and said:

"Well, Brothers, what *is* happening to you? I thought that I'd got you all nicely Settled!"

" Your Rules are too Strict," said one of the Brothers rudely, " it's all very well for *you* because *you* made them up, but what about *us*? "

" *What* about you? " said Gilbert.

" Well, we have to work and pray and all that all day, with only One Hour for recreation," said the Rude Monk.

" What is your work? " asked Gilbert.

" I'm a Weaver, and I make the cloth for the Monks' habits," said the Rude Monk.

" What did you do before you were a Monk? " said Gilbert.

" I was still a Weaver," said the Rude Monk.

" Well, why did you become a Monk? " asked Gilbert.

" Because people didn't buy enough cloth, and so I hadn't enough to eat. I was Starving," said the Rude Monk.

" Nothing about God? " asked Gilbert.

" No," said the Rude Monk.

" Well," said Gilbert, " I should have thought that you were better off now. You never Starve, you have a bed, and a dry, warm house, and all your weaving is very useful. Try to settle down, Brother, and love God as God loves you."

" What about me? " said another Unruly Monk. (If you think for one minute you will see for yourself what Unruly means.)

" *What* about you? " said Gilbert.

" Well," said the Unruly Monk, " I am the Monastery Blacksmith, and I have to work Frightfully hard. Much harder than the Weaver."

" What were you before? " asked Gilbert.

" A Blacksmith," said the Unruly Monk.

" Why? " asked Gilbert.

" Because I wanted to be one," said the Unruly Monk.

" Why weren't you a Weaver? "

" Because I'd rather be a Blacksmith," said the Unruly Monk.

" Well, what are you Grumbling about? " said Gilbert, " you *are* a Blacksmith and you're *not* a Weaver, which is what you chose yourself. Now you settle down, too, but if you don't want to be Monks any more, go away and don't make Trouble here! "

But the two Monks (the Rude one and the Unruly one) didn't want to go away. They were sure of their meals and bed at the Monastery. And so they stayed, and after a time they got Worse than ever. They went out into the Villages and said how Awful the Monastery was, and how badly they were treated, so that at last the people began to believe them. Then they behaved so Badly that Gilbert Excommunicated them! And that meant that they couldn't go to any of the Sacraments, even Confession, until they promised to Behave themselves Properly. Which, when you think about it, is a Very Fierce Punishment. But no doubt they deserved it.

So when Gilbert Excommunicated the Brother Weaver and the Brother Blacksmith, they were very Angry indeed (not sorry, because they had not learned to love God), and they said to each other:

" Let's go and tell the Pope."

So they started off to Rome to see the Pope, and when they got there they told a Long and Sad story. They said that Gilbert had Excommunicated them for nothing at all. That Gilbert had a Spite against them. That, although the Pope mightn't know it, Gilbert was an Awful man, and that the Monastery was a dreadful place. That all the other monks were Wicked, and that no one kept any of the Rules except themselves.

Now, perhaps because they were poor working men, the Pope believed their Story. He undid the Excommunication for them, and he wrote a Stern Letter to Gilbert telling him to take back the two Brothers into their Monastery. And telling him that he ought to be Ashamed of having such wicked Monks in his Monastery (except the Weaver and the Blacksmith).

Poor Gilbert was very Upset. But, because of Obedience, he took back the two Wicked Monks and made all his Rules easier, and did everything exactly as the Pope said in his letter.

Now the other Monks, who weren't wicked at all, did not like everyone talking about their Wickedness like this (neither would you). So they turned on Gilbert.

"If only you hadn't Excommunicated those two," they said, "all this wouldn't have happened. It's All your Fault!"

Then, to make things worse, Gilbert's friends (who had heard the stories of the Bad Monks) wrote to Gilbert saying how Shocked they were that he could have such a wicked monastery. Even St. Thomas of Canterbury said that he was sorry that he and Gilbert had ever been friends, and that he hoped that they would Never Meet Again.

Gilbert was so sad that he didn't know *what* to do. Because *none* of it was true!

He went and told Our Lord all about it, and while he was praying he remembered that people had made up things about Our Lord, and had told all sorts of Lies about him when he was with Pontius Pilate and then he felt happier.

"Thank you, dear Lord," he said, "for letting me be like you. It is a very Great Honour, and I am proud to be allowed to have it. Thank you for reminding me about it." But he went on praying for his Monks (they

294

were Canons, really, which is only another Sort, like Friars) and he prayed that the people would stop thinking they were all a Wicked Lot.

And after a time God gave him his prayer, and people began to see that the Canons were good men after all, and that Gilbert was Holy and not Wicked. And everybody came to the Monastery and asked Gilbert to forgive them for being so Mean, and he did. Even the Bishops came. And King Henry.

Gilbert lived until he was more than a Hundred years old, and when he was more than Ninety he used to ask God every day if he could please die now, because he was getting so Old and Shaky. " Please, Lord, don't forget me, I'm still here," he said.

At last one early morning before anyone was up, Our Lord came and fetched him. And tired old Gilbert was very glad to leave his Old and Used-Up body, I'm sure.

St. Gilbert's Special Day is on February 4th. There are a great many boys called after him in England, but in France girls are called after him too. Perhaps because the French people liked him when he was at School there when he was a Mingy little boy.

ST. WILLIAM

Once upon a time there was a man called William and he was French, and he lived in the Country. One day he had some business to see to in Paris (which is the Capital of France), so he put on his Blue Velvet clothes and he saddled his Bay Horse and he rode in to Town. Now the Business took so long that William thought that he would stay the night, and finish the next morning, so he went to an Hotel, and the Hotel man put the Bay Horse in the Stable and showed William his room. After supper William thought that he would go out for a walk before going to bed, so as to have a Look Round Paris.

The Extraordinary Thing was that although there were Churches and things in Paris nearly everybody had stopped being Christians, and were Pagans, and Shocking Wicked ones they were! William's eyes got rounder and bigger as he walked about, he couldn't *believe* what he saw and heard!

" *Well!* " he said to himself, " well, I *say*! Good gracious me! " and he hurried back to his Hotel and went to bed.

Next day when his Business was done, he rode home on the Bay Horse, and all the time he couldn't help thinking about the Wickedness of Paris. He simply couldn't Get Over it at all.

Then he thought this thought:

" Supposing I go and be a Hermit, and use all my time praying and things, I wonder if it would help to make up to God for all the Wickedness of the people of Paris? They are so Horrible to God that they don't even remember that He died for them. Imagine Dying for somebody and they don't even remember that you did it! "

So he went home and gave his house and garden and things to his Family and said Good-bye to them, and went off to be a Hermit. He learned a lot about God all by himself in his little Cell, and every day he told Him how sorry he was about the People of Paris.

One day God said to William:

" William, I want you to go to the Abbey at Citeaux, where St. Bernard was. You would be able to do more things for me there, and you would have the Church and the Blessed Sacrament nice and near."

So William went to Citeaux, and soon he was the Abbot there, and then he was made the Archbishop of Bourges, which is a town in France. (An Archbishop is a Top kind of Bishop, and an Archangel is a Top kind of Angel and an Archduke is the Top kind of Duke in Austria.)

Now in his Secret Self William always wanted to be a poor Hermit and not a rich Archbishop, and so, although he had to wear Soft Clothing and live in a Palace because of his Rank, he stayed very poor and humble inside, so as to be as much like a Hermit as he could Notwithstanding, and he worked hard and got up early. (And so does the Pope, and so does the King.)

One day a priest called Gerald came to see William.

" Please, Your Grace," he said, " may I speak to you about something Important? "

" Certainly, Father, what is it? " said William kindly.

" Well," said Father Gerald, " my right hand has Gone Lame, and I can't use it at all."

" So what? " said William.

" So I can't say Mass any more," said Father Gerald.

"Oh," said William, "how lucky for you."

"*Lucky*!" said Father Gerald. "Did you say *Lucky*?"

"Yes, I said Lucky," said William.

"Why?" said Father Gerald.

"Well," said William, "you go to Confession this evening and to Holy Communion to-morrow morning, and then come back to me and I'll tell you. Or perhaps you will tell me!"

So Father Gerald went to Confession in the evening and to Holy Communion in the morning, and then he went to see William again.

"Good morning, Your Grace," he said, "please may I speak to you about something Important?"

"What is it?" asked William.

"Well," said Father Gerald, "I did what you said, and now I want to know something."

"What do you want to know?" said William.

"How did you know that I had a Mortal Sin?" said Father Gerald. "It's really most Mysterious!"

"*Had* you got a Mortal Sin?" said William. "Well, then, it *was* Lucky that you had a Lame Hand, wasn't it?"

"Yes, it was," said Father Gerald. "How *very* Kind of God to make me so that I couldn't possibly say Mass when I'd got a Mortal Sin!"

"It would have been a Terrible Thing," said William, "for you to say Mass and hold the Blessed Sacrament in your hands when you had a Mortal Sin. It would have been making God, who is Clean and Beautiful, come near to your Dirty, Ugly, Stuffy Soul. Can you *Imagine* it?"

"My hand is a little better," said Father Gerald.

"In three days' time," said William, "when you have told God how sorry you are, it will be as Good as New."

And it was, and Father Gerald could say Mass again, which was very kind indeed of God.

William was a very Cheerful man, and he was always Singing or Laughing, and lots of Rather Sour-faced People disapproved of him.

" Why are you always Singing and Laughing? " they asked him. " You ought to be Grave and Solemn when you are an Archbishop."

" Why? "asked William in a Surprised voice.

" Because Archbishops are supposed to be near to God, and so they ought to be Solemn," they said, and they looked at William as though they couldn't think how he ever came to be an Archbishop at all.

"But it is a Happy thing to be near to God," said William, laughing at them. "It is a Lovely thing, and a Glad thing, and I couldn't be Solemn and Grave."

But the people went away shaking their heads. They were the sort of people who go to Damp Churches that smell of Mothball on Sundays, wearing their Black Clothes. Then they lock up the Churches so that no one can get in on all the Other Days, which is all very Stuck Up and Stuffy.

One of the things that these people were always doing was a Sin called Detraction, which is Telling Tales. Now this was William's Favourite Sin to Hate, and he was always telling them about it.

"Now listen, all you people," he used to say. "If you say that Mrs. Popinjay chews her blankets and spills her food down her Front when it isn't True, well that's a sin, because it's Telling Lies about poor Mrs. Popinjay. But it doesn't matter Terribly because she can laugh and say: 'What nonsense!' and all her friends can say: 'What a shame! Of *course* she doesn't!' and so Mrs. Popinjay isn't Miserable, only Cross.

"But if it *is* True, then it is downright Wicked to say so. First, it is none of your Business if she does chew her blankets, even if it is a stuffy thing to do, and Second, no one else might know about it, and Mrs. Popinjay might be trying very hard to stop doing it (she might even have actually stopped). Then if you tell everyone about it they will say, 'No! Does she *really*? How awful of her! *Well* now!' and they will tell everyone else and poor Mrs. Popinjay will be *Miserable* because everybody knows about her Grubby Tricks, and she may even have to go away and live somewhere else all because of you! So that Detraction is one of the *Meanest* things," said William, and you can see that he was quite right, can't you?

ST. WILLIAM

One day William thought this thought:

" I think I'd like to be a Missionary now, and tell all the people who don't know about God. I'll tell them about Our Lord at Christmas and at Easter and about Our Lady and about the Sacraments, and all, and they'll be Delighted to hear such Good News! "

So he packed up some things ready to start. He took some Camping things, and a Roll-up Bed, and a Kettle and a Cup and a Plate and things, and a Crucifix and a statue of Our Lady to show to the Heathen People, and some Writing things so that he could write home and tell the Others how he was getting on. He worked for two whole days packing up, and when everything was downstairs in the hall ready to start in the morning he went to bed. He was very Tired.

While he was asleep his Guardian Angel came and said:

" Wake up, William, I want to tell you something! "

" What will you tell me? " asked William, rubbing his eyes. He was still very tired after all the Packing, and he could hardly keep his eyes open.

" It is time to stop living in that Tired old body of yours, and come and live with us," said the Guardian Angel.

" Die, do you mean? " asked William in an Interested voice.

" Yes," said the Guardian Angel; " die here and live there."

" But what about being a Missionary? " said William.

" Wouldn't you rather live with God?" said the Guardian Angel; " you are always so happy when he is near you."

" Oh *yes*! " said William, " I'd rather do that than anything at all. I was thinking of the Ages and Ages of Purgatory I should have to have first," said poor old William. " When can we start? "

"I don't think you will have any Purgatory," said the Guardian Angel, and he helped William to stand up, and held his arm. "God loves you very much, and you have always been a poor Hermit inside. We can start now."

And William went away with his Guardian Angel and there was God waiting for him and smiling at him for being such a Happy man.

So when someone came in the morning to tell William that it was time to get up he found that he had gone already, so someone else went to be the Missionary, so as not to waste all that Packing.

There are lots of other St. Williams, and most of them are English, so I thought that I'd tell you about this one who is French. His Special Day is on January 10th, and people called William are all over the World.

ST. DOMINIC

Once upon a time there was a little boy called Dominic, and his father was called Felix and his mother was called Joanna, and they all lived together in Spain.

Well, one night Joanna had an Extraordinary Dream. She dreamed that Dominic was a Dog who was rushing about with a Burning Stick in its mouth, and whatever it touched started burning too. Soon the Whole World was burnt, and then it was Joanna woke up!

"What a very Extraordinary Dream!" she thought, "it must Mean Something!"

She poked Felix and woke him up.

"Don't!" said Felix crossly.

"But I want us to talk about my Dream," said Joanna.

"Bother your dream! I'm sleepy!" said poor Felix, with a huge yawn. "Why can't you go to sleep like a Christian and chat in the daytime? 'Pon my soul, I never saw such a woman!"

"But I like having little Chats in the Middle of the Night," said Joanna, sitting up in bed and looking very Spry, "and I dreamed about Dominic and he was a Dog!" And she told Felix all about it. He got quite interested and agreed with Joanna that it *was* most Extraordinary.

"What does it *mean*?" asked Joanna.

"How on Earth should *I* know?" said Felix, punching up his pillow and settling down again.

"Well, you always say that you know better than I do," said Joanna; "wasn't it Extraordinary though?"

No answer.

" Wasn't it, Felix? " said Joanna.

" YES!!! " roared Felix, and they both went to sleep again.

At breakfast the next morning they went on talking about the Dream, and in the end they decided that it must mean that Dominic was going to be someone very special, and that the Whole World would know about him.

And so it happened. When Dominic grew up he was a Priest, and he found that heaps and heaps of people that he met were Heretics.

Now in case you don't know, Heretics are people who go round saying things like this:

" We are very Good Catholics, but we don't Hold with the Pope." Or:

" We are Excellent Catholics, but we don't believe that Our Lady is the Mother of God." Or:

" We are honest Christians, but, of course, there isn't such a thing as the Trinity."

Well, you can see for yourself how very Silly these things are, can't you? You might just as well say:

" I'm a very Good Sailor, but I've never seen the Sea." Or:

" I had an Excellent Dinner to-day, but there wasn't anything to eat! "

Well, Dominic's Heretics all said that only Souls and Thoughts and Spirits and things you can't see and touch were Good, and everything that was *made* of something like plants or furniture or food or things was Bad. Even people's bodies were bad, they said, and so people couldn't help it if they were Greedy and ate too much, or were Angry and killed people, or were Thieves and stole things. Because, said these Heretics, it wasn't *them* doing all these things at all, but only their Bad Wicked Bodies.

Wasn't that Absurd? How can all the things that God has made be Bad? How can your body be bad when God made it? (Have you started to learn the Catechism yet?) And anyone with any sense knows that your body wouldn't go and steal something unless *you* allowed it to. So, of *course*, people can help it if they are Wicked!

Anyway, all Dominic's Heretics thought that this was a Lovely Heresy because it meant that they could do just what they liked and it wouldn't matter at all, and Dominic said to himself:

" Something's got to be done about it! "

So he wrote a List of all the Wrong things that the Heretics thought, and, although it made a lot of Extra Work, he wrote it in Questions, like this:

1. " Why do you think that it doesn't matter if you are Greedy? "
2. " Why do you think that *Things* are Wicked? " etc.

Then he gave the List to one of the Heretics.

" Here," he said, " now you go and show this List to your Friends and think of Good Answers. Then to-night we will all meet in the courtyard outside the Church and we'll have a Friendly Argument and see who's right."

" All right," said the Heretic, and he went away.

That evening Dominic tidied up the Courtyard; lit a big Fire there to light and warm everybody, and put some refreshments on a side table.

" I wonder what their Answers will be," he thought.

But the Heretics hadn't been able to answer any of the Questions in a satisfactory way. So when they came along to the Courtyard that night the Chief of them said Grandly:

305

" Well, Dominic, we didn't think it was Worth While answering that Enormous List of yours, but we have a much Better Idea."

Dominic was Rather Disappointed, but he said politely:

" Very well. And what is your Better Idea? "

" We'll throw your List in the fire," said the Chief Heretic, " and if it burns you'll be Wrong!" and he laughed in a Sneering way, " but, of course, I never heard of a List of Questions that wouldn't Burn if you put it in the fire!"

All the other Heretics laughed and Nudged each other.

" Ha! Ha!" they laughed, " this *is* a good way of making Dominic Wrong, and of teaching him to Mind his own Business."

" Very well," said Dominic, " just as you wish. Shall I make up the Fire so as to have a bigger and better Blaze? "

" Yes, do," said the Chief Heretic, and he stood Haughtily watching Dominic make up the fire until there was a really splendid Blaze.

" Now!" said Dominic. And the Chief Heretic tossed the List of Wrong Things right into the very middle of the Fire! In about three minutes all the Heretics burst out laughing:

" Ho! Ho!" they laughed, " Dominic's Wrong and we're Right!"

" Not at all!" said Dominic, and a puff of wind blew the List right out of the Fire, and it wasn't even Scorched!

" Well, really!" said the Chief Heretic, looking Rather Upset, " I can't have dried the Papers properly when I tipped over a Flower Vase on them this afternoon. It's not a Fair Test!"

" Throw it in again, then," said Dominic, " after all, it must be dry now! It's been baked for Three Minutes! "

So one of them threw it in again, and after a few minutes it blew out again without a Mark on it!

" It's really too Tiresome! " fussed the Chief Heretic, " you didn't throw it into the very Hot part. It isn't a Fair Test! "

" All right! *you* throw it in! " said one of the Heretics, " and Third Time's Lucky, so we're sure to be Right this time! After all, it can't *not* Burn! "

So the Chief Heretic put the List into the very middle of the Hottest Part and pushed it down with a Stick and held it there. His Stick began to Burn, and soon he had to leave go. Immediately the List of Wrong Things blew out of the Fire!

The Heretics went away in a Pet, and they never told anyone about it. But a friend of Dominic's who had been watching thought that people ought to know, and so he told everyone he met! This made the Heretics Furiously Angry, and they used to follow Dominic about, making a Mock of him. Some of them used to tie bits of Straw to his Cassock when he wasn't looking, and then they'd all laugh at him. When they found that Dominic didn't care Twopence for their Sillinesses they began to throw Stones and things at him, and set Traps for him to trip him up. But Dominic never said a word, and just went on his way, singing a song to himself.

" But aren't you frightened of us? " asked the Heretics. " Supposing we killed you? "

" I'm not good enough to be a Martyr," said Dominic, " so I needn't worry! " And he went on singing happily.

After a while the Heretics gave up bothering him. It seemed such a Waste of Time.

Well, Dominic had several friends of his who went

round with him (Priests and Monks and Friars), and they all preached and tried to stop the people being Heretics, and one day they thought:

" Wouldn't it be nice if we could be an Order all to ourselves instead of some of us being Ordinary Priests and some being Franciscans and some being Benedictines and things? "

So they went to the Pope and asked him.

" No," said the Pope, " there are quite enough Orders as it is without you wanting to make a New one! "

" But please, there isn't an Order of Preachers, like us," said Dominic. " Not Friars whose Job it is to Preach to the Heretics. The other Orders all have Farms; or have Hospitals; or teach in Schools; or Make things; or Tell people to be Poor here so as to be Rich in Heaven."

" No," said the Pope, " you are going on quite all right as you are now."

That night the Pope dreamt that one of the Churches in Rome was falling down and that Dominic came and held it up, so in the morning he sent for Dominic and told him about it.

" So, after all, Dominic," he said, " you can have a New Order of your own. What are you going to call it? "

" The Order of Preachers, please," said Dominic, very pleased. And that is why Dominicans have the letters O.P. after their names. Like Father Hugh Pope, O.P., or Father Vincent McNabb, O.P. All Orders have their own letters so that people can know which Order a Priest belongs to if they see his name written up anywhere. Jesuits like Father Martindale have S.J. for Society of Jesus, and Benedictines have O.S.B. for Order of St. Benedict. You can work out the others for yourself one day, when you've nothing else to do.

ST. DOMINIC

Well there were Dominic and his sixteen friends all with O.P. after their names. But they hadn't decided yet what sort of Clothes they would wear, so they just went about in their old ones. You know, don't you, that all Orders have their own Special Clothes or Uniform? It is called a Habit. (Like Riding Clothes are called Riding Habits. What is the French for Coat?) The Benedictines (like St. Robert) have all Black. The Carmelites (like St. Teresa) have Brown Habits with White Cloaks, and the Franciscans have Dark Brown (like St. Anthony's Statue), and sometimes they have Grey. The Cistercians (like St. Bernard) have All White. I expect you have seen some of these, haven't you?

One day Dominic had a Dream. (There seem to be a good many dreams in this story, don't there?) He dreamt that he was talking to Our Lady and was telling her all about his New Order.

" But how do people Recognise you when you are in Strange Places when you don't have a Habit? " asked Our Lady.

" Well," said Dominic, " we haven't really thought much about it. We haven't even chosen what Colour to have."

" I'll choose," said Our Lady. " A White Habit and a Black Cloak."

" Thank you very much indeed," said Dominic, " that is a very great Honour for us. I wonder, Our Lady, if you would give me some Advice? "

" Of course I will," said Our Lady.

" Well," said Dominic, " you know those Heretics? "

" Yes, I do," said Our Lady.

" Well, I don't seem to get on very fast with them," said poor Dominic, who was getting tired of preaching to Heretics who wouldn't listen. " How can I get them to Learn Sense? "

" I'll tell you," said Our Lady. " Make them think slowly, one by one, of the Fifteen most Important Things there are, and at each one of them say one Our Father and Ten Hail Marys and one Glory be to the Father."

" How *can* they remember all that? " asked Dominic. " My Heretics are rather Turnip Heads, and they can't pray or even think if they are Counting all the time."

" Well," said Our Lady, " then you must make something for them to Count with so that they needn't think about How Many Times." And she showed Dominic a thing Rather Like a Necklace.

"Look," she said, " one bead for an Our Father, then Ten beads for the Ten Hail Marys and when you feel that you've come to the end of the Ten you say a Gloria. You can make it of Knots in String if you like. Anything will do. Once you get the People used to doing this they'll soon stop being Heretics. You'll see! " and Our Lady smiled kindly at St. Dominic.

" One minute more, *please*, Our Lady," said Dominic. "What shall I say the Fifteen Most Important things are? "

" Start at the Very Beginning," said Our Lady, " and go on to the End. First the Annunciation when Gabriel came to see me, and then when I went to see Elizabeth, and then when Our Lord was born at Bethlehem. Go right on to his Passion and Crucifixion. And then Pentecost and all. You will find Fifteen things if you make a List."

And that, as I expect some people will have guessed, was how the Rosary started. And Dominic had much better luck with his Heretics after that.

Such a lot of Interesting things happened to Dominic that I really don't know what to tell you next! I think I'll tell you about how he met the Devil, and Scored Off him!

ST. DOMINIC

One of the Rules in the Order of Preachers was that no one was allowed to talk from after Supper until after Mass the next morning. Well, one night everybody had gone to bed except Dominic, who was visiting the Blessed Sacrament once more before he went up. As he turned round to leave the Church he thought he saw one of his Friars wandering about down at the Other end of the aisle. Dominic nodded at him and pointed at the Door to tell him to go on up to bed. But the Friar waved his hand to Dominic and made a Horrible Face at him!

Dominic was Shocked and went down the Church and said:

"What *are* you supposed to be doing? You ought to be in bed! And why were you Pulling Faces? It's very Rude, especially in Church."

Then he saw that the Friar was really the Devil-pretending-to-be-a-Friar, and told him that he was Behaving abominably and must Be Off at once!

But the Devil was Delighted!

"Ha! Ha!" he cried. "*I* made you talk! I made you break one of the Rules! Fancy our Pious Dominic speaking when he shouldn't!"

"Be quiet!" said Dominic. "I made the Silence Rule myself, so I can break it if I wish to!"

"*I* tempted you!" sang the Devil. "*I* tempted you! *I* tempted you! You know," he said in a quieter voice, "I tempt all the Friars!"

"Do you really?" said Dominic in an Interested sort of voice. "What do you tempt them to do?"

"Wouldn't you like to know!" said the Devil.

"Yes, I should," said Dominic. "Let's go round the house together and you can tell me all about it! First, how do you tempt them here in Church?"

"I make them come in Late and go out Early!" said

the Devil, who was very happy to find someone who would listen to his Boasting. (Boasting is Blowing your own Trumpet.)

Then Dominic took the Devil to the Dormitory where all the Friars were asleep in bed.

"How do you tempt them *here*?" he asked.

"I make them Lazy and stay in Bed too long so that they are Late for Mass!" said the Devil. "I'll do it To-morrow and you'll see!"

"How do you tempt them here?" asked Dominic when they were in the Dining-room.

The Devil jumped up on a table and Danced up and down:

"Now More, now Less!" he sang. "Now More, now Less!"

"What *do* you mean?" asked Dominic.

"I make some of them eat Too Much until they are too Fat and Lazy to serve God," said the Devil. "And I make the ones who are afraid of being Greedy eat Too Little so that they are Too Weak to serve God! Isn't that a Good Idea?"

"It is, rather," said Dominic. "Come on!" and they went to the Recreation room where the Friars could Chat and play Chess and things when they were not Working.

"How do you tempt them here?" asked Dominic.

"Ah!" said the Devil, rubbing his hands with Glee, "now this *is* a Good Place for me! I make them talk too much, so that they Boast and forget God."

Then they came to the Chapter House where all the Friars went to Confession. But the Devil wouldn't go in.

"I hate this place!" he said, "because whenever I get a Friar on my side by making him sin, he comes here to Confession and I lose him again at once! Every bit of Hard Work that I do is undone in here. I'm not going in, thank you!"

"Well, good-bye!" said Dominic, "and now that by your Boasting you have so kindly given away how you Tempt us, I am afraid that you will have Very Hard Work Indeed to get any of us on your side again!"

The Devil was *Furious* and hurried away muttering to himself, and Dominic went to bed laughing to himself at the Silly way the Devil had let out all his Secrets!

Well, I can't use up all the pages of this book on St. Dominic, and so I won't tell you about how he found a Penny in a Boat, or about how he tried to sell himself when he wanted some money for a Poor Man, or about all sorts of Other Things. They are all written in other books, and you can read them one day.

There are not so many people as there ought to be called after St. Dominic. I can't think why. His Special Day is August 4th, and if anyone's Birthday is on that day they can have St. Dominic for theirs even if their name is Michael or something.

ST. FRANCIS OF ASSISI

Once upon a time, in a very old town in Italy called Assisi, there lived a Silk Merchant whose name was Pietro Bernadone. (Pietro is the Italian for Peter.) Well, this Silk Merchant used to spend most of his time in France buying silks to make dresses for the rich ladies in Italy. So, because he was there such a lot and he made his money there, he loved France.

One day, when he went home with his silks to Assisi he found that his wife had got a son for him, called Giovanni (which is the Italian for John). Pietro wasn't very pleased about this because he didn't like the name Giovanni, but he thought that it would be a good thing to have a son who could go and buy silk for him in France when he grew up, so he changed the baby's name to Francis and felt much happier because he had made up a new name.

When Francis was older and went to school, his favourite things to do were Fighting and Learning French. None of the others learned French, so he felt very grand. He was very good at fighting, but he was never very tall, so it was rather difficult. Even when he was Grown Up he was a small man with dark hair and bright brown eyes and a sunburnt face. While he was still a little boy he loved stories of Battles and Sieges and Martyrs and Heroes, and he decided that he would do all these things when he was a man. So when he was Twenty he went with a lot of his friends, on horses, to fight with the next town called Perugia. No one thought very much of Perugia, so

Francis and his friends did not bother to take very many swords and things. And instead of putting on armour and swords and shields and helmets they put on their very Best and Brightest-coloured clothes. Francis' clothes were the Brightest and Best of all, because of his Father being a Silk Merchant, and he had on a Red Velvet Cloak, with a Silver Collar and Fasteners, and he had a Shiny Black Horse with Red and Silver Harness. Well, when they got near to Perugia they weren't really being a bit careful and were telling each other funny stories and playing guessing games instead of Keeping a Look Out. So of course the people of Perugia saw them coming from miles away because of their Bright-coloured Clothes, and they rushed out and took them all Prisoners before they had time to think! They kept all the horses and swords for their own soldiers and put Francis and his friends in Prison for a whole Year.

They were all very sad at being in Prison and having to keep the same clothes on all the time, and they said it was all Francis' fault for starting it. But Francis kept cheering them up and making them laugh, and he made up funny bits of poetry about them all, so they weren't so unhappy after all.

When they had been in Prison for 364 days (how many days in a year?) Francis had a Dream, and the Dream was—He saw Our Lord standing with piles of swords and silks and cloaks all round Him and every sword had a handle like a Cross. While Francis was wondering what it was all for, Our Lord said:

" These are the things that I give to the people who work for Me, and these are the swords that I give to them so that they can fight for Me."

When he woke up in the morning Francis knew that Our Lord didn't want him to have Bright Clothes any more while he was here, but that he must wait until he got to Heaven and he could have them then if he wanted them. Also that he mustn't fight with the Perugians or anyone at all any more but only the Devil, whose name is Satan. Francis felt very sad about this, because he *did* love fighting, especially with Bright-coloured Clothes on and with beautiful Red and Silver Reins for his horse. While he was thinking about the Dream, Satan came up behind him, very quietly so that he wouldn't hear, and put an Idea into his head quickly and went away before anyone saw him. And this was the Idea:

" If I do not dress in my satin and velvet clothes and fight people, all my friends who like doing that too will not be friends with me any more. So I don't think I'll do what Our Lord said, it will be so dull with no friends and no fighting."

The next day (that was 365 days) Francis and all his friends were let out of Prison, because it was the end of the year, and they all started home for Assisi. The Perugians wouldn't give them back their horses, so they had to walk. It took them a very long time; nearly all day. As he was walking along the road and thinking how nice it would be when he got home and could put on his Blue and Gold Cloak after having worn his Red and Silver one for a whole year, Francis saw a very poor old Raggy Man coming along to meet him.

" I *am* so cold! " said the man. " I used to have a fine red and silver cloak like yours, but I lost it. Now I am so poor I can't buy another one."

Now, although Francis did not know it, there were two people watching him, to see what he would do. One was Our Lord, Who was standing behind an Oak Tree quite close to the Raggy Man, and He said to Himself:

ST. FRANCIS OF ASSISI

"If Francis gives his Red and Silver Cloak to that Raggy Man it means that he is going to listen to that Dream that I sent him and that he is going to be on My side." The other person who was watching was Satan, and he was hiding behind a Gorse Bush and hoping that Francis would not see him, because he was so close. He had on a Red and Silver Cloak just like Francis' and he said to himself:

"If Francis *doesn't* give his Red and Silver Cloak to that Raggy Man it means that he is going to listen to that Idea I put in his head and that he is going to be on *my* side."

Francis thought: "I'll give him my cloak, if he really *has* lost his—no, I won't, because people will laugh at me if I go home without one—yes, I will, because I don't really need it, I've got the Blue and Gold one." So he said to the Raggy Man:

"Here you are, change clothes with me, mine are warmer than yours, and I am not a bit cold. And if I have the Raggy ones I can pretend to be you and give the people at home a Surprise."

So they both laughed and changed clothes and Francis went on to Assisi. Satan was so cross that his side hadn't won that he *stamped* on the ground behind the Gorse Bush and hurt his foot on a stone. Then he started to run along behind the hedge after Francis to see what he would do next, but he kept tripping over the Red and Silver Cloak, so he went home, muttering to himself. But Our Lord walked along beside Francis for a minute and said:

"Never mind if your friends won't talk to you if you are Raggy, you can be a friend of Mine, if you like, and that will be much more Special and Important."

So after that Francis always had on plain grey or brown clothes with a leather belt.

One day there was a poor old woman with a heavy bundle of vegetables that kept *on* coming undone. First a turnip rolled out; and then, when she was stooping to pick it up, out fell a beetroot; then four potatoes; then a carrot and three cauliflowers! Then she dropped the whole bundle all over the road and sat in the middle

of everything and began to cry! So Francis cheered her up and did up the bundle and gave her his leather belt to keep it all together. After that he always had a piece of rope instead of a belt, because it was more useful and much cheaper.

Now as soon as it was settled that Francis was going to be on Our Lord's side against Satan, lots of very Interesting and Exciting Things happened to him, and one of them was about a Wolf.

One day as he was walking along in his brown clothes and a rope for a belt he came to some workmen mending the road. So he thought he would stop for a minute and tell them about being very Poor here so as to be very Rich in Heaven.

"Because," he said, "if you were very Rich here it might make you Proud and Haughty, but you can't be Proud and Haughty in Heaven; nobody is, so it is much better to be Rich there. Besides, Heaven lasts so much longer."

But the workmen thought that it was such a long time to wait until they got to Heaven that they'd rather be Rich *now*. And Francis said:

"That is exactly like eating the Sugar on your Birthday Cake *first*, because then you have to eat *all* the Cake and there will be no Sugar at the end. If you eat the Cake first you can be as long as you like eating the Sugar, and you needn't have anything else to Spoil the Taste."

But the workmen thought that Francis was silly to try and make them be Poor when they were trying to be as Rich as they could.

Well now, about the Wolf. When he left the workmen Francis came to a town called Gubbio, where all the people were Misers! And he wanted to tell them about the Good Idea of being Poor. But there was no one there to listen! Francis thought that this was very funny, so he knocked at somebody's door and said:

"Where are all the people? I want to tell them something."

The lady who opened the door said:

"Oh! didn't you know? Nobody goes out of their houses unless heaps of us go together, because of the Wolf."

" What Wolf? " asked Francis.

" There's a Wolf who lives at the end of the Town," said the lady, whose name was Rina, " and every single day he eats somebody. He is the very Worst Kind of Wolf, because you never hear him coming, and suddenly he *Pounces* on you! You'd better mind out."

" How very Tiresome," said Francis. " I *am* sorry for you. I think perhaps I'd better go and speak to it and then perhaps it won't."

" No, don't," said Rina, " he'll only eat you, and that won't be any help at all."

But Francis started off in his Brown Clothes and his Rope and all the people looked out of their windows to see what he was going to do. He had just got to the End of the Town when suddenly the Worst Wolf he had ever seen Sprang out at him! Its mouth was open and its Red Tongue was hanging out, and its Paws were all ready to Knock him Over, and (Rina was quite right) it was Enormous!

Francis said:

" Wait! " in a very loud and sudden voice and the Wolf was so surprised that it stopped right in the middle of its spring. No one had ever said " Wait! " to him so suddenly; he didn't like it; it made him jump. Usually people tried to run away. Then Francis quickly made the Sign of the Cross and blessed the Wolf. This surprised him more than ever; no one had ever blessed him before and he liked it. He shut his mouth and wagged his tail and waited to see what Francis would do next.

" Brother Wolf," said Francis (the Wolf liked that too, no one had ever called him Brother before), " *Why* do you eat all these people? Don't you *know* that they're so frightened that they daren't come out of their houses?

And you've killed all their sheep and cows and things so that they're nearly starving."

"I know," said the Wolf, "I don't much *like* eating them; they're too thin; but there *isn't* anything else to eat, and I must eat *something*, I can't starve to death, can I?"

"Well, no," said Francis, "you can't. But perhaps you didn't know how Perfectly Abominable you are? You are the Very Worst Wolf I ever saw. If *I* promise *you* that you will always have enough to eat, will *you* promise *me* that you'll never eat people again?"

The Wolf wagged his tail and promised. Francis held out his hand and the Wolf put his paw into it and they Sealed the Bargain.

"Come back to the Town with me," said Francis, "and you'll see what I am going to do."

So the Wolf licked Francis' hand and trotted along beside him into the Town. As soon as they saw them coming, the people all ran into their houses and shut their doors, because of the Wolf.

"Come out!" said Francis. "I want to tell you something."

So the people all came out again and Francis said:

"Will you promise me to feed Brother Wolf always, if he promises never to eat anyone again?" And the People all promised and said, "Yes, we will." So Francis said:

"Well, I'll put you and Brother Wolf On Your Honours."

Then the Wolf held out his paw, and he and Francis shook hands again and all the people cheered.

If you want to know what happened to the Wolf after Francis had gone, he used to be like everybody's Dog, and he barked at tramps. But he got rather Fat because he had such a lot to eat.

When Francis went away from Gubbio, some of the young men who lived there went with him. They gave all their things to the very poor people and dressed like Francis did because of his Good Idea of being Poor. Some of them went to some towns and some of them went to others, so that they could tell everybody about the Good Idea.

Well, one day Francis and one of his friends called Anthony were going to a town called Rimini. (Anthony's home was in a place called Padua, like Francis' was Assisi, and he was the same St. Anthony who finds things for you when you have lost them.) But the people in Rimini wouldn't listen to them. They all went away and talked about something else, very loud, so that they could not hear what Francis was saying. So he and Anthony went down to the seashore (Rimini was at the sea-side), and Anthony said:

"Come out, Fish! I want to tell you something!"

And all the fish came and stood on their tails in the water, with their heads sticking out. The little fish were in front in the shallow water, and the middle-sized fish were in the middle in the middling-deep water, and the big fish were at the back in the deepest water, and there were even some Sharks and a Whale at the *very* back. And Anthony told them how lucky they were always to have something ready for them to eat. And they could even choose what coloured water they would live in: some blue; some grey; some green; and some brown like Francis' clothes. And they could live in Rivers if they did not like the Sea being salty, or Lakes, or Ponds. And he told them that it was God Who made it all nice and ready for them. The Fish were very pleased to hear this because they never knew who had made it nice and ready, and they had always wanted to know. Then Anthony

told them some Important Things about what Fish had done. Like the Haddock who brought a penny to Our Lord when He hadn't got one to pay His Taxes with. And now *all* Haddocks have a mark of a Finger and Thumb on their shoulders where St. Peter picked up the one that brought the penny.

While Anthony was talking, all the People of Rimini (who wouldn't listen before) came up behind him to listen now, because they had never seen such an Exciting Thing as those Fish standing up in the water. And they were sorry they had been rude to two people who did such Exciting Things.

Another day, when Francis was walking along the road with some of his friends, all dressed in their brown clothes and their ropes in case anyone's bundle came undone, they saw a flock of Starlings all twittering in a hedge. So Francis said to the Starlings:

" Stop twittering a minute, Birds! I want to tell you something! "

So they stopped and he told them (like the Fishes) how lucky *they* were to have everything ready for *them*, like Trees and Berries and Worms. And all sorts of other birds came and listened, and they sat on the trees and hedges and all over the ground so close together that the Youngest Thrush (the sort that hops about with a very short tail and yellow edges to its beak) hadn't any room, so it came and sat on Francis' head. Francis didn't mind, even though its toes *were* rather Pricky. Then he told them some Important Things that had happened to Birds. Like the Robin (who used to be brown all over) who was so sorry for Our Lord when He was on the Cross that he came and sat so close to Him that he pricked himself on the Crown of Thorns; and now all Robins have red breasts.

And about how the Holy Spirit pretended to be a Dove when He went to Our Lord's Baptism. The Doves liked this story so much that when all the other birds had gone away, they flew beside Francis and his friends all the way back to the house where they all lived together so that they could be as Poor as they liked without Bothering people. So they made nests for the Doves in the Garden, and they stayed there always.

Once Francis was teaching some people at Christmas time about when Our Lord was a Baby, and the people were being very stupid about it and they *couldn't* understand. So he took one of their babies for a minute, and sent a little boy for a big box, and a little girl for some hay. Then he put the hay in the box and the baby on the hay.

"There now!" he said. "Our Lord was like *that* and Our Lady was kneeling *here*, and St. Joseph was *here*, and the cows and St. Joseph's donkey that Our Lady rode on were *There*! *Now* do you see?"

And the people did. But afterwards they always had a Crib in their church at Christmas to remind them of what Francis had told them. Then other people thought that Francis' idea was so good that *they* had a Crib, too. Now everybody does, but it was St. Francis who Invented it. He Invented singing Carols, too, because he thought the Little Baby Lord would like them better than hymns.

St. Francis did lots of other Interesting Things that are written in other books. And he made such a lot of friends who liked his Good Idea about being Poor, that now there are Hundreds and Hundreds of them. I expect you have seen Friars (like French for Brother, like Francis called the wolf) or, anyway, Nuns, dressed in Brown with Ropes round their waists? Sometimes it is Grey, not Brown. Well, they are Franciscans,

called after St. Francis, and they are still very
Poor.

St. Francis' Special Day is on the 4th of October,
and heaps of people are called after him, even some
other Saints.

ST. ANTHONY

Once upon a time there was a priest called Anthony, and he was a great friend of St. Francis, and was with him when he preached to the Fishes.

One day Anthony was going along the road telling people that they ought to be Poor here so that they could be Rich in Heaven.

"It's no use getting Richer and Richer here," he said, "because when you die you've got to leave everything behind. You can't take anything with you at all, not even your own body! *But*," said Anthony, "if you collect Kindnesses and Sacrifices and things here and store them up in Heaven, when you die there they are all waiting for you, and all turned into whatever sort of Richness you like best, and *those* Riches you can keep for ever and ever and ever!"

And some people thought it was a Very Good Idea but some people thought it was Perfectly Ridiculous.

Well, as I was saying, Anthony (who is the same Anthony who finds things for you) was walking along the road when he came to a Stable Yard.

"I'll just go in and see if the Stable Man is a Christian," he thought, "but I won't actually ask him in case he's cross, but I rather want a drink of water so I'll ask if I can have one from the Stable Tap."

So Anthony went in to the Stable Yard and wandered about until he found the Stable Man.

"May I please have a drink from the Stable Tap?" he said. "It is Rather Hot, walking along the dusty road all day."

SIXTY SAINTS FOR BOYS

" Of course you can," said the Stable Man. " I'll get you a glass. There," he said, coming back, " you'll soon feel cooler now."

" Thank you," said Anthony, " it *is* nice of you to bother."

" Not at all," said the Stable Man politely, and he drew patterns on the ground with the toe of his Boot. After a bit, when they had Got Chatting, Anthony just happened to mention the Blessed Sacrament.

" There now," said the Stable Man, " there's a thing I never can believe. How can a round white piece of Bread turn into God just because the Priest says so? Silly, I call it."

" It would *be* Silly if you believed that," said Anthony, " but it isn't because a Priest says so but because *God* says so, and that is the Whole Thing."

" Even so I don't believe it," said the Stable Man, " it *couldn't* be true. If it was, anyone could go and talk to God in any church at any time."

" And so they can," said Anthony, " and that is what is so nice about being a Christian, if you don't mind my saying so."

" No, I don't mind," said the Stable Man, " but I *can't* believe it, somehow."

" Well, even that Horse that is looking over the Stable Door believes it," said Anthony.

" Rubbish! " said the Stable Man.

" If that Horse saw the Blessed Sacrament and bowed down and worshipped It all by himself, would you believe it then? " said Anthony, Keeping On at it.

" Yes, I would," said the Stable Man, " but if that is going to be your Proof, I must arrange it all my own way."

" All right," said Anthony.

" Well," said the Stable Man, " first I'll starve the

Horse for two whole days so that he will be very hungry. Then I'll stand one side of the Stable Yard with a Sieve of Oats, and you'll stand on the other side with the Blessed Sacrament and we'll let the Horse loose and see what he does."

" All right," said Anthony, and he went away to ask God to tell the Horse about the Blessed Sacrament so as to prove to the Stable Man that it was True.

After two days Anthony came back, carrying the Blessed Sacrament in a little Golden Box. He walked very Carefully and Quietly because he was carrying God, and he kept wishing that he was good enough for such an Honour, and he kept talking to God and saying he wished someone better was carrying Him.

Anthony went and stood at one side of the Stable Yard and went on loving Our Lord. Presently the Stable Man came along and stood at the other side. He was carrying a Sieve full of Fine Fat Oats. Then a Stable Boy opened the stable door and everybody who had come to see the proof craned their Necks and tried to see over each other's heads.

The Horse came slowly out and stood a minute, blinking in the Sun. Then he walked over to Anthony and Knelt down and put his Forehead to the Ground!

Anthony Blessed him and told him to go back to his Loose Box, which he did, without even looking at the Oats!

Anthony watched him go in at the Stable Door, and then turned round. There was the Stable Man, kneeling in front of him, because now he knew that God really is in the Blessed Sacrament. Anthony Blessed him, too, and he got up and went to feed the Horse while Anthony carried our Lord back to the Church and thanked Him very much for showing the Stable Man that it was True.

God did lots of other things for Anthony, and sometimes the Baby Jesus used to come and Visit him in his Room while he was Reading or Saying his Office. And that is why, in Statues of him, St. Anthony is nearly always carrying the Baby Lord and a Book.

St. Anthony's Special Day is June 13th, and I can think of Many People who are called after him.

St. Anthony

St. Anthony said:
" Now listen to me.
Here or hereafter
Poor you must be.

On earth or in Heaven
You may be rich,
But not in both.
So now choose which."

" Simply ridiculous,"
Some people said,
" Who wants to be rich
After they're dead?

" Make money now,
Never mind then—
This is the counsel
Of sensible men."

" Perfectly Splendid,"
Other folk cried,
And came out strong
On Anthony's side.

ST. ANTHONY

" Poverty now,
And riches then,
Is an excellent plan
For sensible men."

And which were right
Quite plain appears,
Now they've all been dead
Six Hundred Years!

ST. HERMAN JOSEPH

Once upon a time, in Cologne, which is a town in Germany, there lived a Very Poor Woman. And she had a little boy called Herman who was Five and who had Our Lady for his Special Person.

Every day on his way to School, Herman used to pass the Church of St. Mary in the town, and, whenever he could, he used to start out early so as to have time to go in and kneel in front of her Altar and talk to her. There was a Specially Nice Statue of her in that Church, with a Crown on and holding the Baby Jesus with His head on her shoulder. Herman loved that Statue and he used to wonder if Our Lady really looked like that.

One morning, while she was getting him ready for School, his Mother said:

"Look in your Satchel, Herman, and see what you have got for dinner to-day!"

Herman looked, and there, instead of his usual Crust of Bread (they were *very* poor, remember), was an Enormous Apple! It was all Rosy on one side and Yellow on the Other side and it had three lovely Leaves on its little stalk!

"Oh! Mummy! How *lovely*!" cried Herman, jumping up and down. "It will Spoil it to eat it, but won't it taste Gorgeous!" And he stroked his apple and kept looking at it until his Mother said:

"Hurry up now, darling, or you won't have time to visit Our Lady before School."

Herman put his apple carefully in his Satchel and

started off. But when he got outside he had a little look to see if it was quite all right. It was, quite.

He ran all the way to the Church partly because he was so happy about the apple, and partly because he wanted to have as much time as possible to tell Our Lady about it. When he got there he knelt and said his prayer and then sat back on his heels and looked at the Statue.

How lovely Our Lady looked! With her Crown, because of being Queen of Heaven, and her lovely Blue Cloak with stars round the edge, and her white and gold dress. She had such a Kind face and she was holding the Baby Lord so lovingly.

"Oh! Dear Our Lady!" said Herman, "I do wish I had something to give you. I have only got myself, and I don't suppose I could be much use to you, but you can have me if you like. I wish I could give you something more useful, because you are so Beautiful."

Then he had a Sudden Idea! And opening his Satchel, he took out his lovely Red Apple and held it out and said:

"Would you like my dinner, Our

333

Lady? It's a very Specially Nice one, and perhaps the Baby Jesus would like it."

And then Our Lady stretched out her hand and took the Apple and gave it to the Baby Lord, and they both smiled at Herman because he had given up his Very Best Apple.

You see, Our Lady had come herself to take the place of the Statue because she loved Herman visiting her before School, and Herman never knew that it was really Our Lady and not a Statue until the Very Last Moment!

When Herman grew up he was a Monk and he still had Our Lady for his Special Person. And one day he saw her again, only this time it was *she* who gave *him* something. It happened when he was praying and she came and gave him a Ring, to show that he belonged Very Specially to her, and she put it on his finger for him.

After that the other Monks called Herman " Herman Joseph," because St. Joseph specially belonged to Our Lady, too.

St. Herman Joseph's Special Day is on April 7th, and there are lots of people called after him, especially in America and Germany.

St. Herman Joseph

Herman Joseph, five years old,
Sometimes hungry, often cold,
I wish I'd seen you give away
Your special lunch that special day,
When Our Lady made herself
Like a statue on a shelf
To take your gift and help you pray
And send you happy on your way,
Herman Joseph, five years old,
Sweet as honey, good as gold.

LITTLE ST. HUGH

Once upon a time there lived a little boy called Hugh, and he was six years old. He lived in a house alone with his Mother, because his Father had died such a long time ago that Hugh could not remember him, even though he could remember when he was two.

Well, at that time the Christians and the Un-Christians were horrible to each other, specially the Un-Christians, so horrible that they lived in different parts of the Town; half for the Christians and half for the Un-Christians, so that they needn't see each other too much. They even had their own special shops and hotels, which was very silly because, after all, they were all *People* even if they were Un-Christians and Christians, so they weren't so different as all that. But a funny thing was that the Christians' School was right in the middle of the Un-Christian half of the Town; I can't think why, because you'd think that they'd have it in their own part. So, when the Christian children went to School they had to go through the Un-Christians' half, and no one liked that very much, but it couldn't be helped.

Hugh, although he was only six, used to go to School and back by himself because his Mother was very poor and couldn't take him because she had a lot of work to do. She used to give him some sandwiches for his dinner and sometimes an apple or a banana as well, done up in a parcel which he carried in his satchel. She always wanted him to put the parcel in last so that it would not get squashed with the books, but Hugh often forgot and put it in first. Usually he had beef sandwiches and honey sandwiches, but on Fridays he had egg ones because, although he did not *hate* fish, he liked egg much better.

At school, before they came home, the children used to have Compline, exactly like we do on Sundays (only, as they didn't go to school on Sundays, they had it on weekdays), and at the end the Bigger Boys used to sing a Latin hymn called " Alma Redemptoris Mater," which means " Kind Mother of our Redeemer." (Redeemer is another name for Our Lord.) Hugh had not got up to doing Latin yet, only the Bigger Boys did it, so he did not know what it meant, but he *loved* the tune and he used to hum it on the way home. Soon he began to know the words because they sang them so often at school, and so he sang them too, and hummed the part he didn't know. One day he asked an Older Boy called Clement, who used to walk home with him sometimes, what the words meant, and Clement, who lived near Hugh's house, told him that they were about Our Lady.

" Is it *all* about Our Lady? " asked Hugh.

" Yes," said Clement, " it's all about her being God's Mother and how she helps us when we can't do things ourselves."

Hugh was very pleased about this because when he was happy he always wanted to sing very loud, and he did not know any songs about Our Lady. He specially wanted to sing about her when he was going to and from school because he always asked her not to let him get Run Over at the Crossings, and she never did. So Clement taught him the song called " Alma Redemptoris Mater," and Hugh sang it all the way to school and all the way back again, every day, just as loud as he could.

Now the Un-Christians used to hear him singing when he was going through their part of the Town and they hated it because they thought that Our Lady wasn't a bit Special and that she couldn't help anyone, and anyway Hugh was a Christian and they hated Christians. So one day, when Hugh was on his way to school and was going along a very Dark and Narrow Street with bumpy cobble-stones all over it, some of the Un-Christians came out and told him to " Stop singing that silly song because they didn't like it in their part of the Town." But Hugh Knew that Our Lady *was* very Special, so he said:

" No, I won't stop singing, because it is *not* a silly song at all but a song about Our Lady-who-doesn't-let-me-get-run-over-at-crossings, didn't you hear the words? Besides, she *likes* me singing that song."

This was very brave of Hugh because the Un-Christians were all Grown-up, and he was Only Six, but just before he had answered the Un-Christians he had said to Our Lady:

"Would you please tell me something to say, *quick*, so that I needn't stop singing your song?" And so she did.

Next morning when Hugh came past, singing his song, the Un-Christians did a horrible thing. They caught Hugh when he was Walking along the Dark and Narrow Street and Killed him in the Throat and put him in a deep hole behind their houses!

When he didn't turn up at school that day no one minded because they thought perhaps he had got a cold and was Staying in Bed for Breakfast. And when he was late coming home for Tea his Mother didn't mind either, because *she* thought that he must have gone to have tea with Clement like he often did. So it wasn't till he was late for supper too that she began to wonder Where he Was. So she got supper all ready, and set Hugh's place at the table with his back to the fire in case he was cold coming in late. Then she put on her outdoor things and went to Clement's house to see Clement's Mother about it.

"Is Hugh staying to supper with you as well as tea?" she asked. "Because it is getting late and it is nearly his bedtime."

"But I haven't seen Hugh all day," said Clement's Mother. "Clement said he thought he must be Staying in Bed for Breakfast as he did not see him at school."

"But he *did* go to school," said Hugh's Mother. "I *know* he did because I remember that he forgot *again* and put his books on top of his sandwiches. I do wish he would not do that, it makes them all squashy."

" What a very Extraordinary Thing! I think we had better go out and look for him," said Clement's Mother. " Perhaps he has been Run Over at one of those nasty Crossings."

" I don't expect so," said Hugh's Mother, " because he always asks Our Lady not to let him be, and she never does."

Anyway, they went out and they looked *every*where and they couldn't find him. At last they asked some of the Un-Christians, but the Un-Christians were very frightened because they had killed Hugh, and so they said:

" No, we haven't seen him since he came past this morning, singing that silly song of his. Perhaps he has been kept in at School."

So Hugh's Mother said to Our Lady:

" Do you know where Hugh is? Because if you do, would you mind telling me, because I'm getting rather bothered, it is so late? I thought you might know because he sings your Special Song and you don't let him get Run Over at Crossings."

Our Lady did not *say* anything, but just then Hugh's Mother heard him singing " Alma Redemptoris Mater " quite close by. She looked about and found him in the deep hole behind the Un-Christians' houses and singing away like anything. She and Clement's Mother got him out, but they were very surprised that he kept on singing when he was killed, but they were very glad he did or they would never have found him.

When people heard that Hugh was still singing his song after he was dead they were very excited and everybody wanted to see. The Christians were very pleased that God had made Hugh do such a Surprising Thing, but the Un-Christians were very angry because they had been Found Out and would be put in Prison.

Then they took Hugh to the church and the next morning the priest said Mass for him before he was buried, like we always do to people when they die or are killed. But as soon as Mass was finished Hugh began singing again in the church! So the priest came and said to him:

"Hugh, *why* are you singing when you have been killed? Or aren't you dead at all?"

Then Hugh stopped singing and said:

"Yes, Father, I *am* dead, but God is letting me sing so that everybody will know how Special Our Lady is. She was always my Special Person because she looked after me on the way to school, and when the Un-Christians Killed me in the Throat and put me in a hole, of course my Mother could not find me. So Our Lady came to me and said, 'Sing my Special Song so that your Mother can find you, she has just asked me where you are. And then the Un-Christians will know that I really do look after you.' And then she put a grain of rice under my tongue so that I could sing when I was dead, and when a priest takes it out again she will come back, and take me to Heaven with her."

So the priest took the grain from under Hugh's tongue, and he stopped singing, and as soon as he had stopped Our Lady came for him and he went away to Heaven with her, and she looked after his Mother until it was time for her to go to Heaven too.

St. Hugh's Special Day is on the 18th of August, nice and near one of Our Lady's Special Days.

ST. RICHARD

O nce upon a time there were two Brothers, and they lived in Worcestershire, and they were Orphans. When the Older one was Twenty-One he had all the house and land and things that had belonged to his Father. But the man who had been looking after everything until he was Old enough had let everything go to Rack and Ruin. Well, the Elder Orphan did all he could to tidy things up, but there were too many Weeds and things, and he was Distracted.

"I *would* ask my Brother," he thought, "but he is such a Bookworm that he wouldn't be any Good." (A Bookworm is always Reading and Studying and all that. The Bookworm's name was Richard.)

Well, at last one day the Elder Brother came and said:

"Richard, I'm in an awful Muddle."

"Are you?" said Richard, "How?"

"Well, I simply can't Cope with all these Weeds," said the Elder Brother, "and the Pigs are thin and Miserable, and the cows are Weak. What *shall* I do?"

"I'll come and help," said Richard, and he put away his book.

"But you don't know *anything* about Farming!" said the Elder Brother.

"I can learn," said Richard, pulling on his Boots. "Come on!"

Richard weeded and ploughed and sowed and reaped and mowed until he was a proper Farmer's Boy. As

342

a matter of fact he got much better at it than the Elder Brother because of being a Bookworm. He knew all about what to give Thin Pigs, and the difference between Turnips and Mangolds, and why Horses mustn't eat Wheat, and the proper way of Shouting at Plough Horses. But he never learned how to keep Rooks from pulling up the corn to see if their Roots are all right. And nobody has, to this Very Day.

Once the farms and things were in Working Order Richard said to the Elder Brother (I have to keep calling him that because I don't know what his name was) —Anyway, Richard said:

"I should think that you could get on alone, now. I would like to go to Oxford and get my B.A." (a B.A. is a kind of exam. called a Degree).

So he did, and then he went to Paris and was a Priest, and then he came back to Oxford to teach. One day a very Interesting thing happened to him.

One of Richard's students, who lived at Abingdon, gave an Enormous Party to celebrate his passing his Exams. And Richard was there and heaps of other students, and they were all having a grand time. Suddenly, in the middle of the Feast, someone knocked at the Front Door.

Bang! Bang!

One of the servants went and opened it, and there was a Man on a Horse, looking very Majestic but not Stiff and Proud. (No, it wasn't the King.)

"May I speak to Richard, the Master?" he asked.

"Certainly, Sir," said the Servant, "won't you please come in? A boy will hold your Horse."

"No, thank you. Ask him to come out and speak to me," said the Man on Horseback.

"But he is the Guest of Honour at a Party we're having," said the servant. "I don't like to fetch him out. I'm sure he would wish you to come in and Rest and Eat."

" Ask him to come out here and speak to me," said the Man on Horseback.

" As you please, Sir," said the servant, and he went into the big Dining Hall, wishing that the Visitor wouldn't be so Difficult.

He told Richard about it, and Richard got up and went to the Front Door, wondering who it could be. But when he got there, no one was to be seen!

Feeling Puzzled, he went back to the Dining Hall and found everyone All Agog. What *do* you think had happened while he was out of the room?

A heavy piece of the ceiling had fallen bang on to his chair! If he had been there he would have been Killed Dead! Which was very Kind of God, wasn't it?

Well, Richard did heaps more things for years and years, until one day, when he was being a Parish Priest at Deal, in Kent, a Message came to him from the Archbishop of Canterbury, which said:

" Dear Father Richard,
    " Come to Canterbury Cathedral next Thursday, I am going to make you a Bishop.
                                    " From
                " Edmund, Archbishop of Canterbury."

Now Richard did not want to be a Bishop very much, he liked being a Parish Priest at Deal. But Orders are Orders and so, the next Thursday, he went to Canterbury Cathedral and he was made a Bishop.

" Now," said the Archbishop of Canterbury, when they were having lunch at the Archbishop's Palace, " how do you feel? "

"I feel rather Anxious," said Richard. "I suppose I must be Bishop *of* something? What place do you want me to go to?"

"Chichester," said the Archbishop of Canterbury; "you will find things a bit Tiresome there but you'll be all right."

So Richard went to Chichester, and found things a good deal Worse than Tiresome. This is what was happening:

Chichester and its Cathedral and all its houses and things belonged to King Henry III, and King Henry specially wanted a friend of *his* called Ralph to be the Bishop of it. So that he could have the money from the rents and things. Now that money was supposed to be the Bishop's for Expenses, to pay to have the Churches cleaned and mended, and the Cathedral organ kept oiled and to buy candles and incense and have the Priests' white things washed, and to buy food for the Poor-and-Raggies and a Thousand and One other things.

King Henry was very Angry with the Archbishop of Canterbury for sending Richard to Chichester instead of his friend, Ralph (who was a Greedy, Horrid sort of man, anyway), and he said:

"All right. *But* the Palace and the houses and things belong to *me*. So *I* will have all the rents, and my friend shall live in the Bishop's Palace. And no one in Chichester must let Richard live with them, and no one must lend him money."

So there was poor Richard. A Bishop with no money and not allowed in the Cathedral or anything! All the Priests round about were on his side, all the same, because they couldn't Abide Ralph.

Well, Richard, who was *very* poor now, found a very nice Priest called Simon, who was Parish Priest of Ferring. (I expect some of you have been to Ferring for your holidays, so you will know that it isn't very far from Chichester.) Simon was very kind to Richard, and proud to be able to look after his Bishop. In return Richard did the Gardening for him. (You remember how good he was at growing things and all that?) He was Especially Good at Budding and Grafting, which is making Grand-but-Weak plants grow better by joining them on to Common-but-Strong roots. (Like nearly all Roses are budded on to Wild Rose roots.)

One day Richard budded a very Special and Juicy Apple on to a Crab apple root.

"There, Simon!" he said, "I hope you'll have a fine apple tree in time. It won't die like it used to, now that it's got a Common Root." And he went away for some weeks, visiting all his Villages that were in his Bishopric. (A Bishopric is the land and people belonging to a Bishop. Like a Kingdom is the land and people belonging to a King. And an Empire to an Emperor.)

While he was away Simon had to do the Gardening, and every day he went to the new Apple Tree to see if the Bud was Growing. And it was. It grew well, and made a nice little Sprout on the top of the Crab Apple root.

And then . . .

Simon left the Garden Gate open! And when he was having his dinner some Sheep got in and Ate Off the Sprout!

Poor Simon! He *was* so Fussed.

"*What* will Richard say?" he thought, "and it was growing so beautifully, too." And he went to shut the Garden Gate.

When Richard came back he Consoled Simon.

"Never mind," he said, "I'll do another." And he

did, and this time it grew so fast that by the end of the Summer they had the most lovely Baked Apples for Supper.

Well, all this time King Henry was very Peevish about all the Bishop business.

" I want my friend to be the *only* Bishop," he said, " and not have that Richard going about, being a Bishop too."

So he wrote to the Pope. " I'm the King," he thought, " and the Top of England, and so the Pope will listen to me, and will do what I say. He will tell the Archbishop of Canterbury to take away his silly Bishop and let me have mine."

But the Pope wrote back a letter saying:

" Unless you take away *your* Bishop at once, I will Excommunicate you. And in future see that you obey the Archbishop of Canterbury."

King Henry had a dreadful Shock when the Pope's letter came!

" *Well!* " he said, " to think of writing like that to *me!* "

But he didn't want to be Excommunicated, and so he took away his Bishop.

Then the people of Chichester got ready for a Grand Procession. They all liked Richard very much, and were very sorry that he had had such a Mingy time. They hung Flags out of their windows and Decorated the streets and had a Band playing. And they sent a White Horse to Ferring for Richard, and he rode to Chichester in Pomp and Glory. Everybody cheered and the Organ in the Cathedral played and the choir sang the Te Deum (which is the special Thank you thing that we sing on Coronation Day, or when we don't have a War that we thought we were going to have, or something like that).

So, after all, Richard was the proper Bishop of Chichester, and he lived there happily ever afterwards.

St. Richard's Special Day is on April 3rd, and it is still one of our Favourite Names.

ST. SIMON

O nce upon a time there were a Mr. and Mrs. Something, and they lived at Aylesford, in Kent. No one seems to remember what their name was or anything about them except that they had a little boy called Simon.

Now Simon wanted to be some sort of Priest or Monk or something, but he couldn't think what kind to be. So he asked his Mother:

" Mummy, what sort of Priest shall I be? "

" Well, darling," said Mrs. Something, " I don't want you to be any sort just yet. You aren't old enough."

" But, Mummy," said Simon, " what sort shall I be when I *am* 'Old Enough? " Mrs. Something thought a minute:

" Be a Hermit," she said, " in the woods at the bottom of the Garden, Simon. Then you can come and sleep at home if it rains."

Simon didn't say much, and when he was a Little Older, but not Old Enough, he went down to the woods and found himself a Hollow Tree for a Cell. (A Cell is a tiny little house with only One Room in it.) He took a considerable time arranging his Cell, and when it was finished Simon said:

" Mummy, I am Nearly Old Enough now, so can I go and live in my Cell and be a Hermit to see if I like it? "

" All right, darling," she said, " don't Catch a Cold! "

So Simon went and lived in his Cell-which-was-a-Hollow-Tree, and he liked it so much that he never went home any more, even when it Rained. And his Mother soon got used to the idea.

Simon made a little Garden and grew cabbages and things and he talked to God nearly all the time because there was nothing much to take his thoughts off.

Now while Simon was being a Hermit in his Hollow Tree near Aylesford in Kent, there was a lot of Trouble in the Holy Land (which is Palestine). A lot of Enemies, called Saracens, were driving the Christians away from Jerusalem and Bethlehem and Nazareth and all those places. Now, of course, the Christians wanted to stay in the Places where Our Lord lived. " Why should we be driven out? " they said. So it turned into a War between the Saracens and the Christians. (Which was a very Bad Thing, all that quarrelling in Our Lord's Country.)

Well, two English Knights thought that they'd make a Pilgrimage to Mount Carmel (which is a Mountain not very far from Nazareth). They thought that if they went and prayed there perhaps God would give some Extra Help to the Christians. (Like he gave some Extra Help to a man called Elias there, but that is Another Story.)

So the Two Knights went to the Holy Land, and at last they got to Mount Carmel. After they had prayed for a Goodish Time they thought that they'd go for a walk and See what they could See. And they found several English Hermits there and chatted to them.

" I wish you'd all come back to England," said One of the Two Knights. " We are in rather a Muddle there just now, and if all you Holy Men come and live there God might be more pleased with England and give *us* some Extra Help, too! "

ST. SIMON

Well, after a time the Hermits decided that they *would* go back with the Two Knights, and they sailed home in a very Tossing kind of Ship and they all felt very Seasick.

When they got to England they were Rather Lonely because they'd been away for such a long time, and so they decided not to be Hermits any more, but All to Live Together in One House, and so they did. They built a Big Monastery at a place called Newnham, outside Cambridge, and they lived there and the people called them the Friars of Mount Carmel, or Carmelites.

Now while the Hermits were building their Monastery that they were going to Live Together in, Simon had stopped being a Hermit in a Hollow Tree Trunk and had gone to Oxford to get a Degree at the University. (A Degree is a thing you get if you pass your Exams nicely.)

The Carmelites had settled down by now and they wanted someone to go round and to start new Monasteries with more Carmelites in them, and they couldn't think who to send!

" Why not have that Holy Man called Simon? " said one of the Friars, " he's clever and has got a Degree at Oxford! "

" Which Simon? " asked the Head Carmelite, " there seem to be a lot of Holy Simons. What is his Surname? "

" No one seems to know his Surname," said the Friar, " he is the Simon-who-lived-in-a-Hollow-Tree, and he is living in Oxford now."

" Well, we can't very well call him The-Simon-who-lived-in-a-Hollow-Tree, can we? " said the Head Friar, " it would take Ages if we had to say that every time! Shall we call him Simon Tree? "

"Or Simon Trunk?" said another Friar (because the *Trunk* of Simon's Tree was Hollow).

"Or Simon Hollow?" said another Friar.

"Or Simon Stock?" said yet another Friar (a Stock is another word for a Trunk. Like Stalk and Stem, for Flowers.)

"Yes!" cried all the Friars. "Let's call him Simon Stock, the two S's go so well together!"

So Simon Stock went from Oxford to Newnham, in Cambridge, and was a Friar there, and one day an Interesting Thing happened to him. And this was the Interesting Thing:

He was praying for the Christians in the Holy Land when suddenly he saw Our Lady standing and watching him!

"Well, Simon," she said, "I've brought you something!"

"What have you brought me, Our Lady?" asked Simon.

"This!" said Our Lady, and she showed him a long piece of rough Brown Cloth with a Hole in the Middle. "You put your head through the Hole," she said, "and one end hangs down in front, and the other end hangs down behind. It is called a Scapular because it goes over your Shoulders." (Scapula is the Latin for a Shoulder.)

"But what is it for?" asked Simon.

"It is my Uniform," said Our Lady, "you haven't got a Habit yet for your Order, have you? Or a Name for it?"

"No!" said Simon.

"Well," said Our Lady, "you must call it the Order of the Blessed Virgin, after me. And whoever wears this Scapular, or one like it, will never go to Hell, because I always look after people who wear my uniform and who belong to me!"

Simon thanked Our Lady very much, and while he was looking at the Scapular Our Lady went away.

Simon hurried out of the Chapel and told the Others, and they were Overcome with Pleasure when they heard about not going to Hell. One of them went out and bought heaps of Brown Stuff and they all made Scapulars for themselves and put them on. And now all Carmelites (we still call them Carmelites even though their Real Name is the Order of the Blessed Virgin), well, they all have Brown Habits and Scapulars with White Cloaks, the Friars and the Nuns the same, except that the Nuns have Black Veils as well (like the Statues of the Little Flower). You did know that St. Thérèse of Lisieux was a Carmelite, didn't you? I expect a lot of you have been in Carmelite Churches and have seen the Friars at Mass or Benediction, haven't you?

Well now, about the Scapular. Of course everyone wanted to have one, even the people who weren't Friars or Nuns. So lots of Ordinary people had little ones to go under their clothes. You can have one if you like, but if you do you must keep some Special Rules, so perhaps you'd better wait, like St. Simon Stock, until you are a Little Older!

St. Simon Stock's Special Day is on May 16th. And girls called Simone can have him as well as the boys called Simon and Simeon.

ST. RAYMOND

Once upon a time there was a young man called Raymond and he lived in Barcelona in Spain, and he learned a lot of very Learned Things at the College there.

After a time he got so clever that he began teaching instead of learning, and he taught so well that the other Teachers used to come and ask him things!

Now this was an Unusual Proceeding (which means that it did not usually happen) and so Raymond began to get Vain!

" *I'm* teaching the Teachers! " he said to himself. " The poor teachers have to ask *me* before they go and teach Other People! " But although he was Vain he was still very Clever.

One day he met a young friend of his who was Pretty Clever, too, and he said to him:

" Why don't you be a Teacher yourself? You could earn Any Amount of Money? "

" Well," said the friend, " I had thought of being a Priest."

" What on earth for? " said Raymond. " Don't be so silly, my dear boy, you'll never have any money and you'll never make a Name for yourself! "

" I don't want to make a Name for myself, specially," said the young man, " I want to work for God." (Making a Name for yourself, in case you don't know, is when Everybody has Heard about you and lots of them Talk about you and some of them remember your Name.)

ST. RAYMOND

"Everyone knows *my* Name!" said Raymond, Grandly, "and I like it! Have you actually *decided* to be a Priest?"

"Not Actually," said the young man, who hadn't much Backbone (which means that he was Rather Spineless), "but I've been thinking of it for Ages!"

"I shouldn't if I were you!" said Raymond. "Come with me and I'll make you a Teacher of Teachers!"

So the young man did, and he never was a Priest, but he got very Vain and Selfish.

One day Raymond was thinking about the young man.

"He isn't much use as a Teacher," he thought, "he's too Selfish, and that makes him Rather Stupid. If only I'd left him alone he'd probably have made an Excellent Priest by now."

Then he thought:

"I wonder if God minds me having taken a Priest away from him?" Raymond hadn't thought very much about God up to now, he had been too Busy teaching. But he began to get Rather Worried about the young man, and so he went to Confession and asked the Priest about it.

"Well," said the Priest, "it was a very Bad Thing to do that! If the young man had been a Priest he would have had a better life and pleased God. Now he is Vain and Selfish, and he has forgotten God, and it's all your Fault!"

"What must I do then?" asked Raymond in a Fright. He hadn't thought that it was as bad as that!

"You must give God something to Make Up," said the Priest, "now go in Peace and God Bless you!"

So Raymond went to another part of the Church and said his Penance, and then he thought:

"What *can* I give to God? I haven't got anything

355

so valuable as a Priest. The only thing that is as valuable as a Priest is another Priest, and I haven't got one!" He got up; knelt to the Blessed Sacrament and walked slowly out of the Church.

"I know!" he thought as he went down the steps outside. "I'll be a Priest myself, and God can have me instead of him!"

So Raymond went and was a Dominican (which as you know is a Friar of the Order of St. Dominic), and he had a White Habit with a Black Cloak, and he was a very holy man when once he got Used to it.

But although he was only a Friar now, Raymond was still a very Clever man and soon the Bishop heard things of him and came to ask his Advice. Then he became the Head Dominican of All, and Kings and Councillors did what he said.

Now King James of Aragon in Spain liked Raymond very much and wanted him to be in the Palace always, and Raymond was whenever he could, but he hadn't much time.

One day King James said to Raymond:

"I'm sure that you need a Holiday, you work so hard. Come with me to my Palace in Majorca for a few weeks. The Queen can stay here and look After things until we get back."

Raymond was very tired, and so he thanked King James very much and said that he'd love to go. So they and some of the Courtiers and Councillors got into a boat and sailed to Majorca, which is an Island not too far from Spain.

But when they got there a Pretty Lady met them in the Palace and King James said:

"My dear, allow me to introduce my great friend Father Raymond, O.P.!" and he turned to Raymond and said:

"Raymond, this is my Queen!"

"But," said Raymond, "the Queen is in Barcelona in Spain! Don't you remember that we left her behind to Look After things?"

"I know," said King James, "*that* Queen is in Barcelona. But *this* Queen is the Queen I have in Majorca!"

"But you *can't* have two Queens!" said Raymond, making a Shocked face. "No one is allowed to have more than one Wife. Even Kings. It is a Mortal Sin, your Majesty, and you must stop it at once!"

"Well, I'll send her away to-morrow!" said King James, and they went in to Supper.

But the next day the other Queen was still there, and Raymond reminded the King about his promise to send her away.

"I will to-morrow," said King James.

But he didn't.

"If she hasn't gone by Supper time, your Majesty," said Raymond, "I shall go back to Spain and leave you."

"Oh, no!" said King James, "*Please* don't, Raymond. Because if you do, who will help me when I get in a Muddle?"

"You're in a Muddle now," said Raymond, "but you aren't listening to me."

"I know," said King James, "but please don't go!"

"Well, send her away, then," said Raymond, in a Stern Voice, and he went to say his Office.

After supper the Queen was still there.

"Good-bye, your Majesty," said Raymond. "I'm going, as I said I would."

King James was very angry.

"You can't go because I won't let you have a Boat!" he said, and he commanded that anyone who helped Raymond to leave the Island of Majorca should have his head Chopped Off!

357

Raymond laughed.

"If the King of Aragon won't help me," he said, "I'm sure the King of Heaven will!"

He went across the Sand to the edge of the Sea.

"Now, dear Lord," he said, "*please* will you help me because I told King James that you would!"

"Certainly I will!" said God, "put your Black Cloak on the water and stand on it. If you hold up one corner of it, it will work like a Sail!"

"Will it really?" cried Raymond, very Surprised. And he took off his cloak and Spread it on the Sea and then he stood on it. It didn't sink or even get wet. It felt just like a boat. He stooped down and picked up a corner of the cloak, like God said, and he held it up in front of him. The wind filled it like a Sail and he sailed across the Sea to Barcelona Ninety Miles away!

When King James heard what had happened he sent away the Other Queen and came home at once. He built a Chapel at the place where Raymond landed and he made a high Tower beside it so that people could see it from a long way off. Perhaps you will see it for yourself one day if it hasn't been Knocked Down by all the fighting that they have had in Spain.

St. Raymond's Special Day is on January 3rd, and lots of people are called after him, especially in Spain.

ST. PHILIP

Once upon a time there was a doctor and he lived in Italy and his name was Philip. His surname was Benizi, so his patients called him Doctor Benizi when he went to see them while they were ill, but we don't.

Now a doctor's work is very much God's work, and Christian doctors and nurses and people of that kind pray a good deal, not so much in Churches and things as when they are actually working. If they are not sure what is the matter with anyone, and especially if they are afraid of hurting anyone, they ask God to stand beside them and use their hands to do whatever it is, and He does, and it doesn't hurt nearly so much that way. And that is Quite True.

Philip was always a bit worried that he hadn't very much time *only* for God.

"If I had a little more time to myself," he thought, "I could get to know God so much better. When I am working with my ill people I know he is there very often, but I have to think of what I am doing. I would really much Rather be a friar or a monk or a priest or something."

One day Philip was praying in a Church, and he was looking at a Crucifix there.

"I wish, God," he said, "I knew whether you wanted me to go on being a doctor, or to go and live only for you. I do wish I knew."

And then a very Unusual Thing happened.

The figure of Our Lord on the Cross spoke to Philip and said:

359

" Philip, if you go to my Mother's servants who live on the hill you will be doing what I want you to do."

So Philip thanked God very much for telling him what to do and he went out of the Church and up the hill to the Priory that was there. Now the friars who lived there were the sort who are called the Order of the Servants of Mary (but we call them Servites for short, and they have an All Black Habit. I hope you remember what a Habit is?)

When Philip asked the Father Prior if he could please live with them and be a Servite the Father Prior said:

" Of course you can. But you will find it is a Hard Life, and it will be Some Time before you can be a priest."

" But I would rather not be a priest, please Father Prior," said Philip, who had not a very great opinion of himself, " I would like to work here and be a servant of the Servants of Mary."

So for a long time Philip was the Gardener, and he was very happy. He used to ask God to help him to grow vegetables for them all, and a fine Kitchen Garden he made. But when people came and admired the rows of cabbages and carrots and things he said:

" Yes, don't they look lovely? All the vegetables are God's work, but I am afraid all the weeds are mine! "

Well, one day the Prior found out that Philip was really very clever, and he said that he must be a Priest. So Philip, (although he still thought that he was too Unimportant) worked very hard and passed his examinations and was a Priest, but he was very shy of saying his first Mass.

" But Father Philip," said the Father Prior, " you must begin sometime. After all, that is one of the Chief Reasons for being a Priest."

" I know, Father Prior," said Philip, " but it is such

a Great and Wonderful thing to say Mass. I am not good enough to hold Our Lord's Body in my hands."

"Nobody is," said the Father Prior, "but we must just be the best we can, with God's help."

But Philip kept putting it off and putting it off and weeks went by, and he still felt that he couldn't touch the Body of Our Lord at the Consecration because he wasn't even good enough to *think* of it.

At last the Father Prior sent for him.

"Now Father Philip," he said, "you will say Mass on Whit Sunday, we will all pray for you, and it will be quite all right."

"Yes, Father Prior," said Philip, because of obeying the Next One Up.

So at Pentecost, Philip, in his red vestments, began to sing a High Mass, and the other friars sang in the choir. When he got to the Sanctus which is the beginning of the most important part of Mass, a whole Choir of Angels sang the Sanctus so beautifully that the friars and all the people in the Church stopped singing to listen. Which was very Kind of God, because it made Philip feel much less Nervous and Worried, and he loved saying Mass after that, but that was the only time they heard the angels singing.

Although Philip always had a very poor opinion of himself, the other friars had not. And as time went on, although he would really Rather Not, Philip was the Head Servite of all and he used to go about visiting the different Priories to see how all the Brothers were getting on.

One day, he visited a priory in a part of the country where there had been a lot of fighting, and all the friars came to the door to meet him. Philip (who was a doctor you remember) was Horrified at their Pale Ill faces and their thinness.

"Really," he thought, as they all went into the Refectory at supper time, "it's all very well to be poor, and it's all very well not to be Greedy, but I *must* tell them to eat more or they will all Die of Starvation and be no use to anybody."

But when they were all in their places Philip saw that the table was Set ready with plates and spoons and things, but there was nothing at all to eat! He looked at the Prior, who said:

"I am very sorry, Father that we have nothing to offer you, we have had scarcely anything at all to eat for some time, and yesterday we ate the Last Crumb!"

"But why?" asked Philip, "where's your Brother Gardener? and where is the Brother who ought to go and buy flour and things?"

"We have no more money to buy even cabbage seeds," said the Prior, "and even if we could get seeds the cabbages would not grow in time. You see, Father, because of the fighting, all the people have gone away and the fields are spoiled."

Now I don't know if you know that Friars have nothing of their own. All they have is what people give them. And if no one gives them anything, well then they don't have anything. Carmelites are Friars and so are Dominicans and so are Franciscans and so are the Austin Friars and so are the Servites. And so these poor Servites had used up all they had, and they had nothing left and they were Starving.

As soon as Philip found out that it was not their fault that they had got into such a Parlous State, he looked down the long table at all the thin faces and said:

"Brothers, come with me to the Chapel and we will ask Our Lady if she will please remember her Servants and look after them."

So they all went to the Chapel and Philip asked Our Lady to come and help them or else to tell them what she wanted them to do. While they were praying they heard somebody knocking at the Front Door and the Brother Doorkeeper went to see who was there.

When he opened the door he couldn't see anyone at all, but there on the doorstep, were two great hampers

full of loaves of bread! He was so surprised that he left them there and ran back to the Chapel.

"Father Philip!" he said, "there's bread! Bread on the Doorstep!"

The other friars looked at him and thought:

"Poor Brother, Starvation has gone to his head!"

But Philip said "Thank you" to Our Lady and said:

363

" Well Brothers, don't look so surprised, haven't you just been asking Our Lady for something to eat, did you think she wouldn't listen? "

And they all went back to the Refectory and had a good Supper of new White Bread.

Sometimes God did miracles for Philip with Ill People (because he was a doctor as well as a priest), and one day he cured a man with a very Catching Illness called Leprosy. But he did not want anyone else to know about it in case they might think he was very holy, so he and a priest called Father Victor, who was travelling with him, hurried on to the next town. As soon as they got there they could see that something unusual was going on because of all the Noise and Chatter.

" What is happening? " they asked a Man in the Street.

" The Cardinals are going to choose a new Pope," said the Man in the Street, " and we can think and talk of nothing else, it is so Exciting."

" Thank God for that," thought Philip, " now they won't hear about the Man with the Leprosy and think that it was *my* Holiness that cured him. They never seem to see that it is God who does it and just uses my hands." Philip was still Shy and Humble, you see, and he couldn't bear it when people said that he was Good.

" I'm not! " he used to say. " If only you knew what I was really like you would never say that again."

But in spite of everything the Cured Man came into the town and of course he began to tell the people about Philip's miracle. Soon the Cardinals heard about it and they began to wonder if perhaps God had sent Philip to the town just at that time because He wanted him to be the next Pope. So one of the Cardinals went to Philip and asked him whether he would agree if they elected him to be the next Pope.

"No!" said Philip. He was quite Horrified at the idea. "I couldn't possibly be the Pope. I am not holy and I am no good at governing, and I would be no good at all if I were Pope. Really, I was happiest of all when I was the Gardener of the Servants of Mary."

And quickly, before the Cardinals could make him be the Pope, he left the town and went to a cave that he knew about and he hid there for three months. (That is why statues of St. Philip generally have a Pope's Crown on the floor by his feet to show that he could have had it to Wear, but didn't.)

While they lived in the cave, Father Victor used to go and collect food for the two of them and people thought that he was alone, and nobody suspected, for a long time, that Father Philip was there too. He was very happy in the cave on the mountain side; it reminded him of the time when he was a Gardener.

Philip did so many interesting things, and so many Extraordinary things happened to him that I would use up too many pages even if I told you some of them. But if you really want to know, you will find them all in other books.

But one thing I *will* tell you: Every year on August 23rd, before Mass (in Servite Churches), a little pile of loaves of bread are put on the side of the Altar and they are blessed and then Handed Round to the people to remind them of the bread that appeared on the doorstep of the Starving Friars. Did you know that? And water is blessed too because of another miracle that I haven't told you about, but somebody else will I have no doubt. And another thing is that Servites are all very humble and have No Great Opinion of themselves, and that is why we never hear very much about them. But I think that at the End of the World we will all hear a Good Deal.

St. Philip's Special Day is on August 23rd (the day that the Bread and Water are blessed) and hundreds and thousands of people are called after him, even other Saints. Girls named Philippa may, if they like, belong to Doctor St. Philip, but there is a St. Philippa.

ST. ALOYSIUS

Once upon a time there was a little boy called Aloysius whose Father was a Marquis and a Soldier.

On his Fourth Birthday his Father gave him a Whole Army of tin soldiers, with their Swords and their Tents and their Cavalry and their Infantry and their Cannon and their Gun-carriages and their Different Regiments. Like Hussars and Dragoons and London Scottish and the Grenadiers. (Only they weren't really those actual Regiments because the Gonzagas were Italian, so they had Italian regiments.)

The Cannon really Worked. I mean they were made like real Cannon and they had tiny Cannon-balls which knocked over the soldiers, but they didn't really explode in case Aloysius hurt himself, because he was Only Four.

Aloysius *loved* his Army. He used to have Battles all day long all over the Nursery floor. He used to divide them in half and have one half for the Enemy, and His Side always won because the Enemy had no one to fire off their Cannon for them.

Aloysius got so good at making Battles, that his father the Marquis said that he would take him with him when he was Five, to gather together a Real Army to fight with the Tunisians.

So, on his Fifth Birthday, Aloysius began to ask his Mother if he could go yet? Now his Mother did not want him to go away, with only the soldiers to Look After him and Bath him and Cut up his Dinner, so she always said:

"Not yet, Darling, wait till your Father sends for you." Because she hoped that his Father would forget. And every day Aloysius asked her the same thing, and every day she answered the same thing.

At last, one evening, just when Aloysius had gone to bed, the Marquis came Home.

"Where's Aloysius?" he shouted, "I want him," and he Stamped About with his sword clanking on his Armour and all the ornaments on the mantelpiece shook and rattled.

"Hush, dear, don't make such a noise," said Aloysius' mother, "he's gone to bed, you'll wake him up!"

"I can't help that," said the Marquis, who was a man of Stern Qualities, "I really must see him now!" And he Stamped About some more.

So Aloysius came downstairs in his dressing-gown and bedroom-slippers and his hair all untidy, to see why his Father wanted him.

"There, my boy!" said the Marquis, very loud, "what do you think of that, eh?" And he showed Aloysius a very Big Parcel. His Mother helped him to undo the string, and there, inside, was a little suit of Armour, just the right size for him, and a Helmet to match. Aloysius was so Enraptured that he did not know what to do next! He put on the Armour and the Helmet and then he ran about the room, and made noises like a Bugle and a Drum, until his mother said he was getting Too Excited and he Really Must Go Back to Bed. Aloysius didn't want to go a bit, but his father said very loud:

"Now, my boy, Orders are Orders in the Army! Up you go!" So he had to.

Next day the Marquis went away to gather together the Army to fight the Tunisians, and Aloysius went too!

The first thing Aloysius did when he found himself alone at the Barracks (a Barracks is a big place where soldiers live) was to find an Arquebus, which is an old sort of gun, and to Fire it off. He didn't know that it would fire backwards too, his toy ones didn't, and he burnt off all his hair and eyebrows, and his face was covered with black Gunpowder and he looked like a Bald-headed Golliwog! The soldiers all laughed at him, but the Marquis wasn't at all pleased, because he said the Child Might have Killed Someone! So Aloysius left the Arquebuses alone after that.

One day, all the soldiers were having their After-dinner Rest, and Aloysius was too. But he got tired of lying down, so he got up and wandered about the Barracks Square where the Cannon were, with their piles of Cannon-balls beside them.

" Well, how funny! " he thought, " these guns look just like the ones in *my* Army! I wonder if they load the same way? "

The Cannon-balls were very heavy and Aloysius nearly couldn't lift one, but at last he managed to load the Cannon.

" I wonder if it Fires Off the same as my ones? " he thought, and he tried to see if it would. It did! There was an Enormous Explosion and Aloysius was knocked over backwards and rolled under the gun-carriage.

When he felt a little better he looked out through the wheels and saw all the soldiers lining up and the officers putting on their swords and the Marquis shouting orders and the sentries running about and Everything all very Hurried and Exciting! Suddenly the Marquis looked across the Barracks Square and saw Aloysius' Cannon still smoking! He rode up and saw Aloysius hiding underneath! He pulled him out, and in a Terrible Voice asked him what had happened. Aloysius told him, and the Marquis was very Roaring and Angry and said he must be Punished very Severely for giving them all such a Fright. They had thought that the Enemy had Suddenly Attacked them! But all the soldiers, who thought it was very Funny, asked if he might be let off, so he was. But the Marquis said he Couldn't Possibly have him at the Barracks any more, and he was sent home, but he talked like the soldiers, very Loud and Ordery, and his mother was shocked.

Aloysius then lived at Home until he was old enough to be a Marquis and a soldier like his Father, but when he was Grown-up, he became a different sort of soldier, and this was the sort:

Did you know that the Pope had an Army? Well, he has; a proper Army with a proper General. Most of the Soldiers in it are Priests as well. And the Pope sends them out to All the Countries in the World to fight for Christ the King against Satan and Heresies and Paganism and Heathenism, which are all very long words for things that hurt Our Lord very badly. So you see why these Soldiers have to be Priests as well, because if they happen to be fighting in a country that is on Satan's Side and some of the people suddenly want to Change Sides, well, there is a Priest all ready to tell them about it! These Soldier-Priests are always being Killed by their Enemies, but one of their rules is that *they* are not allowed to kill their Enemies in case God is not quite ready for them yet. The name of the Pope's regiment or Army isn't the Coldstream Guards or the East Yorkshires or something, but the Society of Jesus. And the Priest-Soldiers are called Jesuits and they are Very Brave Men.

So when he was eighteen Aloysius became a Jesuit, and he loved God so much, and did so much for Him, that when he was twenty-three God let him go to Heaven so as to be nearer to Him, instead of having to wait until he was an old man. If he hadn't gone to Heaven so soon, people thought that he would have ended by being a General, he was so good at being a soldier. But Aloysius was glad, and went one morning just after having had Holy Communion.

St. Aloysius Gonzaga's Special Day is June the 21st, and if anybody is called Louis or Lewis or Louisa or Louise, then it can be one of their Special days, too; specially if it is their Birthday.

ST. CHARLES

Once upon a time there was a boy called Charles, and he lived in Lombardy in Italy, and his surname was Borromeo. His father's name was Gilbert Borromeo, and his Mother's name was Margaret Borromeo, and his Uncle was Pope Pius IV! (What is the name of the Pope we have got now?)

Well, the Borromeos were very Rich Indeed, and they lived in a Castle, and Charles had Velvet Top clothes and Silk Underclothes, and he had a Handmade Carpet in his Sumptuous Bedroom. (Sumptuous is very Fat and Rich-and-Rare.)

But in spite of their wealth, Gilbert Borromeo wanted Charles to be a Priest and so he was sent to a Seminary (which is a School for Priests) when he was only Eleven.

When he was Twelve Charles's Uncle Julius gave him Thousands of pounds every year for his own to keep.

"I suppose," said one of his Teachers, "that you will stop going to be a Priest and be a Gentleman of Leisure, now?"

"I don't see why," said Charles. "A Rich Priest would be useful because he could put lots of money in the Poor Boxes!"

So he went on learning to be a Priest, and when he was Twenty his father, Gilbert Borromeo, died and left him Half of all his money, and the other Half went to Charles's brother Frederick.

So now Charles was Very Rich Indeed and his Teacher said:

ST. CHARLES

" Well, Charles, now that you are Very Rich Indeed, are you going to be a Priest next year, or would you rather be a Gentleman of Leisure? "

" I'm going to be a Priest," said Charles, " a Very Rich-Indeed-Priest needn't always be asking for money before he begins the Sermon."

So Charles was a Priest, and he went to a Village and looked after the people.

But when he was Twenty-three King Philip II gave him Four Thousand pounds a year and made him a Prince! Then another Uncle whose name I don't know, died, and left him a Fortune!

Then, because he was Rolling in Money, his Uncle the Pope said:

" Really, Charles, you would be much more useful in a Town than in a Village, with all that Money! " and he made Charles into the Cardinal Archbishop of Milan and gave him a lovely Red Hat! (Cardinals always have Scarlet clothes and hats.)

So Charles went and lived in a Palace, and when he was all Settled in, his brother Frederick died and left him the Other Half of his Father's money, *and* the Castle that he lived in when he was a little boy!

Charles was now as Rich as Crœsus (who was the Richest Man there ever was) and all the people said:

" Really, a Cardinal has no business to be so Rich! Look at all the Poor-and-Raggies round about who need help! "

They didn't know that Charles gave *all* his money away to Poor-and-Raggies, and that, although he lived in a Palace because he had to, he lived on Bread and Water and slept on the Floor. Under his Scarlet Robes he wore very Rough-and-Ready Clothes.

And why do you suppose he did this when he could have lived in Clover? Because of St. Francis. Do you remember St. Francis and how he said that people ought to be Poor on Earth so as to be Rich in Heaven?

Our life, said St. Francis, is rather like having Suet Pudding and Treacle. If you eat up your Treacle first you've got to Stodge through all the Suet Pudding which has been getting cold. And all the Others will have finished their Dinners and perhaps even have Left the Table and will have started playing something Exciting. And there you sit with your Horrible Cold Pudding while Nanny clears the table round you and leaves it all Bare and says:

" Now hurry up! You've got to stay there till you finish up Every Bit! " (I wonder if that ever happens to *you*? It used to happen to me when *I* was little.)

But if you eat up your Suet Pudding while it is still Hot it isn't so bad as all that, and then you have the Lovely Treacle all melting and runny on your Hot Plate, and you forget about the Pudding because the Treacle is so Sumptuous!

So if we Grab all the Nicenesses while we are here on Earth and never mind about being unselfish and things, when we die, God will say:

" And now what about the Suet Pudding? " and we will have to go to Purgatory for Ages and Ages while the Others will have finished theirs and will be having a Gorgeous time in Heaven.

On the Other Hand, if you share your things and do things for Other People, specially when you don't want to, and all that Sort of Thing, when you die God will say:

" No more Suet Pudding! " and you will be able to have a Sumptuous time in Heaven for ever and ever!

All that is what St. Francis said, and Charles thought that it was such a Good Idea that he always ate his Suet Pudding first. So that is why he didn't buy heaps

of things for himself, but was really very Poor and
Humble.

Charles was very Tall and Thin, and he was always
smiling. The Poor-and-Raggies loved him, the Jews
blessed him and the Protestants adored him. Only
the Rich People (Jews, Protestants or Catholics) hated
him because he made them feel as Selfish as they
were.

Now in Milan (which, you remember, was the town
where Charles was Cardinal Archbishop) there were
some Franciscans. You know what they are, don't
you? They are the Order invented by St. Francis and
the Friars wear Brown Habits with bits of Rope for
belts and bare feet and Sandals. And they are very
Poor here on Earth so as to what? Yes! Well, one day
Charles went and visited the Franciscans in Milan,
and he found that they were not Obeying Rules!

"What's all this?" he asked, "I've *never* seen a
Franciscan Friary like this one! Why have you got
Cushions on your Chairs, and nice Warm Socks and
lovely Hot Dinners and a Sumptuous House?"

"Well," said the Head Franciscan, "we tried all
St. Francis's ideas at the beginning, but we were *so*
Cold and Uncomfy, and we were getting Rather Thin,
so we thought that we'd just live like Ordinary People!"

"Well, you can't!" said Charles. "You *must* obey
the Rules or else you must stop being Franciscans. I
never *heard* of such a thing!"

Most of the Friars were sorry because they hadn't
really wanted to be Rich, but they had Copied the
Others. But four of them were Raging!

"Turning us out of our Comfortable Home!" they
said. "*He* is Rich enough, but no one turned *him*
out! Fancy making us obey those stupid Rules of St.
Francis!"

So they packed up their Traps and left the Friary that very day. As they tramped along the road one of them, a Fat one, said:

" People like Charles oughtn't to be allowed! "

" Well, we can't do anything about it. He's the Cardinal! " said Another who was Rather Thin.

" I wish someone would Kill him," said a Tall Friar. " Couldn't we pay someone to? "

" I should think we could," said a Short one; " isn't it lucky that we saved all our Money and brought it with us? "

" It would be Cheaper if one of us did it," said the Fat one, " because then we could keep all the money! "

" Let's Draw Lots! " said the Rather Thin one, and he picked Four Pieces of Grass and made them all different lengths.

" Whoever has the Longest must do the Killing! "

The Rather Thin Friar held the four bits of Grass in his hand with the ends sticking out.

" You first! " he said to the Fat One. The Fat Friar pulled out a piece:

" It looks Rather Long! " he said sadly.

" Now you! " said the Rather Thin Friar to the Tall one.

" Mine's shorter than yours! " he said to the Fat one, " so I won't be the one! "

" Now you! " said the Rather Thin Friar to the Short one.

" Mine's Very Short! " said the Short one, and he waved it happily.

Then the Rather Thin Friar opened his hand and looked at his own piece of Grass. Then they measured them.

" Mine is the Longest," said the Fat Friar, " I knew it was! " And he looked a bit Worried.

So they all went on until they came to an Armourer's Shop and there they bought a Gun. They gave it to the Fat Friar, whose name was Brother Farina (which means Flour like you make Bread with). It seems an Extraordinary Name, but then he was rather an Extraordinary Friar.

When they got to the Cathedral at Milan it was just time for a Procession of the Blessed Sacrament, and they went in quickly and kept close together so that people wouldn't see the Gun.

The Organ began to play and Charles came in in a beautiful Cope with lots of Gold Embroidery on the back. (You have often seen Copes, so I needn't tell you what this one was like except that it had very heavy Knobby sort of gold Work on it.)

Charles knelt in front of the Altar, and while the people were singing "O Salutaris Hostia", Brother Farina pulled the Trigger of his gun and it went off with a Terrific Report! The Bullet whizzed down the Nave and hit Charles in the middle of his back! It really was a very Good Shot! But it hit one of the Knobbiest bits of gold embroidery on the Cope and bounced off and buried itself in the wood of one of the Front Pews!

Now the bullet had hit Charles with such a bang that all the breath was knocked out of him, and he Fell Over on his face.

"I wonder if I am Mortally Wounded?" he thought to himself. "I'd better keep still a minute and see." So he lay quite still while he recovered his Breath.

But all the people thought that he *had* been killed and they all got up and Rushed About and looked for the Murderers and picked up Charles.

By this time Charles knew that he wasn't a bit Hurt, and he was Shocked at the way that the people were behaving in Church!

"Remember where you are!" he said Sternly. "Even if I *had* been Killed you shouldn't make all this Noise! Go back to your places, and we'll go on with the Procession!" And they did, and at the end they said a Special Prayer of Thanksgiving to God for stopping Charles from being Killed.

But it happened that some policemen had heard the Loud Report and had come running up to the Cathedral to see what it was all about. And Brother Farina and the Tall Friar and the Rather Thin Friar and the Short Friar ran right into their arms and were Bundled into Prison!

Charles did a lot of other things that you can read about another time, and perhaps one day you will go to Milan in Italy where he was Cardinal Archbishop, and there in the Cathedral you will see a Statue of him made of Solid Silver.

St. Charles Borromeo's Special Day is on November 4th, which is easy to remember because it is the day before Guy Fawkes' Day.

BARNABAS OF COMPIÈGNE

Once upon a time there was a dear little man called Barnabas. He was frightfully good at playing a Special Game with balls and knives called Juggling. He dressed in a very funny way, too. Everything was blue or white (you will see why in a minute). One shoe was blue and the other white, and so were his stockings and sleeves. His hat was white, and he had a blue handkerchief, and he had little golden bells on his sleeves so that they tinkled when he was juggling. There were six copper balls and twelve sharp shiny knives, and he used to throw them all up in the air and catch them, and he never dropped a ball or cut his fingers. He was so clever at being a juggler that people used to give him pennies to see him do it, so he used to go from town to town collecting his pennies and humming to himself, and being very happy, except when it rained. When it rained the balls and knives were slippery, and then he did drop them sometimes, and people thought he wasn't a bit clever, and wouldn't give him pennies. So he was nearly always hungry on wet days.

His Very Special Person was Our Lady (so *now* you see why he dressed in blue and white, don't you?), and every time he passed a church he used to go in and ask her to look after him and not let it rain too often.

One wet day he was walking along looking for a barn to sleep in when he caught up with a monk, and they walked along together.

" Why do you have to dress like that? Are you a clown? " asked the monk.

" I don't *have* to, and I am *not* a clown," said Barnabas. " I am Barnabas the Juggler. To be a juggler is the Grandest Thing in the World."

" Oh, no," said the monk, " it may be a very nice thing to be, but it isn't as Special and Important as being a monk, because monks live with God and Our Lady as much as they can."

" I wish *I* could do that! " said Barnabas. " Our Lady is my Special Person. Can I come and be a monk with you? "

" Yes," said the monk. " As it happens, it is very lucky you asked me that, because I am the Prior of that monastery over there. Come and be a monk with us! "

So Barnabas went to be a monk with the Prior, and he dressed in black instead of blue and white, which was rather sad for him, but he didn't mind *very* much.

In this monastery all the Brothers had a Special Thing to do for Our Lady.

The Prior wrote very clever books about her. Brother Maurice painted beautiful little pictures of her for the books, in red and blue and gold. Brother Denis grew special lilies in the garden for her altar. Brother Marbode used to make marble statues. His black clothes were always covered with little chips of marble, and his hair was all dusty. His Most Important statue was a beautiful one of Our Lady that stood in the chapel. She had a crown on and the little Baby Jesus was asleep on her shoulder, and Barnabas (or Brother Barnabas, now he was a monk) used to go and look at this statue and feel *very* sad, because all the monks could do something very clever for Our Lady except himself. And he couldn't do *anything* nicely except juggle. So he got sadder and sadder, and the Prior thought perhaps he didn't like being a monk after all.

One day, before it was time to get up, Barnabas had an Idea. He jumped up and ran quickly to the chapel before any of the others got there. After dinner he went again, *and* after tea. Each time he came back so happy that the Prior couldn't *think* what he had been doing, because usually he was rather sad. So, after supper, when Brother Barnabas had gone to the chapel *again*, the Prior and Brother Maurice (who painted the pictures) followed him and looked through the door to see what he *was* doing. And what do you suppose he *was* doing? Well, he was standing on his head and juggling with his six copper balls and twelve shiny knives, *right* in front of Our Lady's Altar!

You see, it was the *only* clever thing he could do, so he did it for Our Lady and hoped she wouldn't mind.

382

The Prior and Brother Maurice (who painted the pictures) were so surprised that they just stood and stared for a minute. Then the Prior said:

"Poor Brother Barnabas must have gone mad! Quick, go and tell Brother Marbode (who makes statues) to help us to get him out. It is a Calamitous Thing to do things like that in the chapel!"

They were just going to go in to take Brother Barnabas away when he stopped juggling and knelt in front of the statue that Brother Marbode had made of Our Lady, and looked at it. Then they saw her come down from the Altar and wipe Barnabas's hot forehead and smile at him! *She* knew he wasn't at all mad, and she loved him doing his juggling for her, because it was the only Special Thing he knew. So the Prior and

the Brothers went quietly away, and Barnabas never
saw them.

After that the Prior let Brother Barnabas do it always,
and never told him that he knew what the Beautiful Idea
was, because it would have spoilt it all. It was Brother
Barnabas' Own Special Secret.

ST. VINCENT

O nce upon a time there was a young priest and his Christian name was Vincent and his Surname was de Paul (My surname is Windham, what is yours?) and he lived in France in a town called Toulouse.

One day Vincent heard that a friend of his had died and left him a good deal of money just when he was wanting to build a school. So he packed a few things in a parcel and set off to fetch it from Marseilles which is by the sea. He had to walk most of the way (that is why he did not take any luggage) because there were no trains and he couldn't afford a horse. Well after some time he got to Marseilles without any special adventures and he collected the money from the Lawyer who was looking after it for him. He was just going to start on his long walk home when a friend of the lawyer's came in and said:

" I am going part of your way by Sea in my own boat, would you like to come with me? It would save quite half of your long walk."

" Thank you very kindly," said Father Vincent, " I was just thinking that I feel a little less spry going back than I did coming. When is your boat sailing? "

" Tonight," said the lawyer's friend. So Vincent went on board at once. He sat in the sun on the deck and rested his tired feet and watched the seagulls and the other ships in the port. The wind smelled of the sea and he smiled happily at the thought of his nice Sea Holiday instead of his long Hot Walk.

Soon after it was dark the ship sailed out of the Harbour on its way to Narbonne which was where

Vincent was going to land and walk home. But they had hardly got out of sight of Marseilles when three African Pirate Ships sailed towards them and as soon as they were near enough they shot hundreds of arrows at the French ship and one of them went through Vincent's arm and wounded him.

Three against one was too much for the French sailors who weren't ready for a battle and all of them (Vincent as well) were Taken Prisoner.

They were all chained together and put in the dark Hold of one of the ships. (The Hold is like the basement or cellar of the ship and it usually has Rats and Luggage and Black Beetles in it. I don't know why.) The Pirates sailed about for a few days looking for some more prisoners, and when they had enough they sailed back to Africa and unloaded Vincent and the others on to the land.

The Captain came and looked at them.

"What a miserable-looking lot!" he said to his Mate. "I never saw a poorer collection."

"Well, Sir," said the Mate, "a good many of them are wounded, and they have been in the dark hold for six days without washing. They didn't have much to eat either."

"You ought to have seen about it," said the Captain; "they're no use like that. Tidy them up and Fatten them." And he went away.

Vincent couldn't imagine what they were talking about. "I do hope they're not Cannibals," he thought. "Why should we have to be clean and fat, I wonder?"

He asked the lawyer's friend who was chained next to him.

"We will be sold for Slaves," said the lawyer's friend sadly; "that is what they always do with their prisoners. No one will give good prices for us if we look thin and shabby. They would think we couldn't work."

"Oh, I see," said Vincent, "like buying a good fat shiny horse instead of a bony one."

"Yes," said the lawyer's friend.

So for a few days the prisoners lived up in the sunshine and had plenty to eat and then they were marched through the Town to the Market Place to be sold. Most of the people in this African town were not Christians but Mohammedans.

After a time a Fisherman, who was looking for someone to help him with his boat, bought Vincent and took him away and the first thing he did was to take off his chains.

"I don't want you all tied up like a mad bull," said the fisherman, "you don't look angry or anything. Are you going to Escape?"

"No," said Vincent, because he thought to himself, "if God doesn't want me to be here he will soon get me out of it, and if he *does* want me here I must just make the best of it."

So Vincent went out in a little bobbing boat every day with the fisherman who was quite kind to him and who was glad he had found such a helpful slave. But he soon wished he had bought a different one because Vincent was *so* seasick.

"You'll soon get used to it," said the fisherman, but Vincent didn't. He tried eating nothing and he tried eating something and he tried going backwards and he tried going forwards but he just went on and on being seasick.

At last the fisherman got tired of it.

"It's no good," he said; "you are a very nice slave and all that but you are absolutely useless as a Fishing Slave. I shall have to sell you."

Vincent was glad he wouldn't have to go out in the boat any more, but he was sorry to leave the fisherman.

His next master might be very fierce and cruel, you never could tell, if you were a slave.

But the fisherman sold him to an old chemist who lived in his little shop and whose eyesight was not so good as it used to be. Vincent's work was to measure out the pills and medicines for the old man, who gave him some ointment for his wounded arm.

The chemist took a great Fancy to Vincent and was rather proud of having a French priest for a slave. One day he said,

" You know, if only you weren't a Christian, Vincent, I would adopt you for my son. I would teach you to be a Chemist and I would leave you my money when I die. After all, we both worship the same True God."

" No," said Vincent, " that isn't possible for me because you don't believe that Our Lord is God, and the second Person of the Trinity."

" No, I don't believe in the Trinity," said the old chemist, " just in One God."

" But the Trinity is One God, not three Gods," said Father Vincent, and he explained to the Chemist all about it but the old man didn't believe him.

" You'd do far better if you were a Mohammedan," he said. " I would set you free and you would be my son. You would be rich when I am dead and then you could go back to France if you wanted to. Nobody round about here is a Christian. It would be so much more friendly for you if you were the same as we are."

" But I am a *priest*," said Vincent. " You don't understand."

" What is the good of a Priest if he hasn't any People or Church? " asked the old man.

" I've got God," said Vincent.

" So have I," said the Chemist.

" Oh *dear!* " thought poor Vincent, " I'll never get him to see."

And so they used to talk day after day and each of them hoped that the other would Change Over, but neither of them did.

At last the Chemist died and he left all his possessions to his nephew and, because Vincent was one of his possessions (he had bought him, you remember), he had to belong to the nephew too.

But the nephew didn't want Vincent, so he sold him to a Rich Man who sent him to work on his farm in the country.

Now the Rich Man was a Frenchman, and long ago he too had been Captured by Pirates and had come to Africa. And when he saw that as long as he was a Christian he would be a slave he Changed Over and was a Mohammedan. I expect you know why this is one of the Worst Sins there is, don't you? Mohammedans (and Pagans and Heretics) generally don't know about Our Lord properly and so usually it isn't their *fault* if they are not all Christians. They can be very Good Kind people, doing all that their religion tells them to do. And God loves them because he made them and he died for them as much as he died for you and for me. Even though they do not know that he did. (That is why missionaries and people go all over the world to tell them about Our Lord.)

But people who *do* know about Our Lord and who have lived in the Church and who have been to Holy Communion and have learned to know God, for *them* to turn their backs on Our Lord and say that they can't be bothered with him any more, and that they'd rather be something else, is a Very Terrible and Frightening thing to do. And that is what the Rich Man who had bought Vincent had done. But sometimes he wasn't quite sure if he was as happy as he thought he would be.

Mohammedans are allowed more than one wife and this Rich Frenchman had three wives and one of them was a young Turkish lady who did not like living in the town. So her husband used to let her go for visits to his farm. On one of her visits she saw that there was a new slave, and she watched him working, and she saw that he was always singing. So she went out to see him and ask him where his home was and where the Rich Man had bought him.

So Vincent told her about France and the lawyer's friend and the ship and the pirates and the fisherman and the chemist and the chemist's nephew and the Rich Man. And he told her that he was a priest.

" What is a priest? " asked the Turkish Lady.

So Vincent told her about that too and every day, when she went out for her morning walk she found Vincent somewhere on the farm and he told her a little more about Christians and the Church.

" Is that what you always sing about? " said the Turkish Lady.

" I sing all that I can remember of my Office," said Vincent, " and of Mass and the hymns and Psalms. And so sometimes I forget that I am the only Christian round about here, and I feel at home."

When the Turkish Lady went back to town she said to the Rich Man:

" I've been talking to your new French slave. He is a good slave and works hard even when he is alone. He told me about his religion; it is the same religion that you used to have before you Changed Over. That was not a good thing to have done."

The Rich Man had often wondered himself if it was such a good thing as he had thought it was going to be, but he had got himself into a Fix. Because if the Mohammedans found anyone Changing Over from being a Mohammedan they killed him.

"What shall I do?" he thought. "Even if I do change into a Christian I shouldn't think that Our Lord will want to have anything more to do with me after the way I have treated him."

Suddenly he remembered that Vincent was a Priest.

"How lucky for me that I bought him," he thought and he went out to his farm.

When he told Vincent about the Fix, Vincent said:

"It might be that God would want you to be a Martyr so as to make up for your Terrible Sin."

"But will Our Lord ever have anything to do with me again?" said the Rich Man.

"The first thing for you to do is," said Father Vincent, "to see a Bishop. And when he takes you back into the Church you must go to Confession and then you will be able to Start Again. God will not hold it against you," said Vincent.

The Rich Man said that he would much rather be a Christian again even if the Mohammedans did kill him, and after some talk they decided to try to Escape from Africa and get back to France. They disguised themselves as Vegetable Sellers and Vincent carried a basket of cabbages and the Rich Man carried a basket of beans and they walked through the country until they came to the sea. There they saw a little boat but they daren't go near it until it was dark, so they waited about and bought food and some bottles of water which they hid under the Vegetables until the night. Then, very quietly they piled their things into the boat and set off.

Luckily they didn't meet any Pirates and at last they reached France and Vincent thanked God that he wasn't a slave any more.

The Rich Man went to the Bishop who took him back into the Christian Church and then he heaved a huge sigh of relief and went to Confession. Vincent waited for him and found him some work because he wasn't Rich any more. The work was in the Hospital and he liked it very much.

Now that Father Vincent was back in France he went on with his work as a priest and one of the first things that he did was to find out about the slaves who worked in ships. These slaves were called Galley Slaves and most of them had been sent to work in the Galley ships instead of being sent to prison for something wrong that they had done. Vincent knew what a dreadful time they had. No beds; always chained; no room to lie down at night; very little to eat; no daylight.

So Vincent found a house in Marseilles where the slaves could go when their ship was in the port, and where they could sleep and eat and wash their clothes. The slaves could hardly believe it! They were so much happier and worked so much better that the Bishop told Vincent to make houses for the galley slaves in all the sea towns, and after he had done that he started a Hospital for the ill ones. And even now one of the biggest Sailors' Hospitals in the world is in Marseilles.

You might have thought that by now Vincent would have had a bit of a rest. But not at all. He went to Paris and he found that some of the people there were so terribly poor that they could not feed their children when they had them. So they used to leave the babies on people's doorsteps, or in Churches, or even in the road or a shop for anybody who might come along to find. If no one found them or if it was a very cold day the poor babies died, and hundreds of them did die. So Vincent used to go out at night and walk round the streets and when he found a baby he would wrap it in his cloak and bring it home. Then of course he had to have someone to look after them. He found a lady and asked her if she would start a Home for the Foundling Children with her friends and she did. And that was the beginning of the Daughters of Charity. We often call them St. Vincent de Paul Sisters and they are those nuns in blue dresses and Enormous White Hats and umbrellas. They have schools and homes for Orphans and for Foundlings, and they have Hospitals too. They work harder than anyone I know and they get up at Four O'clock in the morning. (Did you say " Why do they have umbrellas? " Well just imagine what would happen to a starched linen hat in the Rain! Did you never see a Sister with her Corners hanging down?)

I haven't told you nearly all the things that St. Vincent de Paul did, but you can find a good deal more in other books. His Special Day is on July 19th, and people all over the world are called after him.

ST. GERARD

Once upon a time there was a little boy called Gerard Majella, and he lived in Italy. His father's name was Dominic Majella, and his mother's name was Olivia Majella. (Majella was their Surname, like Smith or Johnson or something.) And his father was a Tailor.

When he was Five years old Gerard was playing outside the Church when it began to Rain. So he pushed open the Heavy Church door and went inside to shelter. He walked about and looked at the things until he came to a Statue of Our Lady with her Baby Christ in her arms. Gerard stopped and began to talk to them. He told them that he had come in out of the Rain, and that he hoped that it wouldn't make him Late for Tea. And he told them that he would soon be going to School like his sister Bridget, who was Seven. And he said that while she was at School he had to play by himself, and he said he wished that Little Jesus would come and play with him.

As he said this, the Statue of Our Lord came alive in Our Lady's arms and climbed down and was a little Boy just about as old as Gerard. And they played in the Church until it stopped Raining and Gerard had to go home to Tea. (He wasn't Late.)

Well, after this, Gerard used to go to the Church every day. And every day the same thing happened.

One day Gerard felt Hungry while they were playing, and Jesus gave him a little Loaf of Bread, Just about the size of a Roll, it was. Gerard put it in his pocket until he went home. He showed it to his mother.

"Where did you get that, Gerard?" she asked. "I've never seen any bread like that, it is so White."

"The little boy that plays with me in the Church gave it to me," said Gerard.

"Which little boy?" asked his mother.

"He never told me his name," said Gerard.

The next day when Gerard had gone out, his mother sent Bridget after him. (It was a half-Holiday.)

"See what he does and who he plays with," she said; "he is Rather Little to be out so much by himself."

Bridget followed Gerard into the Church and got there just in time to see the Statue come alive and climb down to Gerard.

She ran home and told their mother, who didn't tell anyone because she didn't want Crowds of people coming and bothering and Staring.

When Gerard was Twelve he was sent to a Tailor's Shop to learn to be a Tailor like his father.

Now Tailors always sit Cross-Legged on a Table when they sew. (I don't know why.) And so Gerard sat with some other boys in a row and learned to Sew and Cut Out and Tack and things. But the Tailor who taught them was an awful Bully and, although Gerard learnt a lot more quickly than the Other Boys who were learning, he beat him and jeered at him every day. Now the Master Tailor, whose shop it was, didn't know how badly Gerard was treated until one day he heard a lot of noise going on, and he went to see. He found Gerard lying on the floor in a Faint. The Bully Tailor had hit his head and Stunned him.

"What's all this?" asked the Master Tailor.

"You'd better ask that Lazy Lump!" said the Bully Tailor.

When Gerard woke up the Master Tailor asked him, and Gerard, who didn't want to be a Tell Tale, said:

"It's all right, Sir! I somehow managed to fall off the Table!"

The Master Tailor thought that this was Rather Funny, and so he Watched and Waited for the next few days, and soon found out all about it and Dismissed the Bully Tailor.

When Gerard had learned to be a Tailor he went to another shop to work, but all the time he wanted to be working more for God. So he went to an Uncle of his who was a Franciscan called Father Bonaventure and told him about it.

"My dear boy," said Father Bonaventure, "you wouldn't be Strong enough. You say that you don't want to be a Priest, but a Lay Brother." (A Lay Brother is a Monk or Friar or something who isn't actually a Priest-who-can-say-Mass, but who does the work like Cooking and Cleaning and Gardening and looking after the Chickens.) "But never mind," said Father Bonaventure, "you are a very good Tailor, you know. Work at your Tailoring for the love of God." And to cheer him up he gave Gerard a New Suit of Clothes because his own were very Shabby.

On the way home, though, a Poor-and-Raggy asked Gerard for a Little Something. And the only thing that he'd got was his New Suit. So he gave it to the Poor-and-Raggy and went on with his Old things. Now you might say that there was nothing very Special in that. In fact you expected Gerard would do that! *But* if people come to the Door and ask for things, what do *we* do? We run upstairs and look out any Old thing that we may have, and perhaps we give them a meal (outside the Back door), but do we ever give them anything that we *Want*? So you see, Gerard *was* Rather Special, wasn't he?

Because he couldn't be a Servant in a Monastery or

a Friary, Gerard became a Servant to a very Crusty Military Gentleman. And, although he did his work very well, his master's Temper was very Fiery.

One day, when the Crusty Gentleman was away for the Week-end, Gerard went to the Well for some water to Wash Up. As he leaned over to reach the bucket all his master's Keys fell out of his pocket and went down the well with a tinkling sort of Splash!

Gerard was *Distracted*! What could he do? What would the Crusty Military Gentleman say when he found himself Locked Out?

Then he had an Idea. He went to the Church and asked the Sacristan to lend him the Statue of Our Lady and her Baby. (The one that used to come alive when Gerard was a little boy.)

"What do you want it for?" asked the Sacristan. People don't usually Borrow statues out of Churches.

"I want to let it down the Well to find some Keys I've dropped in," said Gerard.

"Don't be so Babyish!" said the Sacristan. "Only Children would believe a thing like that, not Grown Ups!"

"All the same," said Gerard, "I would be glad if you *would* lend it to me."

"Oh, all right!" said the Sacristan; "I'll go with you to see how Silly you'll look!"

So he and a crowd of other people all went back to the Well with Gerard. Most of them were Sniggling at anyone believing such nonsense.

Gerard tied some Rope round the statue and dangled it down into the water.

"Please, dear Jesus," he said very quietly so that the Others couldn't hear, "will you find the Keys for me? I said that you would, so please do, so that the people won't think that you can't!"

Then he pulled the Statue up again, and there, round the Baby's arm, was the Bunch of Keys!

So the people stopped Sniggling and prayed instead.

When he was Twenty-two Gerard tried to be a Redemptorist Lay Brother. (Redemptorists are an Order started by St. Alphonsus Liguori. Like St. Simon

Stock starting the Carmelites and all that.) But at first the Redemptorists said the same as the Franciscans, that he wasn't Strong enough. But at last he was allowed to try.

"But you will be no Use at all," said the Father Rector (who was the Head Redemptorist).

But he was wrong. Gerard did all his work properly, and no one could make any Complaint.

Gerard loved Animals, and he hated to see Birds in Cages. In those days, Two Hundred years ago, people weren't so Kind to animals as they are now. I expect that people forgot that animals were made by God just as much as they are themselves. And God must like them very much or he would never have made them at all. After all, he *needn't* have. And animals' Souls don't go on living after their bodies are dead like ours do, and so we ought to be Extra nice to them because they haven't got very much time.

The people in Gerard's time used to keep Birds in Tiny little cages. And they often Blinded them so that the birds thought that they were in the Dark and that made them Sing more so that the Other birds could find them and try to set them Free.

One day, Gerard saw a little Girl carrying a Bird Cage with a Bird in it along the road. She put it down in the sun and turned to get a Drink of Water from a Stream that was beside the road. Gerard stooped down and let the Bird out.

"There!" he said, "now, my poor Bird, *you* can get a drink too. Fly away now, quick!" And the Bird flew away. But the little Girl turned back and, seeing the empty cage, she began to cry.

Gerard was Surprised. He hadn't thought that the little Girl might love her Bird. Not many people did. So he called:

"Come back, Bird! The little Girl loves you!"

And the Bird came back and flew straight back into the Cage!

Another time, Gerard was riding along on some message for the Redemptorists, when his Horse cast a Shoe. So they went to a Blacksmith to have another one put on. The Blacksmith in his Leather Apron bellowed up his fire with the Bellows and hammered the Red Hot iron into a Horseshoe. Cling! Cling! Cling! went the Hammer, and then he put it back into the Fire again to get it soft enough to make the Holes for the Nails. Then he fitted it on to the Horse and there was a Loud Smell and Smoke. Then he cut the Horse's hoof a bit and then he nailed the Horseshoe on Firmly.

"There!" said the Blacksmith, "that will be Six Shillings, please!"

"But that's terribly expensive!" said Gerard, "I haven't got as much as that!" Then he said: "It isn't usually so much!"

"Can't help that!" said the Blacksmith, "that's my Price!"

"But couldn't you make it a *little* cheaper?" said Gerard, "the Redemptorists are not Rich, you know. Won't you do it for the love of God? I can pay you *nearly* Six Shillings."

"If you don't pay, I'll fetch the Police!" said the Blacksmith, making a Threatening face. (Threatening is like saying: you *must* do it, or else. . . .)

"All right," said Gerard, "I'll give you back the Shoe, then!"

"But you can't do that!" said the Blacksmith. "I've done my work properly. It *won't* come off until it *wears* off!"

"Kick it off!" said Gerard to his Horse. And the Horse kicked his foot and the Shoe flew off and Gerard rode off down the road, leaving the Blacksmith standing in Astonishment.

Gerard worked very hard as a Lay Brother for the Love of God. And God loved him very much. So, when he was Thirty, God sent for him to go to Heaven so as to be nearer to him. And now Gerard works even harder because, when he was on Earth he could only do things for the people round about him, but now he serves anyone who asks him things, all over the World. And when you remember that working for God was his Favourite thing to do, you can imagine how happy he is now that he works so near to him.

St. Gerard's Special Day is on December 11th, and Hundreds of people are called after him.

ST. MICHAEL

Once upon a time, right at the Very Beginning of Things, there was a Battle in Heaven, and this is how it happened:

God had made Heaven and all the Angels and all the extra Important Angels called Archangels. (Like an extra important Bishop is called an Archbishop.) The Archangels were God's very Special Friends, and were Shining and Strong and Powerful. One was called Gabriel. He was the one that God sent to tell Our Lady about being the Mother of God. Another was called Raphael. He was the one who helped Tobias in the Bible. Another was called Michael. He was "the Angel of the Lord," who was sent to Moses and Jacob and Abraham and people. Another was Lucifer, who was so beautiful that the other Angels called him the Son of the Morning.

Well, everybody was very happy because they were with God, and they all loved Him because he had made them so Strong and Shining and Lovely.

Then one day Lucifer, Son of the Morning, said to himself: "Why should God be the Most Important Person in Heaven? Why shouldn't *I* be? I can fly and I can change into other things, and I am beautiful and I am powerful. In Fact, I am *just* as Important as God, and I shan't do what He tells me ever again. I shall fight Him and have Heaven for Mine!"

This was really very Stupid of Lucifer, wasn't it? Because he wouldn't have been there at all if God hadn't made him, so of Course he wasn't so Important.

Also he was being Vain and Proud and Treacherous, which is Plotting against the King.

So Lucifer went round Heaven and he collected a lot of other Angels who didn't want to be less Important than God, until he had a Great Army.

Then they marched up to the Throne of God and said Proudly:

" We are just as Important as You. Why should *You* be the King of Heaven any more than one of us? We are Strong and Proud and Beautiful, and we will Fight You for the Kingdom of Heaven."

God looked at them. Then he said:

" Lucifer, I thought that you were My Friend and I trusted you. Be sensible, now, and *think* what you are doing."

" I *have* thought," said Lucifer, " and I'd rather not be in Heaven at all than have You for my King, and so would all of us! "

And behind him all the Rebel Angels shouted with a great shout:

" We will follow Lucifer! Long live Lucifer! Let *him* reign over us in Heaven! WE DO NOT WANT GOD! "

" Very well," said God, " if you don't want Me, you needn't have Me. But if you want to fight for Heaven, you can if you think it will be any good."

And He called Michael the Archangel and made him gather together a Mighty Army of Angels who were on God's side.

Then there was a Great Battle in Heaven, Michael and his Angels fighting with Lucifer; and Lucifer fought; and *his* angels; but they did not win. And Michael drove him Right Out of Heaven and he fell down, and down, and down to Hell, and all his angels were driven down after him, and, as the last one disappeared from

403

sight for ever and the Gate of Heaven clanged shut, a great Shout went up from Michael's Army.

"Heaven has won! Rejoice and be glad all you Angels! The Good God always wins!"

So now you know why we sometimes say in our prayers, "Holy Michael the Archangel, defend us in the Day of Battle," because he is so good at battles.

But what happened to Lucifer and his Rebel Angels? Well, he was so Furious and Enraged at having lost his Battle with God that he has never got over it. You see, he is never allowed inside Heaven any more for ever and ever and ever, and now that he *can't* go he is angry about it. So, in Revenge, he does everything horrible to God that he can. His worst Feeling is Jealousy. Who do you suppose he is jealous of? *Us!* Why? Because when Our Lord was Crucified He opened the Kingdom of Heaven for *us* to go in! So Lucifer, whose other name is Satan, or the Devil, is *Furious* because we Ordinary People are allowed in, and he, an Archangel, isn't. So he and his angels try always and always to stop us going in by giving us bad Ideas, and making us do things that we Know are wrong so as to hurt God. So whenever you want to do or say something horrid, think of the Great Battle in Heaven, and remember that it is Lucifer trying to keep you on his side. If you don't do or say it, you have won and have stayed on God's side.

St. Michael's Special Day is September 29th, and it is called the Feast of St. Michael and All Angels because of all the Angels who helped him in the Battle..